TULIPS & ASHES

Lament, Resilience, and Hope in Ukraine

Iryna Kapitonova

Edmonds Press
Berlin

The **Deutsche Nationalbibliothek** lists this publication in the Deutsche Nationalbibliografie; detailed bibliographic data are available in the Internet at https://dnb.dnb.de

Author: Iryna Kapitonova
Interior Illustrations: Julia Ilkova
Cover and Layout Design: Justin Siemens

Initial costs for this book was funded by many contributors through Kickstarter. Publication credits are given to two executive tier supporters:
      Viktoriya (Vika) Dzyuba
      Bethany Johanson
Thank you for your support. Special thanks as well to J. Pharr, E. Picconatto, A. Rousseau, and other friends of Envision Berlin who helped make this book possible.

ISBN Paperback for Global Distribution: 978-3-98999-000-5
ISBN Paperback in Germany: 978-3-98999-004-3
ISBN Limited Edition Hardcover: 978-3-98999-001-2

Sachbücher/Geschichte/Biographien,Autobiographien
THEMA Classifications: DND: Diaries, Letters, and Journals | DNXM: True war and combat stories | DNBX1 Autobiography: religious and spiritual | 1DTN Ukraine | 3MRBH ca. 2020 to ca. 2029
BISAC Classification: BIO026000 BIOGRAPHY & AUTOBIOGRAPHY / Personal Memoirs | HIS067000 HISTORY / Europe / Ukraine | HIS027130 HISTORY / Wars & Conflicts / General | REL012170 RELIGION / Christian Living / Personal Memoirs | Regional Code: 1.6.17.0.0.0.0 Ukraine

To the people of Ukraine,

may your resilience never run dry.

To our defenders who make every day possible for us,

may God bless you and keep you.

To all the fallen heroes,

may you rest in peace and may your sacrifice not be in vain.

Invitation from the Editor

When our family moved into our last house in the US, we found that the yard had once had beautiful gardens, but that it was now nearly barren. The previous occupants (or their family) had removed the gardens as they had grown too old to care for them. They were almost successful in removing the memory of the beauty that had once been there.

But we were surprised, after our first winter, to discover three tulips in the yard – each isolated, but beautiful. As happens with tulips, the beauty was soon gone and by the time summer had run its course, we had forgotten all about the tulips. But they were still there, invisibly tending to their own survival.

The next year, we had more tulips, and by the end of the third year, there were enough to transplant some of the bulbs to other parts of the yard. By the time we moved out, there were reliable, beautiful, stands of tulips that we looked forward to as winter faded into spring.

It's with this experience in mind that I found myself drawn to a picture Ira Kapitonova, had made us aware of, from April of 2022. She said, "Spring comes to Mariupol despite the war as a powerful statement that life will win over death."

Reflecting on the picture later, Ira said "When I look at [it], I see God working through nature to bring beauty from the ashes. That's my number#1 association with the book."

> *"I want it to communicate hope and resilience so that the initial response to the image would be not pity but respect. For decades, Ukraine was perceived as a victim (and that's the meta-narrative we were taught at school), but this past year has shown us that it is not so. We surprised ourselves with this readiness to resist oppression and injustice and learned to believe in ourselves. That is why I would like the images to communicate the idea that even though Ukraine*

is hurting now, it is not broken, but it is eager to live and ready to recover, rebuild, and restore."

As we worked through how to present Ira's work in this book, we wanted to find a narrative that would help us, and the reader, to make sense of the senselessness of this war. We had originally hoped that the war would be over by the one-year mark, but it was not, and Ira continues adding every day to her writing. As I write, it has been 480 days since the 2022 invasion (and of course much longer since the 2014 start of the war). Along with Ira we are angry, we weep, and we look for hope as we see the destruction of life, the disruption of community, the interruption of dreams, the losses temporary and permanent.

As humans do, we are looking for a story in the midst of the pain. And so, we decided to look to the story of the tulip, much like the ones I had back behind my home. Tulips spend most of their lives engaged in invisible work beneath the ground. They briefly interrupt our world with a reminder of goodness, and then fade back out of memory to prepare for next year's interruption. Left to their own, they will often spread that beauty so that each time one emerges it more fully captures our attention – an eruption that draws our eyes away from the surroundings – even when those are bombed out apartment buildings, evidence of man's capacity for evil.

With this story in mind, we've decided to organize Ira's story to follow the life of tulips. The life of these beautiful flowers can be understood in seven stages,[i] and these form the organizing principle for this book.

1. A season to plant: The first step is to plant tulips. Unlike the casual sowing of wildflower seeds, which scatter with the pleasure of the wind and rain, tulips are buried in the ground, far from the light and unlikely to be moved. The initial planting of a tulip is intentional and requires forethought. The rootless bulbs are buried – based on the belief that these onion-cousins will bring beauty into the world.

Planting tulips is an expression of hope, based on past experience. After a bulb is placed in the ground, half a year passes before the gardener knows whether their hope is realized. For these sections of the book, we have selected entries in which Ira has similarly expressed hope based on past memories.

2. A season to make roots: In the dark and cooling earth, the bulbs start to grow roots. This is a remarkable time, where the bulb, unseen and often forgotten, reaches out for survival. Reaching out from its own resources, the bulb finds what it needs in its environment to prepare for the cold ahead.

Having planted our tulip bulbs, we move forward into the busyness of preparing for winter. This is a practical time, built around survival. For these sections of the book, we have selected entries in which Ira is focused on the experience of survival.

3. A season to cool: Winter buries the memory of the hopes that we had planted with our tulip bulbs. Our tulips were often forgotten deep beneath snow drifts. This is not the season for tulips – the environment is harsh. The bulbs rest in the cool earth, and although it is perhaps an unlovely time for the tulips, it is important.

Winter buries the memory of the hopes that we had planted with our tulip bulbs. In these sections of the book, we have selected entries when hope felt distant.

4. A season to grow: As the cold fades, the tulip bulbs – still alive after winter – convert their resources into the food they need to begin growing. Still invisible from the surface, the tulips push against the dirt – extending leaves upward and roots further down into the soil. In spite of the sometimes-returning onslaughts of fading winter, tulips start growing below the surface.

This is a time of defiance and hope. In these sections, we have selected entries when Ira expresses defiance in the face of aggression.

5. A season to bloom: The crowning season for the tulips arrives as their flowers reach to the sky. They share their beauty with us and pollinators find food, and sometimes refuge, in the beautiful, cupped petals. This is a practical time as well as a joyful one. The flower generates seeds. But celebration is vulnerable – the tulip has used huge amounts of the bulb's resources in the hope of future goodness.

Ira expresses celebration and rejoicing, and it is beautiful to see. In these sections, we join her in celebrating, while also aware of the costs.

6. A season to regenerate: Far too quickly are the days of the beautiful flowers gone. Visually, we have reached one of the least lovely times of the tulip; yet also one of the most important times. After the bloom fades, the seeds form above the ground, while the tulip begins to replenish its stores under the ground. This stage is not lovely to look at, but if the stage is cut short, tulips are at risk of dying.

In this section, we see loss and lament at the same time that we find the seeds of future goodness.

7. A season to multiply: Once the tulip has replenished its stores, it begins the hidden work of multiplying, as some seeds slowly make their way into the ground, and as the tulip bulbs themselves begin to multiply and prepare for the following year. This work is invisible, but crucial. Resilience is a characteristic of those who thrive in spite of conflict and aggression. Their commitment to goodness brings life into the world, even as much of what they do is invisible.

We conclude in this section with seeds of future hope and the open question of who will plant and tend them.

Ira's own experience was, due to the war, more chaotic than a neat 7-stage cycle laid out through the year. Sometimes she experienced all seven of these themes in a single day. But it is our hope that as you encounter her story through this cycle, repeated seven times, that the rhythm of it will help carry you through.

The edit: Our intent has been to bring you into Ira's experience of the world in a way that makes sense within your own world. The darkness, pain, and loss of war are overwhelming. By using the seven stages for each chapter, we hope that you will find the cycle of joy and sorrow, tension and release, to allow you to keep going. In addition to making difficult decisions about what to include and what to leave out, we have made some changes to help with the presentation and understandability of the book. You may still be able to find her original posts on Facebook, if you want to read them in their entirety.

The presentation of the conflict: This war, like any other, has myriad perspectives and distortions. At times, Ira writes something she has heard to be true and later updates it with new information. This book is about her journey and is not intended to be an authoritative source. At the same time, she has done a remarkable job including information about the status of various losses and gains, and some of this is presented in the text. We have included the citations for some of the information, but do not present any of those facts here as authoritative – rather these are illustrative of what information was available to her when she wrote. The war, which has been terrible, also generates moments of deep angst. We are committed to recognizing the humanity of each person, but war drives hard against this commitment. Overall, Ira has done a remarkable job of fighting to retain her view of the humanity of those bringing terror to her land and people. But this is difficult. Should a person celebrate when those defending you take the lives of the enemy? Our goal here is not to render judgment of these hard themes, but instead to present Ira's honest reflections as she struggles. And we pray alongside her: "May the truth never be silenced."

The inclusion of scripture: This book is intended for a wide variety of readers, of many different national and faith backgrounds. Ira writes with regular reference to the scriptures of the Christian bible. Originally, we had asked whether the inclusion of scripture might be off-putting or confusing to some readers. Indeed, it might. However, as we selected excerpts from Ira's writing for this book, we discovered that in many cases the verses that Ira had selected accurately presented an extension of her own voice. Thus, many of the scriptures she had selected do appear here so that you, the reader, may hear her cries and her rejoicing more fully.

The intended effect: We have myriad goals in presenting Tulips and Ashes to you, dear reader. We hope to promote conversations that matter, and to help you and people like you to engage deep and difficult questions about what it means to live as humans. We seek peace, and it is often in recognizing the humanity in the other that we can reevaluate our own claims on the world and our place in it. In this way, the book is intended to be costly. We hope that it costs each of us a little more of our own pride, hatred, and capacity for unlove – that we leave the book with less of those and instead with greater empathy, love and hope.

Thank you for joining us on the journey.

Stephen W. Jones, general editor
Berlin

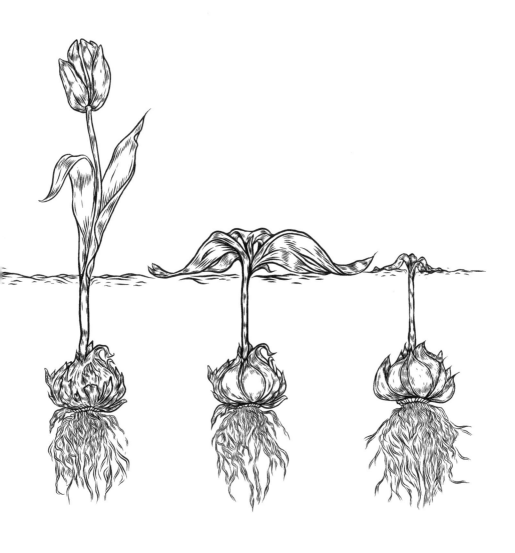

The last peaceful day - February 23, 2022

February 22, 2023: Day 364 of the war

୫ Hear my voice, O God, in my complaint;
preserve my life from dread of the enemy.
(Psalm 64:1)

A year ago today, my son and I were recovering from a cold. We went for a walk in the neighborhood – the weather was sunny and warm, and you could sense the spring in the air. While my son enjoyed himself at the playground, I kept anxiously checking my phone for news. I remember being startled by the sounds of airplanes flying over our neighborhood, even though I was used to them (our neighborhood is not far from the airport). In the evening, when my son was getting ready for bed, someone set off fireworks in our yard, but in the moment's anxiety, they sounded like explosions. My son rushed to the window to watch the fireworks, but I grabbed him and pulled him to the back of the room. We had been reading about safety in the war zone, and the number one rule is staying away from windows and closer to the load-bearing walls. Once I realized it was a false alarm, I let him enjoy the display of lights, but he kept asking me why I didn't want him to watch it from the beginning.

Once he was tucked into bed, I stayed in his room until he fell asleep, and that whole time I felt like a burden was put on my chest. I knew there were words I had to share. I didn't know whom I would share them with, but I knew I couldn't keep them to myself.

So, I sat down and wrote my first daily update. The big war was still 32 hours away, and we still hoped and prayed that God would let this cup pass from us.

As I reread my words from one year ago, I am astounded by their relevance today, so much so that the only editing needed is the numbers.

Below is the updated version of my first daily update when the big war was still 32 hours away. And today's picture was taken on the same day as the picture in the original post – it was one of the last peaceful weekends before the full-scale war.

Posted on the night of February 22, some 30 hours before the invasion
Dear friends,
Thank you so much for your care, support, and prayers!
The war Ukraine is forced to fight now is not for territories or politics. It is a battle for values. Eight years ago, Ukrainians dared to stand up for their dignity, for the value of human life, for the freedom of choice. Even though we had been an independent nation for 23 years, eight years ago, we dared to exercise this independence, and Russia decided that we had to be "punished" for this.

Over the past eight years, more than 14,000 people have been killed (including 4,000 civilians). We can only guess how many more people will have to die, be wounded, or lose their homes in the near future because of the wild ambitions of a crazy man (backed up by his army and supporters) who wants to destroy us not just as a country but as a nation. There is a name for what Putin wants to do, and it is genocide.

It is a war of worldviews and values. It is a struggle "against this present darkness and against the spiritual forces of evil in the heavenly places". Even if you are far from Ukraine, you will still have to fight in this war. Whether you are aware of it or not, you will side with one part or another, so, please, choose wisely.

Ukraine is under attack now. Our army has to defend our homes. We just want to send our kids to school and know they will be safe there during the day. We simply want to be able to make plans without thinking of alternative solutions in case we are under a massive attack. We want to peacefully plant a garden and harvest it in due time. We want to make doctor's appointments without wondering if we'd live to make it. We want our children to have an ordinary childhood, and we want to protect their mental health. Is it too much to ask for?

It is not easy to live in such a time, yet it teaches me to value what I had been taking for granted, and it has made me painfully aware of the truth found in James 4:14-15: "Yet you do not know what tomorrow will bring. What is your life? For you are a mist that appears for a little time and then vanishes. Instead, you ought to say, 'If the Lord wills, we will live and do this or that'."

The only thing we can do now is trust in the Lord, rely on His goodness, and cry out for His mercy. And find comfort in the knowledge that even if evil prevails now, our God is Just, and all those who side with evil today will one day receive their ultimate judgment before His Throne.

Chapter One
Merciless February[ii]
February 24 - 28, 2022

You wake up from birds chirping and bright sunshine coming from the window. You open your eyes, and it takes a moment to understand why you are not home, why your child is sleeping with you in your bed, why the furniture has been rearranged to move it away from the window. It is because yesterday you woke up in hell that your country has been thrown into by its "neighbor."

Day 2 • February 25

Hope Based in Past Memories

A season to plant: *Planting tulips is an expression of hope, based on past experience. After a bulb is placed in the ground, half a year passes before the gardener knows whether their hope is realized.*

A passage that came to mind today as we were praying, and I felt weary, was from Isaiah 40:28-31:

> ❧ Have you not known? Have you not heard? The Lord is the everlasting God, the Creator of the ends of the earth. He does not faint or grow weary; his understanding is unsearchable. He gives power to the faint, and to him who has no might he increases strength.

> ❧ Even youths shall faint and be weary, and young men shall fall exhausted; but they who wait for the Lord shall renew their strength; they shall mount up with wings like eagles; they shall run and not be weary; they shall walk and not faint.

It is with these words that I go to sleep tonight and trust that while I try to rest and regain my strength, the Lord of Hosts who does not grow weary will keep me, my loved ones, and my nation safe.

The Experience of Survival

A season to make roots: *Having planted our tulip bulbs, we move forward into the busyness of preparing for winter. This is a practical time, built around survival.*

Please, pray! Ukraine is under attack. There are sounds of explosion in different cities of Ukraine. We heard them in Kyiv. Please, pray for peace and wisdom for all. May God bless us and keep us.

Day 1 · February 24

At least close the sky and give shelter from the sky...

This night there was a missile attack on Kyiv, on our neighborhood. One of the apartment buildings was on fire.

Another warning about attack from the air coming now.

Please, do something!!! Don't just watch! The war will come to your home and your country sooner than you think if we don't stop it!

Day 2 · February 25

This night is crucial, so the Russians will try an aggressive attack. Please, pray for God's protection over our people, for protection of those who sacrificially stood up to defend us. Pray for Kyiv, our capital city. Pray for repentance of Russian people who came with guns, may they surrender and live rather than murder and be killed. May they flee as they see the army of the Lord of Hosts protecting our nation.

May God give all of us morning.

Please, lift us in your prayers and may God help the oppressed as He is faithful to do.

Day 3 · February 26

Please, keep us in your prayers, especially when it's nighttime here. May we all see the morning.

Day 5 · February 28

When Hope Felt Distant

A season to cool: *Winter buries the memory of the hopes that we had planted with our tulip bulbs.*

Today, people in Ukraine are like a lamb at the slaughter. And it is not enough to give food and clothes to the refugees. It is important to stop the murderers.

Day 2 · February 25

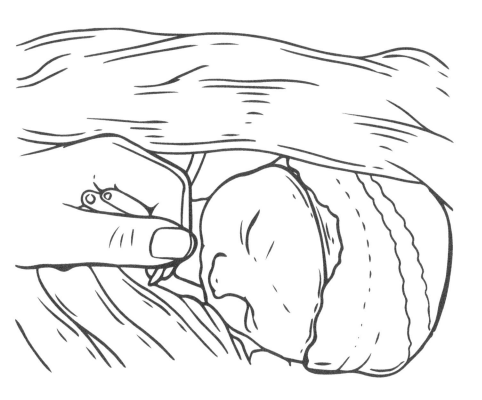

A newborn baby girl, born in Kyiv in a bunker. - Day 2, February 25, 2022

Defiance in the Face of Aggression

A season to grow: *In spite of the sometimes-returning onslaughts of fading winter, tulips start growing below the surface. This is a time of defiance and hope.*

Don't be a silent bystander. Don't sponsor the bombs falling on the homes of peaceful Ukrainian families. Make Russian government pay for their evil.

Day 1 · February 24

We will not give up! There are so many stories of courage! There are endless stories of our people loving on stranded strangers. There are testimonies from our defenders who were rescued from enemy strikes only by the hand of God! We are fighting this Goliath who is drunk with power and who thinks he can mock God, yet we respond with the words of David: "Then David said to the Philistine, "You come to me with a sword and with a spear and with a javelin, but I come to you in the name of the Lord of Hosts, the God of the armies of Israel, whom you have defied" (1 Sam 17:45).

Someone shared this message from our brothers and sisters who are praying for Ukraine: "We're asking God to confuse the enemy and to blind them at the right time. And to let them see the angel armies that are present in Ukraine whom they are fighting against. This is a spiritual war, between good and evil, that has manifested into a physical war." And that's very encouraging as that's the same prayer I've been praying lately.

Day 4 · February 27

But we will also remember countless acts of courage:

• people in the occupied cities of Berdiansk coming into the central square, chanting "Go home!" and singing the national anthem of Ukraine in the faces of armed invaders (caused them to leave!),

- unarmed people blocking the road in their village causing the enemy tank to turn around and leave,
- young boys emptying fuel tanks while the invaders station for a break,

The list can go on and on but I'm too exhausted from monitoring air-raid warnings to continue it. We will remember these stories, we will write books, songs, make movies to make sure these are not forgotten!

Day 5 · February 28

Celebration, While Aware of the Costs

A season to bloom: *The crowning season for the tulips arrives as their flowers reach to the sky. But celebration is vulnerable – the tulip has used huge amounts of the bulb's resources in the hope of future goodness.*

Thanks to your prayers Ukraine stands strong. We see miracles, big and small. Many testimonies, please, feel free to share them in the comments. Let's give God glory and praise He deserves.

Day 3 · February 26

We will also testify about God's faithfulness: Russian soldiers getting lost and confused, running out of fuel and deserting their tanks, missiles hitting just enough "off" the intended target causing minimal damage, Ukrainian defenders get a sudden urge to change their position and are saved from an attack, seven Russian soldiers surrendering to one Ukrainian. Ukraine standing strong against the monster – "What is impossible with man is possible with God" (Luke 18:27).

Day 5 · February 28

Loss and Lament

A season to regenerate: *Far too quickly are the days of the beautiful flowers gone. The tulip begins to replenish its stores under the ground. This stage is not lovely to look at, but if the stage is cut short, tulips are at risk of dying.*

You wake up from birds chirping and bright sunshine coming from the window. You open your eyes, and it takes a moment to understand why you are not home, why your child is sleeping with you in your bed, why the furniture has been rearranged to move it away from the window. It is because yesterday you woke up in hell that your country has been thrown into by its "neighbor".

Day 2 • February 25

However, the situation remains intense. The enemy gets very aggressive in its agony. They attack Red Cross vehicles, children's hospitals, orphanages, civilian evacuation buses. They are attacking peaceful people right now.

Day 3 • February 26

My heart is bleeding with pain. Three hundred fifty-two Ukrainians killed (including fourteen children), 1,684 wounded (including 116 children). Our "safe location" got an air-raid warning. Praise God, we're fine, but our son was scared to go to sleep tonight, and (to be honest) so am I...

Day 4 • February 27

We will never be the same. My close relatives, dozens of dear friends and neighbors with young children are spending night after night in bomb shelters in Kyiv. My niece has been "rescuing" her blankie and favorite toys as they receive an air-raid alert. Peaceful cities are bombed and attacked with cruise missiles (close friends of my neighbor burned alive in their car). Museums are burned down. Civilian evacuation busses are shot down. More than forty million people (not only Ukrainians but from many different nations) who had their lives turned into nightmares.

Tears of thousands of mothers, wives, children, and men. Those will never be forgotten.

Day 5 · February 28

Resilience and the Seeds of Future Hope

A season to multiply: *The tulips begin to multiply and prepare for the following year. This invisible work of resilience is crucial. The commitment to goodness brings life into the world.*

As we were praying today, I saw this image: darkness, explosion flashes on the horizon, anxiety and terror. But then you realize that the flashes change into the bright morning star that brings peace and light. And there was this passage from Revelation 22:12: "Behold, I am coming soon, bringing my recompense with me, to repay each one for what he has done."

I know that the battle belongs to the Lord and that He has already defeated death once and for all.

Day 3 · February 26

Chapter Two

The Spring
that Never Came

March 1 - 31, 2022

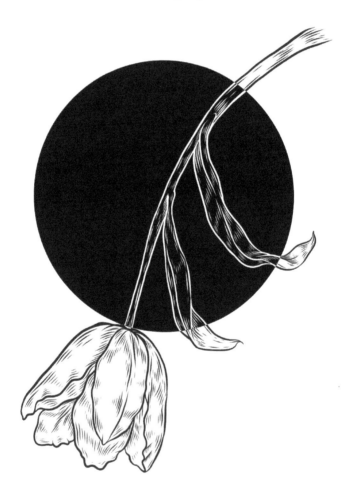

Another day with a whole range of emotions. You go from fear to despair to feeling hopeful to devastation to peace to grief to anger to gratitude to God... And I know that all of these emotions are appropriate and justified but I am still uncomfortable experiencing them...

Day 17 • March 12

Today, I posted a picture of a spring flower. A Ukrainian writer recently wrote that she wouldn't want Ukraine to be known as a place of ruins and devastation but she would rather have it known as a place of beauty and love that we are fighting for. I agree.

Day 30 • March 25

Today was a nice sunny day. I left my phone charging inside and went outside to watch my son play with neighbor kids. It seemed to be such a "normal" day. One of the kids was telling an exciting story that happened to him. "Was it recently?", my son asked. "No, it was when there was no war", was a matter-of-fact response of a 6-year-old.

My heart sank...

Day 34 • March 29

Hope Based in Past Memories

A season to plant: *Planting tulips is an expression of hope, based on past experience. After a bulb is placed in the ground, half a year passes before the gardener knows whether their hope is realized.*

This picture was taken a couple of months ago. It's my balcony garden. I really missed it today. We left home twelve days ago, so I will probably have to start over and plant new plants once the war is over. My comfort for today comes from Isaiah 40:8, "The grass withers, the flower fades, but the word of our God will stand forever."

Love will win. Truth will prevail. Light will defeat the darkness.

Day 13 · March 8

Where is God when Ukraine writhes in pain? He is with us. He is Emmanuel. He mourns with those who lost their loved ones. He grieves with those whose homes have been destroyed. He heals the wounded. He gently carries into safety those who have to flee. He brings food and water to the besieged cities. He keeps his children warm as they spend night after night in bomb shelters. He shields the brave and keeps us safe. He sends His followers to be His hands and feet. He alerts His Spirit to keep praying through the night and He is faithful in answering our prayers. He is in our midst. May we never doubt it!

Do I care about God when I suffer? Do I ask him why? Sometimes I do, but most of the time I just beg Him to be with me through this hard time and give me enough of His grace to remain faithful to Him.

Day 17 · March 12

The war tried to steal our hope – but this is something it will never succeed in. Of course, we may feel desperate, weary, and overwhelmed (to be honest, that's what I've mostly been feeling yesterday and today), but we know that our "help comes from the Lord, who made heaven and earth" (Psalm 121:2),

My balcony garden - Day 13, March 8, 2022

we know that He said, "When he calls to me, I will answer him; I will be with him in trouble; I will rescue him and honor him" (Psalm 91:15). Because if "The Lord is on my side; I will not fear. What can man do to me?" (Psalm 118:6), and that is why we cry out to Him, "In you, O Lord, do I take refuge; let me never be put to shame; in your righteousness deliver me!" (Psalm 31:1).

Day 20 • March 15

Most people in the West have already heard our president speak, and yes, he represents our country, but I would like you to know about people who won't be shown on TV but who are true heroes of Ukraine.

Hundreds of thousands of men and women who joined the Armed Forces of Ukraine and Territorial Defense Forces during the first days of the war – they don't consider themselves heroic, they simply respond to the urge to defend their nation.

Firefighters and rescue teams – they are the ones dealing with the aftermath of bombing and missile strikes, and often they have to do their job under shelling.

Doctors, nurses, and all medical care professionals – they work 24/7, conduct surgeries in bomb shelters, provide assistance over the phone if they can't be there in person. They see pain and death every day, yet they fight them with all their strength.

The often underestimated "working class" – those who make sure we have electricity, heat, water supply, and those who faithfully empty garbage cans. We tend to take it for granted, but we should remember those who make it happen.

All the drivers who help evacuate people, bring in supplies, deliver goods to stores – they spend hours behind the wheels, they go down endangered routes, yet it is thanks to their effort that "ordinary" life continues even under Russian bombs.

People who work at stores and pharmacies – it may not sound like a lot, but would you be able to come to work every day "as if nothing happened" because so many people depend on you?

All volunteers, from those who send supplies from abroad to those who raise funds, to those who manage communication, to those who do whatever has to be done – they do it not because they are paid for doing it, but because they are called to it.

Teachers – they are my heroes in peaceful times but even more so now. Imagine finding time in all this craziness to prepare a lesson, and then gracefully conduct it online when your students are scattered all over the world or perhaps you have new students who had to flee from their homes and end up in your class. Today, teachers offer our children not only knowledge but the much-needed love and support.

Everyone who has a job and keeps working – we desperately need those who would keep our economy going despite the war. I admire those who choose to focus on doing their job well when they'd rather check the news, I applaud those who pay the bills, pay their taxes, and financially support our army and those in need.

Moms – another category of everyday heroes who shine even brighter in these dark days. All the moms of young children who make staying in bomb shelters fun (one mom told her children that the sounds of explosions are actually giants farting), who literally cover their children with their bodies, and all the moms of adult children who send their sons to war and spend days worrying about them and praying for them. Is there greater love?

Zoo activists and pet owners – it is so easy to forget about animals when so many humans are in pain, yet there are those who rescue pets that were left behind, provide food for them and organize evacuation.

Thousands of people who opened their hearts and homes to welcome refugees – 6.5 million people within Ukraine and over 3 million Ukrainians abroad have been welcomed into (temporary) homes, have been offered support, have been shown solidarity. Even the least "significant" help says "I care", and this in itself brings us closer to our victory.

Millions of people across the globe who daily pray for Ukraine – the prayer warriors who stand by us and wage the war with darkness. The true unity of the body of Christ. Living out Philippians 2:1-2: "So if there is any encouragement in Christ, any comfort from love, any participation in the Spirit, any affection and sympathy, complete my joy by being of the same mind, having the same love, being in full accord and of one mind." It is an incredible blessing to experience it.

Please, pray for these heroes and other "ordinary" people doing extraordinary things amid war.

Day 24 • March 19

Learning more about God's character, I realized that His mercy and justice come hand-in-hand. It was both His mercy and His justice that brought Jesus to the cross. Without His mercy, I myself deserve as severe judgment as those tormenting my people today. This realization gave me peace and helped me trust God in situations where the pain is too raw and it seems impossible to forgive.

I took the liberty and paraphrased Zephaniah 3:14-20. May this passage encourage you as it encouraged me: "Rejoice and be glad. I have cleared away your enemies. I, your King, am in your midst, so fear not. I am in your midst, and I am mighty to save. I rejoice over your faithfulness. I exult with loud singing over the fact that you walk with me. Let my love comfort you and quiet you. I will remove your mourning and deal with all of your oppressors. I will change your shame into praise and renown. I will bring you home. I, the Lord your God, will be your shelter and your hiding place."

Day 35 • March 30

The Experience of Survival

A season to make roots: *Having planted our tulip bulbs, we move forward into the busyness of preparing for winter. This is a practical time, built around survival.*

People in Sumy have been under continuous attack this whole time. Today they had no electricity and no running water. But God gave them snow! People were melting snow and collecting water from drainpipes outside. I choose to praise God for giving them this idea and sending them a source of water despite the siege (snow also helps confuse the enemy army).

Day 9 · March 4

What day of the week is it? They say it's Saturday, but it feels like Thursday to me. Because it was on Thursday morning, 10 days ago, that Russia started its massive attack on Ukraine (the initial invasion was in 2014 with Crimea and Donetsk and Luhansk regions). That's when time stopped, and it will resume after God grants Ukraine victory in this horrible war.

Day 10 · March 5

My friend's sister managed to get out of an occupied suburban town that's almost leveled with the ground.

My friends managed to get in touch with their family in an occupied town in the south of Ukraine. They didn't have cell phone reception for two days. They have no heat, but they have running water and are alive and well.

My friend's family lived through the night in the city that was bombed last night (Sumy). They keep strong in the spirit and help others in need.

My friend was able to get in touch with her family in Mariupol. The city has been under a siege for over a week. No heat and no electricity. They are running out of food and supplies. Her family stays there to help those in need.

Day 14 · March 9

Mariupol remains under siege, and the Russian officials recognized they intentionally bombed the Maternity hospital yesterday under the pretense of it being used as army headquarters. They don't allow any humanitarian aid into the city and keep bombarding and shelling the city. People don't have heat, electricity, food, or water. At least 71 children died, and 100 children have been wounded over the course of 15 days of the war.

Day 16 · March 11

"Are you safe?" "Why are you staying? Don't you know you can leave Ukraine?" I can't tell you how many times I heard these questions over the past 18 days...

I realize we may be forced to leave if our "relatively safe" location isn't safe anymore. I also know many families who have left the country, and I know that their decisions were right for them, and I know that their lives as refugees or "foreigners" (depending on the status they choose) aren't necessarily easier than lives of those who stay in Ukraine, and I don't judge them. I pray for them every day.

Why don't we leave? Because Ukraine is our home. I never thought I could be this attached to a country, but as I read news reports, I feel the deep strings in my heart resonate with pain because there are connections that turn out to be stronger than I thought.

Kyiv: It's been my home since 2005. That's where I studied in the university, met my husband and where our son was born. There are so many memories that wouldn't fit in a dozen of books! My heart is still there with my friends and colleagues (especially YWAM Kyiv), my neighbors, and loved ones. I check air-raid alerts for Kyiv and my heart tightens every time. I can't be there now but I can't leave it behind.

Kherson: It's temporarily occupied by the Russian forces, but every day hundreds of people come into the streets with Ukrainian flags and sing Ukrainian songs in the face of armed invaders. My grandma comes from Kherson region. That's where my dad was born. That's where I spent the first year of my life as my parents, being young teachers, started their career at a boarding school in a remote village there. I grew up listening to the stories about locations that were far away geographically yet felt very close to my heart.

Mykolaiv: My grandpa comes from Mykolaiv region. As a child, I would often giggle when he mentioned a small town Kavuny (Watermelon). I thought it was a ridiculous name for a town. Marianivka, Agronomia, Arbuzynka – those small towns would usually come up with names of some distant relatives I never met, and I thought I didn't care about them that much. Now, I know that the towns that mattered so much to my dad and his parents in my childhood are less than 50 km (30 miles) away from Voznesensk (active fighting took place there last week).

Kharkiv: I've been there only once. I went there to meet with a dear friend who was there on a business trip. We spent a weekend there, watched a ballet, it was 9 years ago, but I still remember the magnificent central square that was hit by a missile rocket on March 1. Our friends still have family members there. I can't stop thinking about Kharkiv even though I can't call it my city.

Mariupol: I've never been there, but I've been earnestly praying for this city for the past two weeks, and now I feel that they are my family. They are my heroes. I remember artillery attacks on Mariupol in January 2015. I couldn't stop crying. Firing rockets at civilian residential areas seemed to be the climax of cynicism. I couldn't even imagine that 7 years later, the same city would be under a siege and constant bombing with civilians starved to death. It breaks my heart to know that family members of my friend are in the city.

Crimea, Luhansk, Donetsk: You could think that those "territories" have been forgotten since 2014. Well, you can forget territories but you can't forget people. My brother-in-law is from Donetsk. My best friend from university is from Crimea. Our church friends are from Luhansk. They've been separated from their homes or even family members for years! I'm longing for the day when we will be able to visit those places again.

Day 19 · March 14

I want the world to know and remember the name of this city – Mariupol.

It could be known as the tenth-largest city in Ukraine, a center for the grain trade, metallurgy, and heavy engineering. It could be known for its resorts, parks, and notable people. But today the world must know it as the epicenter of war crimes of Putin's army.

The city with a population of over 400,000 people has been under siege for over two weeks. The Russian army is specifically targeting hiding places of women and children – a Maternity hospital (on March 9) and theater (on

March 16) are just the two most prominent examples, but there are hundreds of them!

Constant shelling, nonstop bombing, artillery attacks on cars trying to escape this hell. No electricity and no heat. People cooking food over fires. No water supply. People melting snow and taking water from puddles in the street. Children dying from dehydration. An attempt to exterminate a nation. Genocide. Those seem to be horror stories of WWII, but unfortunately, they are taking place in Ukraine, in the heart of Europe, right now.

Day 21 · March 16

Our internet connection was down for most of the day but thankfully we managed to find a way to have a cell phone reception. What does it mean? We're still in a "relatively safe" location, but for the whole day we were cut off from the news reports, communication with our friends and family, and we weren't even able to get air-raid warnings on the phone app (but my sister faithfully kept us updated on those). It felt as if God wanted us to fully rely on Him. He reminded me that He is in control even when I don't check the news and that He is capable of knowing who needs help even when I can't be very specific in my prayers.

Day 23 · March 18

I don't know how much you know about WWII, but we grew up listening to many first-hand accounts, and it is horrifying to see so many similarities today.

Back in school, as we were memorizing all the dates in our history class, I would always make mental notes which of my relatives were born before or after the war. My son was born in 2014, as Russia was starting the first stage of the war. Will his children and grandchildren also be making similar mental notes when they study about this war years after it ends?

I was born 43 years after the end of WWII, yet it was still fresh in the memories of my grandparents. My grandmother always made sure she had some nonperishables stocked up in her home – because you never know what may happen tomorrow. She would often wish others "a peaceful sky". I always thought it was a cliche or "an old lady thing", but now I know that would be my wish to all those I love.

I remember one summer in middle school. There was a wedding or another celebration in my small town, and they decided to fire fireworks at midnight. It was the first time I saw fireworks, and I was so excited, I loved it. I remember hearing my grandmother and a few other old ladies talking to each other in the morning, saying they woke up in terror as they thought those were bombs. My friends and I thought it was such a silly statement, so we laughed... Today, we listen to every unusual noise – car doors slammed, loud engine noise from a block away, airplane sound. And I hope and pray no one would ever want to fire fireworks at midnight...

On the other side of the family, my great-grandmother was 22 when WWII came to her home. The Nazis took her and other young people from her village captive – they were to become "Ostarbeiters", slaves to perform forced labor in Germany. She worked in an underground factory somewhere in the Alps. She didn't really like talking about those days unless my mom asked her specific questions. It seemed so distant to me... Today, we read about people from Mariupol forcibly being deported to economically depressed cities in Russia with no right to leave for at least two years, with the obligation to work at the specified place of work. Does it sound familiar? Does it still sound too distant?

There are so many other similarities because even though the Soviet Union ultimately fought the Nazis, its "victory" was also a stepping stone to occupation and oppression. After all, communism was as great a threat. The Baltic states and Poland are some of the most faithful allies of Ukraine today because their memory is still too fresh.

Day 25 · March 20

Mariupol, Chernihiv, and Avdiivka (in Donetsk region) seem to be in the most need today, but there are dozens of towns (big and small) that suffer every day.

Pray for people in temporarily occupied parts of Ukraine (south of Kherson and Zaporizhzhia regions, parts of Luhansk, Donetsk, Sumy, Chernihiv, and Kyiv regions) – people are suffering inhumane treatment there, including pro-Ukrainian activists being kidnapped and tortured.

People who are trying to evacuate need to do so under constant shelling. Today, they shelled a bus that was evacuating children from Mariupol, and this is not the only case.

Pray for all the wounded (both servicemen and civilians) to be able to get the medical care they need and to receive supernatural healing from the Lord.

Pray for the Lord's blessing on all agricultural activities in Ukraine – the time is coming near when they will need to plant the fields. The enemy is trying to ruin those plans by mining the fields, destroying the equipment and storage facilities. Agriculture is an essential part of Ukraine's economy, and if the enemy succeeds, food shortage can become a severe problem not only for Ukraine but also for our trade partners.

We've been in this active state of war for 26 days, and we're getting exhausted (both physically and emotionally) - pray for supernatural strength and the end of this horrible war.

Day 26 · March 21

Every day, before going to bed, I write my daily update here. Sometimes I feel like I am running out of words. Sometimes I think that I shouldn't describe all the horrible things that are happening in my country. Sometimes I'm afraid that we're getting overly used to the terrors of war. Most of the time I want to share the good news, share answers to our prayers but then I wonder if I wouldn't be painting too bright of a picture...

Day 29 · March 24

Did you know that a strong wind sometimes sounds like a fighter jet? I never thought about it until now, when every gust makes you hold your breath and listen.

Today, we were talking with Ivan Kapitonov about how our perception of war changed over the past 31 days. We still care; we are still appalled by what's going on yet we're getting used to it. The reports of new missile hits no longer cause panic but rather a quick evaluation of whether any of our loved ones are in immediate danger and a prayer for God's protection over those who are.

My friend messaged me this evening with the traditional question, "How are you?" My response surprised me, "Praise God, nothing has changed". Could it be a proper response to God's command, "Be still, and know that I am God" (Psalm 46:10)?

Day 31 · March 26

When Hope Felt Distant

A season to cool: *Winter buries the memory of the hopes that we had planted with our tulip bulbs.*

The nightmare continues. The war in Ukraine is not a hot news topic anymore. It is so easy to get discouraged, which is why I choose to praise God for every small and wonderful thing He does!
Day 9 · March 4

As we pray, as we read news reports, as we hear from our friends and loved ones, I want to cry out, "How long, O Lord? Will you forget me forever? How long will you hide your face from me?" (Psalm 13:1)

But then I read His promise just a few verses before: "I will now arise," says the Lord; "I will place him in the safety for which he longs" (Psalm 12:5).
Day 15 · March 10

An apartment building in Kyiv was damaged. It's about a mile away from homes of my friends and family.

I don't want my page to be filled with pictures of destruction. I want my page to be filled with hope. But this is the reality we're living in.
Day 19 · March 14

It seems that I have passed the stage of grief, I have even passed the stage of hatred. All I can do now is pray for deliverance and divine justice of the One who says, "It is mine to avenge; I will repay" (Deuteronomy 32:35 NIV).
Day 21 · March 16

There are more and more reports about the inhumane treatment of people on temporarily occupied territories. Kidnapping, rape, tortures, terrorism, deportation to Russia... Today, they formed groups that inspect libraries and bookstores in the occupied cities and burn all Ukrainian history books as well as "ideologically wrong" books from their blacklists. Are there people who still doubt the purpose of this war? It's not about geopolitics or resources. It is an attempt to exterminate Ukrainians as a nation and erase our history and language.

Day 29 · March 24

Pray for our cities. Just as I am writing this, there are reports of explosions in Kyiv, Kharkiv, Zhytomyr, Lutsk, and Rivne (the latter three being hundreds of miles away from where the fighting takes place). Pray for God to guard our hearts and minds in Him. Every family in Ukraine has been affected by the war. We experience loss and grief, and oftentimes they transform into bitterness and hatred. May God cleanse us and give us His mercy and grace.

Day 32 · March 27

35 days of the war.

The shock wears off, the pain settles in, the intensity and speed of the invasion decrease but we know that the beast isn't defeated and is still bringing death and destruction (and is capable of bringing even more).

I cried a lot during the first two weeks. I almost don't cry now. As I read news reports and hear stories from people I know, I feel numb inside and only beg God for His deliverance and justice.

Knowing even this little bit about the horrible things that are taking place in my country today, would I be able to be obedient to God if He told me to go and prophecy repentance in Russia? I don't know. Do I want God to be merciful to them? I don't know. If I am completely honest, I'd say I would follow Jonah.

Day 35 · March 30

We may be in a relatively safe location, but our hearts are at the frontlines. We may not have much and that's why we generously share what we have with those in greater need. We feel helpless against the enemy and that's why we're doing the impossible in supporting each other and keeping the enemy at bay. We desperately want to live while they are trying to kill us. We are swamped with horrible news reports and that's why we persevere in prayer and find hope even in the darkest of times.

Day 36 · March 31

Defiance in the Face of Aggression

A season to grow: *In spite of the sometimes-returning onslaughts of fading winter, tulips start growing below the surface. This is a time of defiance and hope.*

They say that it's Putin's army fighting for him, but it is God and all of our Ukrainian nation fighting on our side. "What then shall we say to these things? If God is for us, who can be against us?" (Romans 8:31).

Day 7 · March 2

Many cities are in ruins. I saw a picture from Kharkiv today. I've been there only once, yet my heart aches for this city. When I look at this picture, the feeling I have is compassion and a strong desire to clean out the debris and start restoration. So, I choose to praise God for giving me these feelings instead of hatred, resentment and fear.

We visited a local volunteer hub today. Dozens of women were calmly doing what they can – cooking, bringing supplies, making masking nets for the army. Yes, they are quiet and concerned, but they are also resolved. I choose to praise God for these examples of solidarity.

Day 9 · March 4

In Kyiv, a lady threw a jar of pickles from her balcony to knock down an enemy drone, and succeeded.

One of the combatants was helping evacuate children from the war zone. As he was carrying a young girl to a safe place, she was hugging him and repeating over and over again "I love you, Ukrainian soldier. I love you so much!"

The picture below is what struck me today. People were trying to evacuate from Irpin. The Russians blew up the bridge and sent airplanes to bomb

Taking refuge under a destroyed bridge in Irpin. - Day 10, March 5, 2022

the city. People are taking refuge under the remains of the bridge and our defenders shield them by standing in front of them.

Day 10 · March 5

My thoughts run from devastating pain for the atrocities of the war to hopeful joy at every small answered prayer...

• there are a few locations where people are running out of food and are unable to evacuate because of constant shelling YET we (and most of our close friends, as far as we know) lived through another day and had food and water,

• 38 children have been killed in this war (as of this morning) YET our counter-air defense shot down two missiles aimed at the main children's hospital in Kyiv,

• they continue bombing peaceful cities YET we receive many reports about bombs landing without explosions,

• they feed lies and propaganda through Russian TV and media YET the truth can't be silenced. We dearly cherish our friends from Russia (and other oppressive countries that favor Putin's regime) who stand with us and do what they can – we pray for your protection every day!

•   Western governments take their time deciding whether they should help or stay out of it YET we have enormous support from ordinary people and we have God shielding our sky.

Day 11 • March 6

17 days ago, Russia started a full-scale war against Ukraine.

Here are the bits of conversations I had with my son today (he doesn't have free access to TV or internet resources, so we make sure he is shielded from brutality).

Mom, the news showed a house on
fire and its roof collapsing.
Is it in Ukraine?

Yes, my dear.

Mom, I want to pray the same
happens to them.

Do you want the same to happen
to homes in Russia?

No, I want the same to happen to
the spirit of those who caused it.

Mom, you know, the Bible teaches us
that we should love our enemies.

Yes, dear, you're right,
but it's not always easy.

Mom, let's pray for their repentance.
Their eyes are covered with lies as if
with tar. If their eyes see the truth,
I'm sure they would repent. I know God
wants them to be saved.

I'm sure He does.

Mom, do you remember that I want
to build robots when I grow up?

Of course, how can I forget?
You talk about it every day.

Mom, if Russia doesn't stop, does it
mean I would have to build killer robots?
Russia seems to like killing people,
but I don't want my robots to kill...

Don't worry, dear,
Russia will not win.

There were more conversations that just pierce my heart. I am blessed to know that my son has such a gentle loving spirit, and I am ready to do whatever it takes to protect him from the horrible reality Russia wants to throw us into.

And so, I pick up the weapon of childlike faith and prayer, and I will keep praising God for His faithfulness:

Day 18 · March 13

I can't leave, at least for now. The pain of my people is my pain, and it is easier to bear it when you are in their midst. That is why every day I intercede for my people and my country.

Day 19 · March 14

They say it takes 21 days to make something into a habit. It is the 22nd day of war yet it still feels wrong and foreign, and I'm glad it does. It means we're not completely numb and we'll keep on fighting.

Day 23 · March 18

Please, KEEP PRAYING for Mariupol, Kharkiv, Izum, Chernihiv, Mykolaiv as hundreds of thousands of people remain there and face hell every day.

We are blessed that our air-defense system and fighter pilots keep our cities safe (they shot down 4 missile rockets aimed at Kyiv and downed 4 Russian planes). In Hlukhiv, they found a missile rocket that didn't explode – praise God! Please, KEEP PRAYING for God to be a shield over Ukrainian sky especially as people go to bed for the night.

According to US army officials, they are impressed with how well our army uses Javelins. They say it's 100 hits out of 112 fired and that's better than American records (in training; not in the field!) – it is an answer to our daily prayers for God to guide our soldiers. Please, KEEP PRAYING for the Lord's protection over our soldiers, for supernatural strength and endurance, and for God's blessing on their hearts.

Yesterday I shared a story about an airfield in Kherson region where our army has repeatedly destroyed Russian helicopters that keep coming to the same location. They did it again today. They say it's been six successful events so far. You can add to this story an episode with a pontoon bridge that the Russian army was trying to construct. They tried four times in the same location, and every time our army was successfully preventing it. Please, KEEP PRAYING for the confusion of the enemy army.

There are numerous reports about the soldiers in the Russian army being demoralized, deserting their positions, refusing being deployed to Ukraine. Please, KEEP PRAYING the Lord crushes their spirit and makes them flee in terror as they realize what they're doing here.

Day 23 · March 18

As I pray for God's protection for our nation, I often ask Him to turn enemy plans against themselves and to cause enemy weapons to malfunction. Yesterday, learning about more missile strikes on our land, I prayed "God, let their missiles explode where they are fired!" That's how I felt, yet I also perceived it as a figure of speech. Today I read a report from the airfield in Kherson region (the same one where our aviation destroyed enemy forces 7 times!). The Russians wanted to shoot down our aircraft so they launched an air-defense rocket which took off, but then just fell back to the ground hitting their machinery and causing a massive fire. God knew that I needed His reassurance and gave such a specific answer today!

As I saw a video of a man playing cello in Kharkiv square amid the war, I found it very fitting. Even during the war, there's room for music, art, beauty, and hope.

Day 27 · March 22

All military experts expected Ukraine to be defeated in the first 24-72 hours. Now, 672 hours have passed, yet Ukraine keeps fighting. How is it possible? Ask the One who turned water into wine, fed thousands with five loaves of bread, calmed the storm, and rose from the dead. After all, He Himself said, "With man this is impossible, but with God all things are possible" (Matthew 19:26).

By God's grace, we see the enemy troops surrendering or fleeing (in Sumy they reported about Russian units turning around and refusing to go to war), we see them making mistakes (remember that airfield in Kherson region successfully attacked by our army nine times), we see nature preventing them from fulfilling their plans (during the first days of war, the invaders blew up a dam on Irpin river and now the river is flooding which pushes them further away from Kyiv).

However, our enemy is strong, aggressive, and has no moral standards. That's why we must persevere in prayer.

Looking back, I realize that these 28 days have created an insurmountable difference in our lives. Yet I praise God who remains unchanged, for He is yesterday, and today, and forever the same.

Day 28 · March 23

People in temporarily occupied cities keep showing up for peaceful protests. The media reported about people who were forcefully deported to occupied Donetsk to be used in the recording of a propaganda video footage. However, the plan failed because in the morning they discovered "Glory to Ukraine" inscriptions on the places where these people were kept. God is faithful in strengthening the spirit of our people!

I hear from my non-Ukrainian friends in different countries who are volunteering and helping refugees. God is faithful in opening the hearts of people and taking care of his children wherever they are!

Pray for people in Russia. Some of my dear friends are from Russia or currently in Russia, and they know the truth. They are devastated by what's going on, and they do what they can to fight it. May God comfort, encourage, guide them, and keep them safe. I am standing with you, my dear friends, just as you stand with us. Please, also pray for God to open the eyes of those who refuse to see what's going on, may He change their hearts of stone and bring them to repentance.

Day 32 · March 27

We choose life. We choose hope. We choose faith. How else would you explain that starting tomorrow they will reopen some of the theaters and concert halls and relaunch a bike rental service in Kyiv? How would you explain the fact that municipal workers in Kharkiv (that's been severely bombed day after day) prepare their parks for spring by planting flowers in flowerbeds?

Day 36 · March 31

Celebration, While Aware of the Costs

A season to bloom: *The crowning season for the tulips arrives as their flowers reach to the sky. But celebration is vulnerable — the tulip has used huge amounts of the bulb's resources in the hope of future goodness.*

Thank you for your prayers! Last night I felt overwhelmed but today God refreshed my spirit and gave me confidence in His victory (as David said in Psalm 30:5: "For his anger is but for a moment, and his favor is for a lifetime. Weeping may tarry for the night, but joy comes with the morning.")

We see so many testimonies. There are broken families reconciling and coming together, supporting each other in the face of danger. Many people giving their lives to Christ, one man getting baptized right in his bathtub. Thousands if not millions of people are reaching out, offering help, covering us with prayers, "standing in the breach" for our nation. There are bombs and missiles not reaching their targets. Some enemy landing operations failing due to natural causes (air landing troops literally "gone with the wind" back to the enemy territory, sea storm flipping their boats, snowstorm clouding their vision for airstrikes). Our people are standing strong despite the atrocities — we mourn every single life that was lost and promise to make sure it was not in vain. The spirit of the enemy army being crushed, and they surrender or leave when they see the resistance of even unarmed people (unfortunately, a few unarmed civilians were brutally killed in the process, but this did not disperse the crowd but made it even more resolved). An 82-year-old man (born in 1939) from my hometown donating over $13,000 to the army (who knew he had such savings and was willing to give them away!).

Day 7 · March 2

"I will give thanks to the Lord with my whole heart; I will recount all of your wonderful deeds" (Psalm 9:1). Three hundred ninety babies were born in Kyiv over the past eight days. I choose to praise God for this new life, and I believe He will be faithful in taking care of these little ones. Two enemy tank groups destroyed each other with a "friendly fire". I choose to praise God for confusing the enemy and saving innocent lives. The Russian army bombed the city of Pokrovsk (Donetsk region) with cluster bombs. They caused a lot of damage, but I choose to praise God for at least two cluster bombs that did not explode. It may seem like too little but I know that even one life is precious so I will praise God for this.

Day 9 · March 4

Today, they shot down two planes and a few missile rockets aimed at Kyiv. Can you imagine how many lives were spared? I know that God is in control, and He is the one shielding our sky and homes. I know that I can trust Him.

We read numerous reports about the enemy army being demoralized. Tonight, they reported that since the beginning of war, over 2,000 Russian soldiers surrendered or were taken captive. I praise God for lives spared.

Our army reports about the enemy falling into many traps, and I know that it is an answer to our prayers for their confusion. I know that God is faithful.

Day 13 · March 8

God sends cold weather, snow, and a strong wind making it impossible for the Russians to attack from the sea, so all of their ships retreat.

My friends from YWAM Kyiv who are actively serving people in Kyiv keep testifying about God's miracles. They were running out of supplies, but they accidentally ran into the director of the pasta factory at a store, so now they have 1,000 kilos of pasta that will be cooked and served to hundreds of people in Kyiv and neighboring villages.

Every day, we have so many people from around the world praying for our nation, sending us words of encouragement, sharing their love with us. We are beyond blessed.

Day 16 · March 11

According to the State Emergency Service, about one third of missiles and bombs fired at Ukraine do not explode. An interrogated POW reported that 600 Russian marines refused to attack Odesa. Due to cold weather, whole groups of Russian soldiers surrender in hopes to get food and a warm place to stay. During daytime, as the temperature rises, soil and dirt roads turn into mud literally swallowing up Russian machines.

Day 18 · March 13

Here are the answers to our prayers that were found in news reports today:

Russian forces couldn't attack Bilohorodka (Kyiv region) because of an ancient fortification wall that's been there since the day of Kyivan Rus (10-11th century). I praise God for preparing our means of defense a thousand years in advance!

Mariupol remains under siege for twelve days. They didn't let humanitarian aid into the city, but they were able to deliver food and supplies for the army stationed there. Ukrainian soldiers chose to share their portions with local civilians. Of course, it's not enough for everyone but I praise God that He finds ways to provide. I praise God for the love and compassion that came forth in this dire time of need.

A group of Russian soldiers (about ten people) surrendered in Mariupol, yes, the same city that's sieged by Russians. I praise God for crushing their spirit even in positions where they seem to prevail. There are numerous reports about soldiers in Belarus and Russia refusing to go to Ukraine despite promised benefits. I praise God for stopping them where they are.

Russian forces shot down their own investigation drone in Kharkiv region. I praise God for confusing their minds.

Our God is a God of miracles.

Day 19 · March 14

Ukrainian Genesis[iii]

And there was morning and there was evening, the twenty-second day. And the Ukrainians stood on their land, and didn't let the horde in.

And it was difficult for them, they lacked strength.

And they cried out to God, "Lord, how long shall we stand until our victory? We have been standing for twenty-two days! Every day we lose our people, property and strength."

And God said to them, "Do not lose faith. Because with faith you survived two world wars, Holodomor and terror. You won on the Maidan with faith. You will win today. Your sacrifices are not in vain – you save the world from darkness. My punishment will fall on the tyrant, he will pay for the death of the innocent.

And you will live in peace, joy and love."

Our prayers work!

Yesterday Russians threw a heavy bomb on a drama theater in Mariupol. About 1,000 women and children were hiding in its bomb shelter. They specifically targeted civilians and intended maximum damage.

But God is good! Today, as they cleared the debris, they discovered that the bomb shelter withstood the bombing and lives of women and children were spared.

It doesn't mean that there were no victims but even in the midst of tragedy, God shows His power. Glory be to God!

Day 22 · March 17

The bomb shelter in Mariupol drama theater withstood the heavy bombing and they were able to rescue people from under the debris. Please, keep them in your prayers. There were about 1,000 women and children there, not all of them have been rescued so far as the enemy army keeps shelling and bombing the city.

About 3,000 people were able to leave Mariupol today. Please, keep praying as about 300,000 remain in the city. There's been no luck in organizing safe evacuation or bringing humanitarian aid because of constant shelling.

One of the cities got an air-raid warning during our prayer meeting so we stopped right there and prayed for God's shield over that region. In a couple of hours, we read that our air-defense forces shot down two missile rockets. God is good! Please, keep praying none of their missiles and bombs reach the targets and explode.

Two fun stories. There's an airfield in a small village in the temporarily occupied part of Kherson region. A few days ago, Russian forces brought about two dozen helicopters there. Our army successfully destroyed them. In a few hours, they did the same thing, and our army destroyed them again. Today, it happened for the fourth time. Please keep praying the Lord stops the enemy in the way He chooses.

The second story took place on our fertile Ukrainian soil. Two Russian tanks got stuck in the field. They sent two more tanks to get them out but they also got stuck. Now, there were four tanks stuck in the middle of the field and the Russian soldiers had to abandon them and flee. Please, keep praying for God to confuse the enemy army, blind their eyes, make them flee in fear.

Day 23 · March 18

Late at night, there was a breakthrough in our internet connection, and I was able to check the news. And in the midst of horrible and devastating news reports, I still see God's faithfulness. "My mouth will tell of your righteous acts, of your deeds of salvation all the day, for their number is past my knowledge" (Psalm 71:15). Almost 5,000 people (including 1,000 children) were able to evacuate from Mariupol. A total of 9,145 people were able to leave dangerous locations today.

Day 23 · March 18

I often quote Romans 8:31: "If God is for us, who can be against us?" I don't think I fully realized the extent of this statement until I read a report about a Russian plane that was brought down by wild geese. It happened yesterday in Kherson region. The bird(s?) flew right into the plane's engine causing it to crash in a swamp. Did it happen by chance or was it orchestrated by the Almighty Creator of all? It is up to you to decide. As for me, I will say, "Great and amazing are your deeds, O Lord God the Almighty!" (Revelation 15:3).

Day 24 · March 19

Even though Russia keeps attacking more and more cities in Ukraine, our air-defense forces shoot down their rockets and fighter jets. Today, they fired four missile rockets on Rivne region, and three of them were shot down, which means hundreds of lives were saved. Praise be to God!

Remember that airfield in Kherson region where our military forces have successfully destroyed enemy helicopters several times before? It happened for the seventh time today! May God continue confusing the enemy!

In the last 24 hours, in Kyiv, they detained 149 saboteurs and enemy collaborators and neutralized ten explosive objects. May God cleanse our cities from all enemy forces and keep ruining all schemes of the enemy!

Eight thousand people (including 3,000 from Mariupol) were able to evacuate today from dangerous locations. I praise God for every life that was rescued today.

This morning, the Russian army shelled a plant in Sumy, destroying a tank with ammonia. It could have caused massive chemical poisoning in the city. However, the wind sent this cloud away from the city (ironically, sending it in the direction of the Russian border), minimizing the threat and making it easier to neutralize it. I will praise Him "who forms the mountains and creates the wind, and declares to man what is his thought, who makes the morning darkness, and treads on the heights of the earth– the Lord, the God of hosts, is his name!" (Amos 4:13).

Day 26 · March 21

As I was praying this morning, I felt desperate and was begging God to show His power. And He heard my plea. Yes, the war continues, the atrocities continue, more and more locations are shelled or hit with missiles. But God is good. Today, He showed me His love by showing me very specific answers to my prayers:

We have been praying for the besieged city of Mariupol for weeks. Hundreds of thousands of people are still trapped there. But today we heard from our dear friend that her loved ones managed to leave Mariupol and are on their way to their "relatively safe" location. Another friend wrote today that he got a message from his family in Mariupol that they're fine – he hadn't heard from them in 22 days! Those are true miracles even if just for a few people!

The Russians keep attacking our cities with missile rockets that cause colossal damage. Often, our air-defense forces can shoot them down but even the fragments cause serious damage as they fall to the ground. I was praying for God to divert all missiles and their fragments so that more lives would be spared. Today, they shot down a missile rocket that was aimed at Kyiv and its fragments fell into the Dnipro River. Yes, it was just one rocket, but it is such a vivid answer to the prayers!

Day 26 · March 22

Today, I read at least three stories from three different people at the front lines sharing how God saved them when they were in immediate danger (they all got a sudden urge to shelter or change the location of their group right before the attack). May God keep each of our defenders safe and show His power and mercy to them!

Remember that airfield in Kherson region I keep telling you about? It sounds ridiculous and I know it's hard to believe, but our forces made yet another (tenth!) hit on Russian positions in the same location. It's likely that large amounts of ammunition were destroyed. May God keep confusing the enemy.

Day 29 · March 24

Last night, Russia simultaneously launched a record number of 70 missile rockets, but only 8 of them hit ground targets! God is faithful in shielding our sky!

Day 32 · March 27

A small miracle happened to us yesterday. God helped us get our summer tires that were left in a storage facility in Kyiv. Its owner happened to be going past the place where we are staying and offered to bring them to us. It's exciting to see how God works even in small things. Russians accidentally shot down their own plane. Let God send more "friendly fire." The Russians blocked one of the roads in Kyiv region with landmines but our people managed to drive in-between these landmines and come out unharmed. May God protect our people and ruin all the evil schemes.

On the first day of the war, the Russians took over Chornobyl. They also went on tanks across the whole Chornobyl exclusion zone (the most radioactively contaminated area in the world since the disaster in 1986) without any sort of protection. For days our experts kept saying that it's not safe as they disturb radioactive dust and will suffer permanent damage. But they didn't listen and decided to set up a camp there and even started digging trenches in the Red Forest (the waste graveyard). As a result, the special hospitals in Belarus are filled with patients with symptoms of radiation sickness. Today, the Russians left the Chornobyl Nuclear Power Plant. We believe it was an answer to our prayers and we hope our nuclear power plants will not be under immediate threat anymore.

Our army keeps pushing the enemy horde away. Today, they liberated eleven formerly occupied villages in Kherson region (south) as well as some territories in the north and south of Ukraine. May God bless and protect our armed forces.

An unlikely story (short of Biblical miracle) took place in Kherson region last week. I hesitated sharing it because it seemed too wild but it looks like it has been verified. In one of the villages, a swarm of bees attacked a group of Russian soldiers. Three soldiers died from the stings and 25 were taken to the hospital. Indeed, if the Lord of all creation is for us, who can be against?

Day 36 · March 31

Loss and Lament

A season to regenerate: *Far too quickly are the days of the beautiful flowers gone. The tulip begins to replenish its stores under the ground. This stage is not lovely to look at, but if the stage is cut short, tulips are at risk of dying.*

There won't be a long post today. As we go to bed in a "relatively safe" location, Kyiv and other cities are heavily bombed in attempt to level them with the ground. If you ever need to learn about war crimes, we see plenty of them.

Today, I felt overwhelmed with pain for my country, our people, our children... I felt weary. But God didn't abandon me.

Day 6 · March 1

I've never prayed so much or so hard in my life as in the last week. You read every news report, every message from a friend, and breathe a prayer of thanksgiving or supplication. Today God urged me to pray through Psalm 46:10: "Be still, and know that I am God. I will be exalted among the nations, I will be exalted in the earth!"

So, I try to do my best and be still in Him.

Please, keep praying for us. Here is a picture of a bomb that got stuck between the floors and did not explode. I choose to praise God for this miracle despite the horrible news coming from all over my country.

Our God is the God of miracles and wonders.

Day 8 (to tell the truth, all days are blurring together by now) · March 2

So many praise reports and a lot of heartbreaking news. Sometimes I feel numb and exhausted, but get overwhelmed in just a moment...

Day 11 · March 6

A bomb stuck in the floor - Day 8, March 2, 2022

Today Russian army bombed a children's hospital and maternity ward in Mariupol. They are completely destroyed (I am not posting pictures on purpose but it's easy to find them on internet). Yet I will rejoice in the Lord – they reported no killed and seventeen wounded. It's unthinkable but God is good.

They bombed a clinic and a children's hospital in Zhytomyr. Yet I will rejoice in the Lord – no one was killed or wounded.

Tonight, my son asked me if we'll ever come back home and I told him I can't answer this question. Yet I will rejoice in the Lord – we are alive and relatively safe.

Day 14 • March 9

What makes me concerned more and more, is the aftermath of this war. As it's getting closer and closer, as it's getting more and more personal, I'm wondering if we will be able to come out of it and keep our humanity.

It scares me when I watch videos of a captive Russian soldiers talking to his mother on the phone, and the mother calmly says, "Too bad you're captive, you should have been more careful in your assignment." Don't they have a heart even for their own children?

It scares me when a captive Russian soldier reports that they were given orders to kill civilians and kill their own if anyone dares not to shoot. Who would give such orders? How would you justify it?

It scares me that we will get used to these horrible things, or we will get resentful. If we get dehumanized, would it mean that the Enemy wins?

Day 15 · March 10

The Russians have destroyed at least 200 schools, 30 hospitals, eight churches, 1,600 residential buildings, nineteen administrative buildings, 23 factories/warehouses, twelve airports, five power stations. They also ruined 15,000 kilometers of roads, 5,000 kilometers of railway, 350 bridges.

The number of civilians killed during the war is much higher than the total number of Ukraine's personnel losses for all military units. It shows that Russia started this war with the intent to kill us as a nation. A genocide taking place in the heart of Europe in 2022! Twenty-four children were born in besieged Mariupol over the past 24 hours.

Day 16 · March 11

Twentieth day of war...

I try not to think about everything this war has stolen (even if temporarily) but I choose to look for things it has given me.

The war has stolen our sense of security and ever so faint confidence in tomorrow. But we learn to trust each other and put our trust in God and ask Him for His "peace which surpasses all understanding".

The war has ruined our plans and dreams (last week I was to start a course in non-fiction translation, and next week we would have been starting another year of the School of Biblical Studies at YWAM Kyiv SBS) – but we learn what it means to not only say, "If the Lord wills, we will live and do this or that," but actually do it. We also learn that not all of our plans are that important and that we are capable of dreaming even bigger dreams than ever before.

The war has stolen our homes and amenities. But we learn how little we actually need – just to be with our loved ones and to know that they are safe.

The war keeps stealing innocent lives. Those will not be forgotten. There is nothing that can make it right. It's not something you can repair. But we learn to value what we have. We learn to appreciate each other and not to hold grudges. We also learn to share in the pain of others.

Day 20 · March 15

Unfortunately, the war continues and brings more death and devastation. Over 50 civilians were killed in Chernihiv today. Numerous cities and small villages are attacked from the air. Large fires were caused by shelling in Kyiv and Kharkiv. We cry out, "How long, o Lord?"

Today, I feel like lamenting before the Lord. I'm so thankful He can bear our questions and complaints, I'm so thankful He does not reject us when we do it, but instead He comforts us in our grief and helps us remember His faithfulness. I know that it's okay to cry before the Lord as long as it is to Him that we come and as long as we seek Him. My today's lament comes from Psalm 22:

> ✣ My God, my God, why have you forsaken me?
> Why are you so far from saving me, from the words of my groaning?
> O my God, I cry by day, but you do not answer, and by night,
> but I find no rest.

> ✣ But you, O Lord, do not be far off!
> O you my help, come quickly to my aid!
> I will tell of your name to my brothers;
> in the midst of the congregation I will praise you:
> ✣ For he has not despised or abhorred the affliction of the afflicted,
> and he has not hidden his face from him, but has heard, when he
> cried to him.

> ✣ All the ends of the earth shall remember and turn to the Lord,
> and all the families of the nations shall worship before you.

✎ For kingship belongs to the Lord, and he rules over the nations.
(Psalm 22:1-2, 19, 22, 24, 27-28)
Day 23 · March 18

As I read the news today, I realized there didn't seem to be anything big to report. The Russian army keeps destroying our homes, killing our people, bombing and shelling our cities... Our army stands strong and brave fighting the enemy, and our whole nation joins them with every fiber of our being.

In images we can see the pain through art. I was struck by "Stolen lives" by Sasha Anisimova, from Kharkiv; and another image in which 109 empty strollers in Lviv downtown stand for 109 children killed since the beginning of the war.
Day 24 · March 19

When it's quiet, no air-raid warnings, no distant sounds of explosion... When the sky is deep blue and cloudless... When the spring sun brings first waves of warmth... When you are laughing with your friends... When you enjoy a meal with your family... When you read to your child at bedtime... When life seems normal... That's when it strikes you really hard. That's when you realize that your life will never be normal, "as before." That's when you get overwhelmed because you suddenly start appreciating these small things you used to take for granted. And you feel guilty enjoying them because you know that there are those who don't have them now or have lost them forever. Could it be that the disciples of Jesus had similar feelings before Jesus appeared to them in the upper room? I don't know.
Day 26 · March 21

I saw a picture of devastation from Krasylivka, a small beautiful, peaceful town east of Kyiv. May God raise it from the ashes and comfort those whose lives were destroyed.
Day 26 · March 21

Mariupol, Chernihiv, Izum, Avdiivka (along with other towns in Luhansk and Donetsk regions), Kyiv suburbs... These cities are our raw wounds. We pray for miraculous deliverance for everyone who remains there. May God stop the destruction and drive the enemy out of our land!
Day 29 · March 24

Thirty days of the war...

It's not just a popular thing to say that we don't know what date it is but we know which day of the war it is. It's actually true for most people I know.

Over and over again I think back to eight years ago when Russia annexed Crimea and the war broke out in the east. Even with a newborn, the war was at the forefront of my mind back then. I remember waves of refugees (or rather "internally displaced persons"), fundraisers for the army needs, grief for those who lost their lives... Looking back, I keep thinking that we could have done more but perhaps we felt too secure and comfortable being separated from the war by the distance. Do we fully experience it now? Do we really experience what Jeremiah described as "Since my people are crushed, I am crushed; I mourn, and horror grips me" (Jeremiah 8:21 NIV)? I know that even staying in the country amid war I can still be unaware of the depth of the pain my people are going through.

So tonight, I will be crushed and mourn with those whose loved ones will forever stay under the ruins of cities destroyed by Russian bombs. I will be crushed and mourn with those who can't get in touch with their family members and can only pray for a miracle. I will be crushed and mourn with those who had to be uprooted twice and who had to flee from the hands of Russians for the second time. I will be crushed and mourn with those who lost their precious children (both born and unborn) to war. I will be crushed and mourn with those who remain in besieged cities and witness hell on earth. I will be crushed and mourn with those who managed to escape that hell yet are haunted by their experience. I will be crushed and mourn for the orphans, widows, and all "underprivileged" who are left at God's mercy with no one to take care of them. I will be crushed and mourn with those who were forcefully deported from their land by the Russians. I will be crushed and mourn with those who feel desperate and helpless. I will be crushed and mourn in repentance for failing to properly do it before.

Day 30 · March 25

There are so many things that used to be a part of that other, "pre-war" life.

We used to watch movies on Netflix. In the past 33 days, my husband and I haven't been able to watch even one episode of our favorite TV series. It feels wrong.

We used to read books. Now, I only read books to my son. I don't have the mental capacity to focus on a storyline that's not connected to the current war or people who are dear to me.

We used to have hobbies and regular jobs. I used to do written translations as a side job. About two weeks into the war, someone asked me to translate a document for them. As I pulled my laptop out of my "emergency backpack" and turned it on, I was triggered on so many levels! It was something from my "previous life", something that brought forth memories of so many things that we had to leave behind...

There are millions of "ordinary" things that we used to do that are paused, that are put "on hold" until our victory. We will enjoy them again one day, but they just seem too foreign in our new reality.

Yet life goes on. We smile and laugh. We enjoy the warm weather and each other's company. We delight in good coffee and cake. We develop new habits and make jokes about the war. Life has to go on because that's what the Enemy is after. He wants to rob us of our joy, peace, love, and kindness. He wants to crush our spirit, yet it's impossible because "He who is in you is greater than he who is in the world" (1 John 4:4).

Day 33 · March 28

As the Russian forces keep attacking our cities causing massive destructions, we learn about personal stories of people who survived their brutality. In one of Kyiv's suburbs, drunk Russian soldiers shot the man of the house in front of his wife and then repeatedly raped his wife. Her four-year-old son was hiding in the boiler room. When the invaders fell asleep, she took her son and they left the city on foot. In Mariupol, Russian soldiers took turns repeatedly raping a woman in front of her six-year-old son. She died from the wounds. Her son's hair turned completely gray.

Since the start of the full-scale war, 145 children died, over 220 have been wounded. There is no way to calculate the number of kids who lost their parents. Irpin (Kyiv suburbs) was under occupation and is almost completely ruined. The Russian army broke into a ministry center there, made a pile of Bibles and Christian literature and set it on fire.

As the enemy army retreats, they shell and burn down villages and houses along the route. Sometimes they loot houses before burning them down. There was a video clip from one of the villages liberated by our army. They showed a grandma kneeling and crying with gratitude as she saw our soldiers. She lived through WWII as a child. She had to live through this nightmare in her old age.

I am painfully aware that these are just a few stories, and we will never know the full extent of the atrocities of the Russian army.

Day 35 · March 30

We are forced to fight this war, and we will do it with dignity as long as it takes, but we would much rather plant gardens, write books, and create a beautiful future for our children. We choose life. "Oh, continue your steadfast love to those who know you, and your righteousness to the upright of heart! Let not the foot of arrogance come upon me, nor the hand of the wicked drive me away" (Psalm 36:10-11).

Day 36 · March 31

Resilience and the Seeds of Future Hope

A season to multiply: *The tulips begin to multiply and prepare for the following year. This invisible work of resilience is crucial. The commitment to goodness brings life into the world.*

I know that the war is not over.

I know there's still a lot of pain ahead of us, but I am confident that God's mercy is on us and I am eagerly waiting for the day when I would be able to say, "You have turned for me my mourning into dancing; you have loosed my sackcloth and clothed me with gladness" (Psalm 30:11).

Day 7 · March 2

I choose to praise God that He gave us yet another day.

Day 9 · March 4

I think of the end of the war, and Oh, I have so many dreams and plans for that day!

I'm going to praise God and hug my family, my loved ones, my friends who stood with us throughout this time.

I'm going to cry and mourn with those who lost their loved ones.

I'm going to pray for God's healing for the bodies, hearts, and souls of those who had to go through this hell.

I'm going to try to forgive those who were silent when we were begging for help and will remind myself that it is not up to me to judge but all justice belongs to the Lord.

I'm going to honor those who sacrificially defend us today.

I'm going to visit Chernihiv, Sumy, Kharkiv, Izum, Mykolaiv, Mariupol, Kherson, Berdiansk, and the small suburban towns that are in pain today to share in their pain, love them, and help them recover.

I'm going to call all of my friends from all over the world who pray and support us today and invite them to visit our home in Kyiv and enjoy the beautiful country of Ukraine.

I'm not going to forget...

Day 10 · March 5

As we were praying today (it feels like it's the only thing I'm capable of doing these days), God reminded me these verses from the book of Zephaniah: "Behold, at that time I will deal with all your oppressors. And I will save the lame and gather the outcast, and I will change their shame into praise and renown in all the earth. At that time I will bring you in, at the time when I gather you together; for I will make you renowned and praised among all the peoples of the earth, when I restore your fortunes before your eyes, says the Lord" (Zephaniah 3:19-20).

I'm looking forward to the day when God would address these words to my people...

Day 11 · March 6

Tonight, as my seven-year-old son was going to bed, he asked me, "Why did God allow this war?" I know that so many people are asking the same question. I also know that his innocent mind has no idea how much worse it is than what he knows. I know that each one of us will be asking this question again and again.

I did my best to explain to my boy that God didn't want this to happen and He is as grieved as all of us. I reminded him that all of our decisions have consequences and often those consequences affect many people, so it's important to make right choices. We looked at God's blessings even in this horrible time. I also reminded him of the great gift we receive through Jesus and His promise of an eternal dwelling place where He will "wipe away every tear from their eyes, and death shall be no more, neither shall there be mourning, nor crying, nor pain anymore, for the former things have passed away" (Revelation 21:4).

I am sharing these words now not to show off and I'm not asking for praise. I'm sharing them so that once the war is over and life is "back to normal", this post would remind me what really matters.

Day 14 · March 9

Pray for God to hear my son's prayers, for the enemy army to repent, and for the victory to come soon!

Day 18 · March 13

"Give ear to my prayer, O God, and hide not yourself from my plea for mercy! Attend to me, and answer me; I am restless in my complaint and I moan" (Psalm 55:1-2).
"But I call to God, and the Lord will save me" (Psalm 55:16).

Day 19 · March 14

And even if the worse comes to worst, we still can hold on to our greatest hope: "He will dwell with them, and they will be his people, and God himself will be with them as their God. He will wipe away every tear from their eyes, and death shall be no more, neither shall there be mourning, nor crying, nor pain anymore, for the former things have passed away" (Revelation 21:3-4).

Day 20 · March 15

I know that God is at work. I know that He is faithful. I know that it is He who evacuated people from Mariupol (about 30,000 over the past couple of days), Chernihiv, Sumy, Kharkiv, Irpin, Bucha, Hostomel and so many other places. I know that it is He who blinds and confuses the enemy. I know that it is He who gives courage to Russian soldiers to surrender or refuse to go to Ukraine. I know that it is He who opens the hearts of people across the world to pray for us, welcome our refugees, send humanitarian aid, volunteer. It is He who says, "When he calls to me, I will answer him; I will be with him in trouble; I will rescue him and honor him" (Psalm 91:15).
So, I will stand firm on His promises.

Day 21 · March 16

I'm longing for the victorious day when "I will also praise you with the harp for your faithfulness, O my God; I will sing praises to you with the lyre, O Holy One of Israel. My lips will shout for joy, when I sing praises to you; my soul also, which you have redeemed. And my tongue will talk of your righteous help all the day long, for they have been put to shame and disappointed who sought to do me hurt" (Psalm 71:22-24).

Day 23 · March 18

This post may seem a bit too morbid, but let me assure you that we still have hope. When things looked hopeless to Israel, God said, "Remember not the former things, nor consider the things of old. Behold, I am doing a new thing; now it springs forth, do you not perceive it? I will make a way in the wilderness and rivers in the desert" (Isaiah 43:18-19). I believe God can make something new and bring something beautiful out of the ashes again.

As I see my beloved Kyiv on fire again, as I beg God for a miracle for people in Mariupol, Chernihiv, Kharkiv, numerous towns in Donetsk and Luhansk regions, I remind myself of Jeremiah's lament: "The steadfast love of the Lord never ceases; his mercies never come to an end; they are new every morning; great is your faithfulness. 'The Lord is my portion,' says my soul, 'therefore I will hope in him'" (Lamentations 3:22-24).

Day 25 · March 20

But I do know that God is capable of bringing Hope into desperate situations. In Isaiah 61:3-4, He promised Israel "to give them a beautiful headdress instead of ashes, the oil of gladness instead of mourning, the garment of praise instead of a faint spirit; that they may be called oaks of righteousness, the planting of the Lord, that he may be glorified. They shall build up the ancient ruins; they shall raise up the former devastations; they shall repair the ruined cities, the devastations of many generations."

Day 26 · March 21

"I believe that I shall look upon the goodness of the Lord in the land of the living! Wait for the Lord; be strong, and let your heart take courage; wait for the Lord!" (Psalm 27:13-14).

Day 27 · March 22

❧ Yet I will not remain crushed and mournful forever!

❧ I will extol you, O Lord, for you have drawn me up and have not let my foes rejoice over me. You have turned for me my mourning into dancing; you have loosed my sackcloth and clothed me with gladness, that my glory may sing your praise and not be silent.

❧ O Lord my God, I will give thanks to you forever!
(Psalm 30:1, 11-12)

Day 30 · March 25

Tonight, as I was talking with my husband (Ivan Kapitonov), we both agreed that we don't know when the war will end (even though we pray for it to be over soon). We don't know how it will end (even though we pray for our victory). We believe in our victory but we are reasonable enough to admit that we don't know anything about it. And this state when you hope for something yet don't know what's beyond is called faith.

Day 32 · March 27

We can have an abundant life even in the midst of war. It is up to us to choose it. "The thief comes only to steal and kill and destroy. I came that they may have life and have it abundantly" (John 10:10).

Day 33 · March 28

One of the hottest debates I heard over the past couple of days was between village people arguing about whether you should plant flowers in your garden or it's an outrageous thing during the war. These past five weeks seem to be one horrible Thursday that lasts years. Ukrainians seem to be stuck in this sort of limbo, living in two realities at the same time.

Day 36 · March 31

Chapter Three
Burying Seeds
April 1 - May 31, 2022

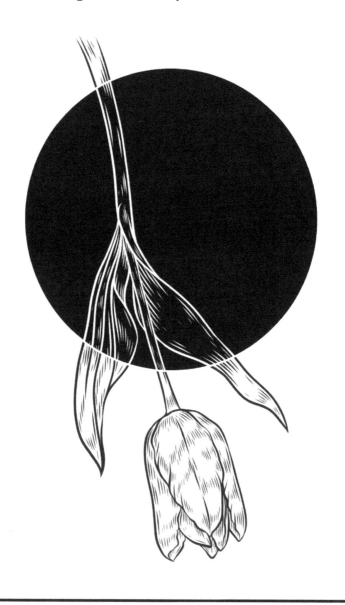

Pray for deep healing for those who were able to get out of hell.

Day 37 • April 1

It seems like there are no words left.

Day 40 • April 4

Do you think it's bad? It gets worse.

Day 62 • April 26

In early March, my friend told me she was reading my daily updates and thought they would make a good book after the war was over. "Oh no," I told her. "Please, not a book. Let it be a thin brochure." Today, I remember her words as I write my entry on the 70th day of the war and think this brochure is getting rather thick.

Day 70 • May 4

My today's post could simply repeat my yesterday's one.

Day 83 • May 17

The horrible events in Ukraine today will also be "embroidered" in our hearts for generations. I pray that God would heal and bring beauty out of this pain.

Day 85 • May 19

It's the last spring day, but Ukraine still lives in February.

Day 97 • May 31

Hope Based in Past Memories

A season to plant: *Planting tulips is an expression of hope, based on past experience. After a bulb is placed in the ground, half a year passes before the gardener knows whether their hope is realized.*

Before the war, different war experts gave Ukraine up to 72 hours to complete defeat and capitulation. We passed that time frame by over 1,000 hours. In the first weeks of the war, we felt that it was a matter of time until Belarus openly joined Russia, but it never did, even though it is still letting Russian troops use its territory to launch missile rockets and station their aviation there. We were fervently praying for Chernihiv and Sumy (and that region in the northeast of Ukraine) as they were under heavy attacks every day. Being close to the Russian border, they took the heat and prevented the enemy army from going straight to Kyiv. These cities went through hell, but they are slowly returning to life. Mariupol has been under siege since the first days of the war. It's surrounded by over 10,000 Russian troops, thousands of civilians have been killed, but the city remains standing. It is the only Ukrainian stronghold in the otherwise occupied region.

Even two weeks ago, I was constantly checking on my friends in Kyiv as there were constant air-raid warnings and shelling in different districts of Kyiv. They were saying that surrounding Kyiv was a matter of time. Today, Kyiv region is free of Russian troops.

"We are deeply concerned over what's going on in Ukraine" was the most we could get from various western governments and organizations for years. Now, they finally start realizing what stands behind Russia. Some had to witness the #BuchaMassacre to give up Russian gas. Others waited until the missile strike on evacuation trains in Kramatorsk to give up Russian oil. There's still a long road ahead, but it's finally moving even though we all realize at what price!

These are just a few "big" or significant answers to our prayers that I overlooked this morning when I was concentrating on the prayers God hasn't answered yet. But there are so many more miracles, big and small, on a personal and national scale.

God, please, forgive me for doubting your goodness. May I never think You are idle! May we keep turning to you in our prayers, and please, let us witness your answers. Lord, bring victory and freedom to Ukraine. May your name be glorified here forever and ever.

"Though the fig tree should not blossom, nor fruit be on the vines, the produce of the olive fail and the fields yield no food, the flock be cut off from the fold and there be no herd in the stalls, yet I will rejoice in the Lord; I will take joy in the God of my salvation" (Habakkuk 3:17-18).

Day 45 · April 9

Christ has risen! Ukraine shall also rise!

This was the traditional Easter greeting among Ukrainian insurgents who were fighting against both the Nazi and Soviet Union in WWII, and then continued underground struggle against the communist regime. In the days when any form of religion was forbidden, when identifying as Ukrainian was deemed as nationalism, they kept celebrating the feast of Christ's resurrection and kept the faith that one day Ukraine will also rise to be a beautiful independent nation.

Today, Christ's resurrection is also our source of hope – the hope of victory over death and evil, the hope of restoration of justice, the hope of new life that springs forth through the ashes.

May the power that brought Christ back to life deliver our nation and bring a bright future to Ukraine.

Day 53 · April 17

Today, someone asked me what gives me strength in this situation. I honestly said that it is God and prayer; otherwise, I would have gone insane in the first days of the invasion. I praise God for His faithfulness and being available and near when we need Him the most. Run to Him when you feel weary and find rest in His embrace.

Day 61 · April 26

I needed a nature walk today. As I was enjoying the afternoon sun and the trees in bloom, I was filled with hope. Every day, God works in mysterious ways to bring forth new life - a tiny seed goes into the ground and is completely transformed into a full-grown plant that yields fruit. It's such an ordinary thing that we fail to be mesmerized by this miracle. I praise God for He is the God of wonders, and so I will trust in Him to provide for everyone in need and restore peace and justice in Ukraine.

> ❧ You visit the earth and water it;
> you greatly enrich it;
> the river of God is full of water;
> you provide their grain,
> for so you have prepared it.

> ❧ You water its furrows abundantly,
> settling its ridges,
> softening it with showers,
> and blessing its growth.

> ❧ You crown the year with your bounty;
> your wagon tracks overflow with abundance.

> ❧ The pastures of the wilderness overflow,
> the hills gird themselves with joy,
> the meadows clothe themselves with flocks,
> the valleys deck themselves with grain,
> they shout and sing together for joy.
> (Psalm 65:9-13)

Day 65 · April 29

When I get overwhelmed with the hard questions, I go outside and look at the nature around me. Seeing the beauty of God's creation always inspires me to worship Him. And I realize that there are so many things I don't know and don't understand, but God keeps them under control.

Just today, as I was walking around, I was wondering how the bees can fly around and find blooming trees yet remember where their hive is. I was wondering how the seeds preserve their growing power through the winter and how the weak plants can break through the hardest of soils. I'm curious how the storks and swallows find their nests after they return from winter migration and if they feel happy to be home. I was amazed at how each plant, animal, and even insect seems to know its order and pattern. If I continue here, my list of questions will get similar to chapters 38-39 of the book of Job.

So tonight, I am humbled by the majesty of the Creator. I am amazed that the One who sets the endless Universe in motion and cares for the myriad creatures is personally involved in my life. No issue is too great or too small for Him. He's got the whole world in His hands, yet He opens His embrace for me to come to Him and pour out my burdened heart.

Tonight, I give all of the uncertainties and anxieties of the Ukrainian people into His hands and choose to trust Him and His timing.

I was thinking about the blooming apple trees in our yard. Their delicate petals and sweet fragrance reassure me that if God cared enough for the fleeting beauty of the trees, how much more does He care for his children.

Day 79 · May 13

Thanks to the numerous testimonies of God's faithfulness, I can hold on to His promises, even when it's hard: "Because he holds fast to me in love, I will deliver him; I will protect him, because he knows my name. When he calls to me, I will answer him; I will be with him in trouble; I will rescue him and honor him. With long life I will satisfy him and show him my salvation" (Psalm 91:14-16).

Day 91 · May 25

As I was wrestling with difficult thoughts tonight, God showed me two passages from the Bible. The first one is from Zechariah 4:6, "Not by might, nor by power, but by my Spirit, says the Lord of hosts." God gave this verse to me (and confirmed it through a couple of other people) during the first days of this invasion, and we've been holding on to it since. I trust that our God is mighty to save despite people's plans and intentions. The second passage is from the book of Esther. When Esther wasn't eager to help her nation (fearing for her life or worried she would lose the comforts she'd already gotten used to), Mordecai confronted her, "For if you keep silent at this time, relief and deliverance will rise for the Jews from another place, but you and your father's house will perish. And who knows whether you have not come to the kingdom for such a time as this?" (Esther 4:14) I trust that God is mighty to bring deliverance and relief for Ukraine, but those who choose to side with Russia (even if they cover it up with words of concern for Ukraine) will be put to shame.

I will be holding on to these verses as I ride my "rollercoaster of emotions" throughout this war, knowing that situations may change and my moods may vary, but our God is the same yesterday, today, and forever. To Him be the glory.

Day 93 · May 27

Today we could be celebrating Kyiv Day. I never really liked the festivities and crowds in the downtown area, but I do love Kyiv. I moved there in 2005 when I entered university, but I fell in love with the city before that. My parents met in Kyiv during their university years. Every summer in my childhood, we visited my grandparents, and our bus went through Kyiv, which was a perfect opportunity for my parents to show us their favorite places. Now, having lived in Kyiv for half of my life, I have my own list of favorites. They may not necessarily be of great significance to the city, but they are to me.

The park in the downtown area where Ivan and I went on our first date and where he proposed. Or the park with a lake not far from our home where we would often go on weekends for a breath of fresh air.

Our small church that's a converted facility in an apartment building. That's where my sister was baptized and where we exchanged our marriage vows.

The Ukrainian Education Center was my first serious job and the place where we welcomed many missionary teams and held outreach events. Some of its visitors have become dear friends.

Many memories come from the first apartment we rented when we got married. It had the most beautiful skyline sunsets (that's one of them in the picture). That's where we brought our son when he was born.

Our favorite coffee place is in our neighborhood. When we didn't need to rush anywhere, we would take a leisurely walk and get croissants and coffee. Our son loves those "family dates."

A small family shop that sells dairy and vegetables. They used to be just a stand and got a shop last fall. We used to go there a few times a week and

Kyiv skyline from our first apartment - Day 95, May 29, 2022

jokingly call it our "Kyiv cow." The owners come from a village north of Kyiv, so I've been wondering about them since the war started.

These places are the first that came to mind, but I could go on and on and share millions of stories. They would probably mean nothing to someone else, but they are dear to my heart. So, when the Russian army was only miles away from Kyiv when artillery shelling and missile strikes were on the city, my heart was wrenched with pain. We must praise God and thank our Armed Forces that our city is still standing today. Because a city is more than just buildings, it is more than the people who live there. It is also memories that are cherished and need to be passed on.

Day 95 · May 29

Another thing that helps me persevere is stories of missionaries who were faithful despite the circumstances. I think about the persecuted church and people who secretly preached the Good News in the Soviet Union and other Communist countries, such as Romania. They didn't know when or if their ministry would be successful. They were risking their lives for the Gospel. They were ready to "[forget] what lies behind and [strain] forward to what lies ahead, [pressing] on toward the goal for the prize of the upward call of God in Christ Jesus" (Philippians 3:13-14). And some of them were blessed to see their reward – spiritual liberation and revival in post-communist nations, such as Ukraine. Many modern-day missionaries to the restricted nations persevere in faith, hoping for the bondages to be broken and for spiritual life to come to their countries.

These examples inspire me. We don't know how long this war will last. I certainly hope to live to see Ukraine's victory and glorious future, but it is not an excuse to give up on prayer today, even if it takes longer than expected.

"And let us not grow weary of doing good, for in due season we will reap, if we do not give up" (Galatians 6:9).

Day 96 · May 30

The Experience of Survival

A season to make roots: *Having planted our tulip bulbs, we move forward into the busyness of preparing for winter. This is a practical time, built around survival.*

Forty-first day of the full-scale war on Ukraine

Today, we went to a slightly larger nearby town. It was the first time in over a month that we traveled that far. Usually, we would only walk to a store (ten to twenty minutes away) and back once a week. Somehow it doesn't feel safe to be far from home. But we needed to get some supplies we couldn't get locally and pick up a package at a delivery service. The whole experience was unusual.

First of all, you drive down a familiar road, you know that it is far enough from the active war zone, yet you feel the war in the air. Almost no cars on the road, some roads closed for traffic, fortified stations along the route, trench shelters – you realize that even though we all hope for the best, we have to be prepared for the worst. As we were driving, the only thing I could do was pray the Lord's blessing over all who defend our land. Once we came to the entrance to that town, there was a checking point. You see uniformed men with machine guns, and you feel tense at first, but then they exchange a few words with you, you see their kind eyes and smiles, and your fear is gone. It's as if they shared some of their peace and confidence with you. You are reassured again when they recognize you on your way back and give you a friendly salute instead of checking your documents.

The line at the delivery service took over two hours. We knew it was the only branch office still working in the area, but we didn't expect it to take that long. It was past lunchtime, so my son and I went to a store to get something to eat before heading home. I was surprised to see that this larger town supermarket had almost empty shelves – they say it's because volunteers purchase food to be sent to the front lines, and many new people are coming to stay in this town since it is currently relatively safe. As we sat down in the car to have our lunch, I wanted it to be fun for our son, so I presented it as an adventure, a "lunch date." While he was enjoying his food (we were able to get some bread, ham, and bananas – a modern-day luxury), I had a million thoughts run through my head. I remembered an interview with people who got out of Mariupol that I read last night. Among other things, they told how they had to ration their food, so one day they divided an egg between fifteen of them and enjoyed it as a high delicacy. As I thought of it, I was overwhelmed with gratitude that today we have a car, we have money, there's food in the store, and it is relatively safe here.

"Relatively safe"? This thought brought in a wave of anxiety: What if there is an air-raid warning, and we are in this unfamiliar location, and we don't even know where the nearest bomb shelter is? I didn't say anything out loud, but it was as if my son read my mind because, at that very moment, he calmly said, "Mom, do you know what we should do if there is an air-raid warning while we are in a car? We should drive home and go to our safe place." Then he smiled his sweetest smile and said, "I love you, mom, and I'm so happy we spent this day together," and I knew that he felt safe because he was with me.

His simple words were what I needed to hear for my anxiety to be gone. No, it wasn't about the "driving home" part, but it was about going to our safe place. Are you safe? Is anyone really safe today? There are natural disasters, uprisings, military threats, terrorist attacks, bullying, and domestic violence taking place worldwide. Even in the safest locations, people may suddenly get into a car accident or discover they are seriously ill. So, is there a safe place here on earth? Not really. But you can always feel safe when you are in your Father's arms. Just as my son said, "I'm so happy we spend this day together," I come to my Heavenly Father every night with these exact words. In Him, I find strength and confidence. I know that when everything else fails, I will still be safe in Him, and it's not because of something I did but because of what Jesus did for me on the cross.

> Therefore, brothers, since we have confidence to enter the holy places by the blood of Jesus, by the new and living way that he opened for us through the curtain, that is, through his flesh, and since we have a great priest over the house of God, let us draw near with a true heart in full assurance of faith, with our hearts sprinkled clean from an evil conscience and our bodies washed

with pure water. Let us hold fast the confession of our hope without wavering, for he who promised is faithful.
(Hebrews 10:19-23)

Please, keep praying for Ukraine. The needs are so great that even people on the ground may not be completely aware of all of them, but let the Spirit of God lead you as you pray for our nation.

This is the beginning of the new stage of this cruel war on Ukraine.

Early in the morning, there were numerous missile strikes on different cities of Ukraine, including Lviv – a city in the West of Ukraine, a safe place many people flee to. The missile strike killed seven people and wounded eleven (including one child). Among the injured, a family had to leave Kharkiv under heavy shelling to run away from war, but the war followed them to Lviv.

Tonight, the air-raid sirens go off in all regions of Ukraine. There are reports of explosions in Kharkiv, and Mykolaiv, heavy shelling along the whole line of fire in Donetsk and Luhansk regions, ongoing clashes in Kharkiv region in attempts to take control over Izum. The Russians are bombing Mariupol with extra heavy bombs to destroy the underground shelter of the Azovstal plant, where over a thousand civilians (including children) are taking refuge.

We also keep learning about the atrocities committed on the now-liberated territories during the Russian occupation. According to recent reports, these monsters were raping not only women and young children but also men and babies. As our security services sweep every inch of the reclaimed territory to make sure it is safe for people to return to their homes, they find booby-trapped children's toys, fridges, washing machines, and even clothes drawers.

As the fighting intensifies in the East, we learn about Ukrainian activists abducted and tortured in the temporarily occupied Southern regions of Kherson and Zaporizhzhia. In addition to "mandatory language camps" for Ukrainian kids to learn Russian, they plan "mandatory teacher camps" to train teachers to teach according to the Russian program. They also keep deporting people to the Russian territory, putting them through filtration camps, separating families, and giving up Ukrainian children for adoption in Russia. All of this seems surreal, like something you would read about in a history book, something that could only take place in some barbarous times, but not in the 21st century in the heart of Europe.

The things I mentioned in this post are just the bits I remembered off the top of my mind. As I turn to God with all this pain, I am at a loss for words. I don't know where to start. I'm not sure I can even list all of the requests before His face. I find myself repeating over and over again, "Lord, have mercy. Intervene, by your grace. We need your miracle!"

In these overwhelming times, I take comfort in knowing that "the Spirit helps us in our weakness. For we do not know what to pray for as we ought, but the Spirit himself intercedes for us with groanings too deep for words" (Romans 8:26).

Day 54 · April 18

Please, keep praying for Mariupol, the occupied Kherson and Zaporizhzhia regions, for the main battle in Donetsk and Luhansk regions. The Russians have announced possible attacks on Ukrainian infrastructure, namely bridges and railroads. There were missile strikes on railroads in central Ukraine today. The Russians are planning terrorist attacks on their territory with many casualties to blame the Ukrainian army. Pray for all enemy plans to fail.

Day 57 · April 21

I remain concerned over the situation in Transnistria (occupied Moldovan territory). Its residents started getting messages saying they needed to evacuate because Ukraine was planning a missile strike on their territory. We know it's another Russian provocation. They may be trying to get "Transnistria" involved in the war on Ukraine, which would put three "relatively safe" regions in immediate danger. Or they may use Transnistria as leverage and a threat on Moldova, trying to expand the occupied territories and get their much-needed blitzkrieg. Either way, the situation is serious, so we need lots of prayers on this front as well.

On April 26, 1986, there was an accident at the Chornobyl Nuclear Power Plant, which turned into the worst nuclear disaster in history in terms of cost and casualties. While the Soviet government tried to cover it up, the radioactive contamination spread well beyond Ukraine, Belarus, and Russia all the way to Western Europe. Today, 36 years later, Russia fired missiles that went really low above three nuclear power plants in Ukraine (Zaporizhzhia, Khmelnytskyi, and Pivdennoukrainsk). I guess they are really keen on repeating all the heinous crimes of the Soviet Union. Please, pray for God's protection and that there would be no nuclear, biological, or chemical threats over Ukraine or anywhere else.

Tonight, I watched a small report about three men who organized burials in Bucha. Somehow, they managed to get permission from the occupational forces and were the only ones allowed to collect and bury dead bodies in Bucha. They would dig graves by hand, about 20 a day, every day during the occupation. They wanted to honor the dead and prevent their bodies from decaying in the streets. At the end of the interview, one of them, a tattoo artist, said, "God saved us dozens of times during shelling or when we were shot at. Why? Why did He let us live? Perhaps so that we could continue what we were doing. It was the first time that I clearly knew my purpose in life. Drawing, painting, all the things I did before are nothing. This is what I had to do, what I lived for."

This may look like a somber statement, yet it seemed powerful to me. It is such a joy to know what God wants you to do and be faithful enough to do His will. I pray that we will know God's will and live according to it. So that in the end, we would be able to hear, "Well done, good and faithful servant. You have been faithful over a little; I will set you over much. Enter into the joy of your master" (Matthew 25:23).

Day 62 · April 26

While the situation at the front line remains mostly unchanged, my heart is burdened with the thoughts that would definitely resonate with any human heart, especially that of a woman and a mother.

As of yesterday, Russia has killed 215 children. Four days ago, on Saturday before the Orthodox Easter, there was a missile strike on Odesa. The rocket hit an apartment building, killing a three-month-old girl, her mother, and grandmother. The baby's father had just stepped out to get groceries for the Easter meal. While numbers alone are devastating, the reality is much worse.

That same missile rocket killed another young couple in this building in Odesa. A few days before, they had announced they were expecting a baby. I don't think this unborn baby is included in the reported statistics. These numbers also won't show how many unborn babies died during this war because of miscarriage or stillbirth as the mothers experienced stress or weren't able to get the medical care they needed. These stories won't be shared publicly, but they will definitely leave their scars and have long-term consequences that we will have to learn to deal with.

Another deep and complex issue with long-term consequences is sexual violence. The Prosecutor's office currently has information about over 400 children and adults who had been raped by the Russian soldiers. This number only represents people who filed paperwork and went through the needed examination. How many hundreds of victims chose to remain silent? How much time will they need to heal?

Do you think it's bad? It gets worse. Dozens of women got pregnant after the rape. Today, there was a report about a fourteen-year-old girl from Bucha who was raped by five Russian soldiers. She got pregnant and chose to keep the baby. She is currently working with a therapist to learn to love this baby whose biological father is an invader and a rapist. I can't imagine what she's going through and what she will have to endure in the future. There were many hateful comments under this report. Some were saying the girl was brainwashed by religious fanatics; others blamed doctors for manipulating her into keeping this baby. The article also contained abortion advice for rape victims. I praise God for this girl's courage, but I must admit that I wouldn't be able to blame her if she chose to do otherwise. I guess this case shows that the aftermath of war contains all shades of gray, and we will need a lot of wisdom to deal with it.

These reports that came on the same day made me turn to God, searching for answers. I know that He is a Giver of Life, that His ways are not my ways. For some reason, He saw it fit to take away those unborn babies yet give pregnancy to an unsuspecting teenage rape victim. I am tempted to ask, "Why?" but instead, I beg God to be faithful and intimately close to those who suffered from this cruel injustice. I pray that He reveals His will amid this pain and turns weeping into praise.

Day 63 · April 27

This year's spring has been unusually slow. It is as if nature itself is stuck in the "February 24" mode and needs time to awaken and come to its senses. While the weather is just a conversation topic and a matter of preference for many people, it is of vital importance to Ukrainian villagers. Many people here have large land plots where they plant potatoes and other vegetables that are canned and preserved in cellars for the winter season. These land plots helped many people survive in the 1990s during a severe economic crisis after the collapse of the Soviet Union, and many people still heavily rely on them today. These land plots can turn into "victory gardens" and solve the possible food shortage problem in Ukraine, but we need God's provision for that.

Usually, most of the planting is done in April and early May. This year, because of rains and a cold front, many people are just starting their work in the garden. Experienced grandmas are worried it will lead to poor crops, and I pray for God to send an abundant harvest despite all circumstances as a testimony of His sovereign grace.

We also need God's miracle to provide a good harvest for all of Ukraine. Kherson, Zaporizhzhia, Donetsk, Luhansk, and Kharkiv regions are under occupation or in the line of fire (it's 27% of Ukraine's territory if you include Crimea, which has been occupied since 2014). Sumy, Chernihiv, and Kyiv regions (another 14%) have been liberated but remain heavily contaminated with landmines which is a significant threat to any fieldwork. And these numbers don't take into account Mykolaiv, Dnipropetrovsk, and Odesa regions which are often shelled as potential targets of the Russian army. Our farmers also lack fuel (due to numerous missile attacks) which also hampers the planting season. While Ukraine may manage to cover the domestic demand, world prices for grains and oils are skyrocketing as Ukraine was among the leading agriculture exporters. According to the UN estimations, up to half a billion people may be on the verge of hunger as a result of the Russian invasion of Ukraine.

While we can rely on humanitarian aid sent by the generous people and governments worldwide, hunger is a serious threat to the occupied territories. The Russians are emptying grain storages and taking the "plunder" to the occupied territories. They have stolen most of the agricultural equipment but are forcing Ukrainian farmers to plant the fields under the fear of death. Today's techniques used by the Russian army remind us of both the Soviet Holodomor times and the Nazi occupation. We desperately need the war to end, and for these lands to be de-occupied as soon as possible to prevent starvation there.

As we're talking about food, please, also pray for the besieged cities (especially Mariupol), towns in the line of fire, and liberated territories – they all experience different degrees of lack of food and medical supplies. Pray for God's provision as He is Jehovah-Jireh.

Day 65 · April 29

Tonight, most of Ukraine was sheltering during air-raid warnings as Russia, in its rage, was spitting out missiles. Eight missile rockets were shot down by our air-defense forces (preventing attacks on Kyiv, Vinnytsia, and Odesa). The other ten brought destruction upon Lviv, Zakarpattia region, Kirovohrad region, and Odesa region. The enemy is targeting railroads to prevent evacuation and interfere with ammunition logistics.

Day 69 · May 3

The other day, I caught myself thinking that I was really wishing for a weekend. It's not like I'm working all the time and have no time for rest (quite the opposite, actually), but I really wish we had a day or two when we could just relax. Unfortunately, the war has no days off, so I come to God to seek rest in His embrace.

I think weariness can be a serious threat. When you are drained (physically or emotionally), you are more prone to despair or ready to compromise.

I've heard someone say, "I'm so tired of this war. I just want it to be over. I don't care who takes control of my city. I just want the war to be over." While I understand the sentiment, I don't think this person realized the full extent of what may come after "whoever" takes control over their city.

I read a disturbing report today about life in the parts of Donetsk and Luhansk regions occupied since 2014. Their supermarket shelves are empty, and the prices keep going up. Many places don't have electricity and running water (or these are provided on a schedule for an hour or two a day). There are almost no men left in the cities – all of them were forcefully "mobilized" and sent to the frontlines without any training or provision. Those who stayed try to hide at home, but the occupational government looks for ways to find them. For example, they would tell everyone to leave an apartment building because of an alleged bomb threat. Once everyone is outside, they would grab men and take them to mobilization stations. They are perceived as cannon fodder and are treated as such.

Please, pray for people who have been under occupation since 2014. Some of them were victims of the Russian propaganda and chose to stay willingly.

Some of them had no opinion of their own and were ready to act to suit the time and occasion at hand. Some people could not leave the occupied territories because of the need to take care of sick family members. Some of them spent months trying to start a new life in the cities under Ukraine's control but chose to go back because they missed their homes too much or felt "too old" to start anew. There are many different situations, but none of them is an excuse for the treatment they get under occupation. Pray for the people not to get weary and indifferent as they don't understand what they are wishing for.

Also, please, pray for the displaced people (both within Ukraine and abroad). People have been away from homes for over two months. They're tired from sleeping on couches or sharing a room or shower with other people. They are exhausted from not knowing how long they will be there and whether they should be looking for a job/permanent place to stay/school for their children/language courses, etc. They are on the verge of despair, tired from feeling useless because they know they don't belong there. Please, pray for God's guidance for them. May He show them how He can use them for His glory right where they are.

People all over the world are getting tired of this war. Even those who genuinely want to help may find themselves unprepared for such a long run. Volunteers may need a break. The supply chains may be getting thinner as the resources are not endless. Those who welcomed refugees into their homes may need their property and/or privacy back. People in Europe may be getting tired of these Ukrainians who seem to be everywhere disturbing their ordinary way of life. And it's understandable. Please, pray for the helpers. May God abundantly bless them. May He replenish all of their needs and refresh their strength. May He send new helpers with fresh energy. May He show them the fruit of their labor.

Please, do not grow weary in praying for Ukraine. Every day, I thank God for each prayer warrior and ask Him to bless you and guide you. We are standing today because you are holding our backs.

"Let us not grow weary of doing good, for in due season we will reap, if we do not give up. So then, as we have opportunity, let us do good to everyone, and especially to those who are of the household of faith" (Galatians 6:9-10).

Day 72 · May 5

They did intensify missile strikes. There were lots of air-raids today.

Day 75 · May 9

These days I keep thinking about Mariupol. Over 150,000 civilians remain in the city, and most of them cannot leave because of Russian "filtration camps." The city lacks medicine and medical specialists. There are problems with the water supply and sewage system, which may cause the spread of infectious diseases.

Those who try to leave the city go through "filtration camps." Everyone who looks suspicious or is found to have connections to the Armed Forces of Ukraine or is an active pro-Ukrainian activist is detained. Over 3,000 people are kept in an overcrowded detention facility (intended for 850 people). They share a jug of water between dozens of them, are given food every other day, are taken to the bathroom once a day, and have no outside time. The confinement cells are packed, and people can't lie down; they can only stand or squat. Add here daily interrogations, tortures, threats, and coercion to cooperation.

Please, pray for God's miracle in Mariupol and Ukraine.

"I cry aloud to God, aloud to God, and he will hear me. In the day of my trouble, I seek the Lord; in the night my hand is stretched out without wearying; my soul refuses to be comforted" (Psalm 77:1-2).

Day 77 · May 11

When I think about our lives during this war, I realize there's very little certainty. Many people have lost their jobs or experienced significant salary cuts. Millions of people left their homes (5 million Ukrainians left the country, and another 7 million became internally displaced) in February or early March, and with the warm weather approaching, they are wondering if they should go on and buy summer clothes or they would be able to return home soon. Millions of children are finishing the school year online scattered worldwide and pray to see their classmates in person in September. We are experiencing severe fuel shortage (Russians have been specifically attacking fuel storage and petroleum processing plants), so there's more anxiety – will people be able to evacuate, will there be enough fuel for the fieldwork, how will people get around? With the prices going up all over the world, more and more people in Ukraine are wondering if they will have enough come winter.

People who have lost everything are wondering how long they will be able to survive on government help and humanitarian aid and what they should do next. People in villages along the Russian border (and all de-occupied towns) are wondering if it is safe to return home and whether they should start rebuilding or if there will be another wave of the destroyers and all of their work will be in vain. Every day we keep thinking about Mariupol and other contested or occupied territories, wondering how long they will have to endure the Russian torture.

Day 79 · May 13

Imagine that you are sound asleep in your nice bedroom in your soft bed. Suddenly, you wake up from screaming coming out of a house next door – someone is raping and killing your neighbor. You feel terrible – you had to wake up from your sweet dreams, and now you can't fall asleep. You need to do something. So, you call this neighbor and ask her to stop screaming because she is being disruptive.

Does this sound cruel, ridiculous, and inhumane? Yes, it does. However, some people make similar statements about Ukraine both on personal and official levels: "If only Ukraine surrendered, lives would be saved." "Both Russia and Ukraine are to blame for the war." "Well, Russia refuses to be reasonable, so let's get to 'business as usual' with Putin, and Ukraine can simply give up the occupied territories. Come on, everyone is tired of this war." It breaks my heart when I hear such statements, and I hope that people who are making them do so out of ignorance and don't honestly think so. Otherwise, it's really sad, and I pray that people who make such statements would never have to live through what Ukrainians are experiencing today.

Last night, we were having dinner when we heard the sound of an airplane (or some say it was a missile rocket) flying over our house. Our son immediately left the table and ran to the hallway (the safest location inside our house). He had fear in his eyes. It broke my heart.

My friend, who currently lives in another country, volunteered at a local church helping out Ukrainian refugees. The church was located close to the local airport. Every time there was a sound of a plane landing or taking off, the refugee children would drop to the ground and cover their heads.

Every person in our country, no matter the age or location, has suffered trauma from this war, and every day, I pray that God would help our people heal and that this trauma would not cripple our children's future.

Right now, there is an air-raid warning for most regions of Ukraine. They just confirmed a missile strike on Lviv (no details at the moment). In times like this, I feel weary, crying out, "How long, O God?" And I know that He hears my cries, and I know He cries with me for all the lives lost. I know He will not delay, and I must humbly wait on Him.

O my God, in you I trust; let me not be put to shame; let not my enemies exult over me. Indeed, none who wait for you shall be put to shame; they shall be ashamed who are wantonly treacherous. (Psalm 25:2-3)

Please, keep praying for Mariupol and the Ukrainian defenders at Azovstal Steel Plant. The Azovstal garrison has successfully completed its combat mission – for 80 days, they kept 20,000 Russian soldiers busy, preventing their transfer to other locations and buying precious time. Due to their effort, Russian troops didn't have enough manpower to capture Zaporizhzhia or surround Ukrainian forces in Donetsk and Luhansk regions. Now, the mission is to save the lives of our defenders. Today, they evacuated 53 seriously wounded soldiers from Azovstal to a hospital in Novoazovsk (a settlement under Russian occupation). 211 defenders were evacuated to Olenivka (Donetsk region, also under Russian occupation) and should be exchanged during the next POW exchange. Please, pray that everything goes according to the plan (we all have learned that you can't trust Russians) and that they are safe. Also, pray for the rest of the soldiers still at Azovstal. This is a huge step. Keep praying for God's miracle and deliverance.

There were reports that people in Mariupol and those trying to evacuate were forced to write a letter stating that they suffered at the hands of the Ukrainian army and were asking Russia for aid. Please, pray for wisdom and protection in situations like this. Also, keep praying for people in "filtration camps" (basically, Russian concentration camps) and those forcefully taken to Russia.

A few weeks ago, there was information about thousands of Ukrainian children from occupied territories who had been separated from their parents. According to some sources, Russia may be trying to use this situation to spread its propaganda. They would return the children to their parents and present it as if the Ukrainian army separated the families and the Russian side was the one reuniting them. Please, pray for these families and for the truth to prevail.

> ❧ Oh, guard my soul, and deliver me!
> Let me not be put to shame, for I take refuge in you.
> May integrity and uprightness preserve me,
> for I wait for you.
> (Psalm 25:20-21)

Day 82 · May 16

Today, reports came from the newly liberated towns in Kharkiv region. Lots of reports of cruelty and rape (the youngest victims under the age of two!) Once again, I will not go into details here not to traumatize anyone, but I'll just say that these stories prove that Bucha was not an exception but rather a "foreshadow" of the Russian army in all its glory. There is no other explanation for what is happening now other than it's an intended genocide. A teenage girl from Bucha said her rapists told her they would do terrible things to her to make sure she never wanted to have children with a Ukrainian man. Now similar reports come from liberated towns around Kharkiv. I'm afraid to think about the territories still under Russian control.

Heavy fighting continues in Luhansk and Donetsk regions. The enemy army tries to destroy and kill as many as possible every day. Town after town turns into a heap of rubble. I do not doubt that we will rebuild all that was ruined, but I can only pray for God to heal the ruined lives and broken hearts of hundreds of thousands who have lost their homes and loved ones.

We keep praying with bated breath for the defenders of Mariupol (both that remain at Azovstal Steel Plant and those taken captive). The international organizations (namely, Red Cross) say they have a complete list of soldiers brought to the occupied territories, so it should prevent Russia from "misplacing" them.

Day 85 · May 19

As I read the news, I'm making mental notes on which stories are worth sharing. Today, I realized that so many stories start blending together.

I read about a girl from Vuhledar who lost her whole family and was severely wounded during heavy shelling. She has pieces of shell stuck in her brain and spine. I thought I had already shared her story, but it turns out that the first girl was from Mykolaiv and her parents are alive.

There was a story of a woman who lost her legs after a missile strike on Kramatorsk. I thought I'd already read her story but realized that the one I already knew was about a girl from Lysychansk who stepped on a landmine.

I read about a family looking for a young soldier who saved the life of their child. I remember reading a very similar story, but it was in Irpin during the evacuation in March. This one was recent and took place in Orikhiv (Zaporizhzhia region) – the soldier covered the girl with his body during an artillery attack.

I know that each story is unique, and I wish we could collect them all to make sure we never forget them. But when I noticed so many stories being so similar, I was grieved, realizing that when we read a news report about one person, dozens of those experienced something very similar. However, each of the stories I read showed me a glimpse of hope. The girls with shell injuries to their brains managed to get the medical care they needed and are going through rehabilitation. The girls who lost their limbs didn't lose their loved ones and are resolved to get back to "normal" life. The soldiers ready to risk their lives to save others are such a vivid example of sacrificial love that I am just speechless and can only praise God.

Day 86 · May 20

"It is the Lord who goes before you. He will be with you; he will not leave you or forsake you. Do not fear or be dismayed" (Deuteronomy 31:8).

This verse came to mind as I was praying tonight. We went outside today to check on our vegetable garden when we heard a loud noise in the sky. A Russian missile rocket was flying over our house. It was low enough to see it very well. At that moment, I felt a whole range of emotions – fear, anger, helplessness. I started yelling at it, "Disappear! Disappear!" I felt the anguish of knowing it will bring destruction to some unsuspecting people and being powerless to do anything about it. The only thing I could do was pray, so I prayed for this missile to be shot down, for it not to bring any destruction and death, for the protection of our air defense forces, and for God's punishment on those who came to kill. The missile was gone in a matter of seconds, but we were pretty shaken and would stop in our tracks from any noise.

When I went inside, I immediately went online to check if a missile attack did any damage. Praise God, there was a report about at least four missiles rockets shot down. There was also a report about another missile rocket that fell into the river, not causing any damage. A couple of days ago, another missile hit an empty toilet at a beach in Odesa. According to the reports, the success rate of Ukraine's air-defense system went from 29% at the beginning of the war to 72%. I know that there are thousands of prayers and hundreds of lives saved behind each of these reports, and I praise God.

Day 88 · May 22

Pray for the temporarily occupied territories. There is a flood danger in Kherson region. The hydropower station in Kakhovka needs repair, but the occupational forces do not allow it. There is already some flooding, but many villages may end up underwater if the situation gets worse. My heart breaks for Kherson region – my grandparents were participating in the construction of the hydropower station in Kakhovka, and my parents spent their first years of marriage (and my first year of life) in a village that is just a few kilometers down the river from Kakhovka. And these are just a few personal connections that we have, but our friends have family members there.

The situation in occupied Mariupol is very sad. The city may be on the verge of a cholera outbreak because of a lack of sanitary conditions. People still don't have electricity or running water, but the first thing the occupational forces did was set up giant screens to broadcast Russian propaganda. They announced that there would be no summer break for schools in occupied Mariupol so that the children could "catch up on Russian language and history" (a.k.a. intense brainwashing). At the same time, the occupational government in Crimea suggested removing the English language from the school curriculum, explaining that it's dangerous (it may get a child interested in other countries) and useless to people who will never go to London. At least they admit they are afraid of open-minded people.

Russia is already known for its use of "scorched earth" tactics when they level everything with the ground. After they occupy the territory, they try to depopulate it by making life unbearable. They persecute, deport, kill, starve, and terrorize until the remaining people leave or are broken and completely submissive. After that, they would repopulate the area with people from Russia as it would guarantee loyalty to the invaders. This approach was used in Soviet times. If you know Bible history, the Assyrians used a very similar tactic. We know what happened to the ten tribes of the Northern Kingdom of Israel – they are considered lost forever, and I guess everyone knows how the Jews despised Samaritans (the people living in the territory that used to be the Northern Kingdom of Israel).

Anyone who cares to know what's going on in Ukraine now would have to call it a genocide, no matter how uncomfortable this statement may be. Why are many people reluctant to call it for what it is? I think they are trying to escape responsibility. If you recognize something, you would also feel responsible for doing something about it, and it's so much easier to pretend it's not so clear.

Day 92 • May 26

It is the end of May, a traditional end of the school year in Ukraine. I remember how it made me feel when I was a child – a little nostalgic yet excited for the endless opportunities of the summer break. That's how the kids should think about it. However, this year is different. Ukrainian children will not have their traditional graduation parties. Most of them are scattered all over the world or are busy sheltering from Russian bombs and missiles. Our children have matured overnight because of the crazy ambitions of the Russian dictator.

Please, take your time to pray for the children of Ukraine. They ask serious questions. They are dealing with anxiety from sirens wailing with air-raid warnings. They are learning to manage their emotions, especially anger at the situation. They experience losses on various levels – loss of security, their home, loss of a friend or a family member, loss of limbs. The war scars their childhood, and we pray for their future not to be crippled by this experience.

In these past three months, whenever I was thinking about the children in Ukraine, I would be reminded of the passages from Deuteronomy where God instructs Moses and the Israelites to make sure their children and their children's children know about the great deeds of the Lord and understand and keep His commandments. Children will grow up to be the new generation, yet their childhood determines which way they will go as adults.

Will our children hate Russia forever? Will they learn to be cruel? Will they recover from the atrocities they experienced in their lives? If they left Ukraine as refugees, will they ever return home, and which country will they call their home? Will they always be afraid of thunder and the sound of an airplane? Will they understand what values their nation was fighting for, or will they take it for granted or disregard it completely?

The answers to these questions depend on what we, as parents, do today. They will learn from our responses and our actions. May God grant us wisdom in fulfilling this responsibility:

> ✠ Only be careful, and watch yourselves closely so that you do not forget the things your eyes have seen or let them fade from your heart as long as you live. Teach them to your children and to their children after them. Remember the day you stood before the Lord your God at Horeb, when he said to me, "Assemble the people before me to hear my words so that they may learn to revere me as long as they live in the land and may teach them to their children."
> (Deuteronomy 4:9-10, NIV)

Day 94 • May 29

When Hope Felt Distant

A season to cool: *Winter buries the memory of the hopes that we had planted with our tulip bulbs.*

"Where was your God? Why did he let this happen? I don't want to hear anything about a god who is blind to this evil!" I already saw quite a few of these comments today. As I was thinking about war before it broke out, these were the questions I was dreading. Is there a satisfactory answer to them?

Day 39 · April 3

42 days, 6 weeks of the war

As we learn about more and more horrible things done by the Russian army on our land, we are afraid to even think about how much worse things could be discovered in the cities still under temporary occupation.

The recent news reports show that the Russians started using mobile crematoriums in Mariupol to cover their atrocities. As the active war zone moves more to the east and south of Ukraine, we add more and more city names to our prayer list and beg for the #neveragain.

Is there any hope left? Is there any light in this darkness? I see glimpses of light and hope when I hear stories filled with absolute love in unspeakable circumstances.

Day 42 · April 6

Every day, as I sit down to write my daily update, I hope that "at this time tomorrow," I will be able to share the great news of Ukraine's victory. However, it hasn't happened yet. "O Lord, how long shall I cry for help, and you will not hear? Or cry to you 'Violence!' and you will not save?" (Habakkuk 1:2)

I don't know how familiar you are with the book of the prophet Habakkuk, but this small book has been on my mind since the first days of the war, and the story that happened today made it even more vivid. I have been translating for the School of Biblical Studies for the past five years, and I'm sure it was part of God's plan to prepare me for this trying time. Every day He brings to my mind different passages from the Scriptures and reveals the depth I might have missed before. Habakkuk was unlike other prophets because he didn't address his people on behalf of God and didn't confront them. He struggled with seeing God's goodness in his circumstances, so he complained to God and lamented before Him. And God answered him. And even though God's answer was different from what Habakkuk wanted to hear, it still encouraged him to live by faith.

Today, God really convicted me in my heart, and I was reminded of Habakkuk once again. This morning, someone messaged me and asked me how they could pray for Ukraine. As I started typing my response, I felt exasperated and started complaining to God: "How long, God? Do you even hear our prayers? Oh, yes, we see lots of testimonies on a personal level, but is it all you are capable of? Is it too hard for you to answer a 'big' prayer request? How long will I keep asking people to pray for Mariupol? How long will we keep getting devastating news from different parts of Ukraine? Will you finally do something?!"

And God's answer came immediately. It wasn't a roaring thunder or blinding lighting. A quiet realization came as I looked at my response to the same "How can we pray for Ukraine?" question that I gave two weeks ago, a month ago, and after the war started. I heard God asking me to examine my prayer requests and see if He was idle this whole time.

Day 45 • April 9

A ninety-one-year-old Holocaust survivor died in Mariupol.[iv] She was 10 years old in 1941 when the Nazis entered Mariupol and killed the city's Jews, including her family. She survived because she was hiding in a basement. Eighty-one years later, in 2022, she had to hide in a Mariupol basement once again, this time – from the Russian "liberators". As she lay dying in a freezing Mariupol basement pleading for water, she kept saying she didn't remember anything like this during WWII and wanted to know only one thing: "Why is this happening?"

According to the reports from our intelligence services, Russian soldiers were given orders to kill all Ukrainians taken captive around Popasna (a city in Luhansk region).

The promised evacuation of women, children, and elderly from Mariupol failed because the Russians didn't keep the ceasefire agreement and didn't let people get to the evacuation buses.

Day 56 · April 20

Easter Sunday in Ukraine. The day was very sunny and the nature was serene. It looked like a perfect day for rejoicing in the resurrected Christ. And we do cling onto the hope we have in Him, because the world we are living in sometimes looks hopeless. There were nine missile strikes on Kremenchuk (Poltava region), a false-flag operation with Russian tanks waving Ukrainian flags and shooting at Ukrainian villages in Kherson region, reports of the Russian Orthodox church actively aiding the Russian aggressors in forceful deportation of Ukrainians by gathering information from the occupied territories and providing their monasteries as deportation bases, continued attacks on Azovstal in Mariupol. Even though these crimes bring devastation, we are not really surprised. We've learned not to expect anything good from Russia.

Unfortunately, there are also reports that are painful because they look like backstabbing: A group of German intellectuals signed an open letter to the Germany Chancellor, Scholz, urging him to stop supplying arms to Ukraine to encourage it to capitulate; the Austrian Foreign Minister said Ukraine should not be offered European Union membership; there are reports about different countries or companies finding loopholes to continue trade with Russia. We know that we have support from the population of those countries, but it is painful to see how the governments use this tragic war for their personal gain. That's one more reason for us to put trust in the Lord.

"Woe to those who go down to Egypt for help and rely on horses, who trust in chariots because they are many and in horsemen because they are very strong, but do not look to the Holy One of Israel or consult the Lord! And yet He is wise and brings disaster; He does not call back his words, but will arise against the house of the evildoers and against the helpers of those who work iniquity" (Isaiah 31:1-2).

Day 60 · April 24

Honestly, I feel weary. We're into the third month of this war, and there's no way to know how long it will last. I scrolled back to a couple of weeks ago and caught myself thinking that I could just copy my previous post and replace the city names, but the rest would remain accurate. This morning, five new locations were hit by missiles – all of them are important railroad hubs (just as predicted a few days ago). More cities and villages are leveled to the ground by the so-called "liberators." The Russians continue torturing the occupied territories, emptying all food and grain storages to starve people and make them more cooperative. I can't even think about Mariupol – satellite images show at least three mass grave sites there that far exceed the gravesites in Bucha.

Today, there was a terrorist attack in Transnistria (Moldovan territory illegally occupied by Russia since 1992). It's one of the expected provocations that would allow Russia to use this occupied territory for the attack on Ukraine. Another provocation to justify mass mobilization and instigate aggression in Russian society is shelling of villages on the Russian territory close to the border with Ukraine. Putin's bloodthirsty regime has demonstrated several times that they put no value on human life, even if it's their fellow citizens. Still, it breaks my heart that more people would have to experience the terrors of the war. In my prayers, I would often ask God to help people stand up for the truth and do something about the current situation before the war comes knocking on their doors. I will keep praying for the war not to spread and for the evil to be stopped soon.

Day 61 · April 25

Another airstrike on Odesa with casualties today. I've lost track of all the places that were shelled today. The 100 people who left Azovstal yesterday still haven't gotten to Zaporizhzhia (the intended location in Ukraine-controlled territory).

On some days, it takes extra effort to remain hopeful, but God sends heartwarming stories which refresh my spirit.

During the siege of Kyiv, one man saw a car with keys parked by his apartment. When the owner didn't show up in a few hours, he packed his family into the car and took them to a relatively safe location. Once they got there, he searched the vehicle and found a note with a phone number in the glove compartment. He called the number and said, "Hello, I stole your car to take my family to safety." He was speechless to hear in response, "Don't worry. I have four cars. I took my family in one and left the other three in different parts of the city with full gas tanks, keys, and my phone number in the glove compartment. You are the third person who called me with this phrase today."

Today, there was an unusual rescue operation in Borodyanka (Kyiv suburbs). Someone saw a cat stuck on the seventh floor of the destroyed building. No one knows how much time the cat spent there without food or water, but it's safe now. Under the rubble of a completely destroyed house in Borodyanka, they found an icon that remained undamaged amidst the total ruin. There was a wedding in one of Lviv hospitals today. The first wedding dance is always a moving part of the celebration, but this one was incredibly moving. After stepping on a landmine in Lysychansk (Luhansk region), the girl lost both her legs and four fingers on one hand, but it didn't stop them from dancing.

A group of soldiers was passing through Mykolaiv when they saw kids waving at them. They stopped, gave them some candy bars, and took pictures. As they were ready to leave, one of them asked the most talkative boy, "Will you join the Armed Forces of Ukraine when you grow up?" – "I will if I don't die here" was the shocking response. The boy smiled, tried the helmet on, took a bite of the candy bar, and ran off to play. An eighty-seven-year-old Holocaust survivor, managed to get out of Mariupol. They had to pass numerous Russian checkpoints until they reached the territory under Ukraine's control. "Were you happy about it?" asks the journalist. "Happy? No, happy is when you have ice cream on a hot day. You don't understand. We reached Ukraine!!!"

These stories are heartbreaking, yet they show God's faithfulness and goodness.

"Blessed be the Lord, who daily bears us up; God is our salvation. Our God is a God of salvation, and to God, the Lord, belong deliverances from death" (Psalm 68:19-20).

Day 68 · May 2

As I read these reports and sat down to write my daily post, I prayed and asked, "God, will this ever end? I know you have your plans, and I believe you will bring something wonderful out of this disaster, but it's so hard to wait. Would you show me the glimpses of you in this mess so that I could persevere with hope?"

"Answer me, O Lord, for your steadfast love is good; according to your abundant mercy, turn to me. Hide not your face from your servant, for I am in distress; make haste to answer me" (Psalm 69:16-17).

Day 69 · May 3

When the full-scale war just started, we wanted to hope it would be over in a few weeks. Then we were praying it would be over by Easter. Now, we pray it will be over by the end of summer, but the time keeps stretching. According to the US Intelligence expectations, Russia is going to prolong the war and switch to a crawl in order to exhaust Ukraine and the rest of the world. Putin thinks that by winter, people will get tired of hearing about the war, and they will be annoyed with the inconvenience of the war (higher prices, food shortage, immigration crisis – all of this will impact the world, not just Ukraine). He hopes to get everything he wants, adding more nuclear war threats.

Please, pray for the world not to give up on Ukraine. If you look at the map, you will see how many European countries immediately depend on the outcome of the war on Ukraine.

Day 76 · May 10

Russia is slowly devouring Ukrainian land. They completely wipe away village after village, town after town. They intentionally aim at bomb shelters with people. They destroy roads, power stations, and water supply infrastructure to make life unbearable for those who chose to stay. They have no mercy.

I check the world news only to see more devastation. A school shooting in Texas (USA) takes away innocent lives. The economic crisis (rising food prices and severe shortages) in Sri Lanka leaves thousands of people insecure and hopeless. The looming global food crisis caused by climate change, poor crops, and broken supply chains makes the world vulnerable.

Today, I want to cry out, "My God, why have you forsaken us?" I guess I take comfort in knowing that it's okay to say this to God. Even Jesus, who is one with the Father, cried out these words on the cross. I know that God can handle my frustration.

Day 91 · May 25

When someone asks me how we're doing, I usually say, "We're fine. We're praying and waiting for our victory." But waiting is hard.... Why does it take so long?

Day 96 · May 30

Defiance in the Face of Aggression

A season to grow: *In spite of the sometimes-returning onslaughts of fading winter, tulips start growing below the surface. This is a time of defiance and hope.*

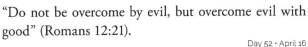

"Do not be overcome by evil, but overcome evil with good" (Romans 12:21).

Day 52 · April 16

It was on Thursday, eight weeks ago, that Russia started its massive invasion of Ukraine.

A couple of years ago, I participated in an interesting discussion upon finishing a course on European Studies. The final debate was about the dominant power in Europe (and in the world in general) – values or interests. It was curious to see how people from different backgrounds think. I remember I insisted that we must do everything for values to prevail; otherwise, everything else would lose its meaning.

In the past eight weeks, we've seen just that. Ukrainians came together and refused to give in to the monster in an earnest attempt to defend what they love. People from all over the world chose to support Ukraine because they recognized the values we are fighting for. While politicians may be hesitant and careful in their statements, we see how even they have to take action moved by the intensity of support for Ukraine demonstrated by their electorate. I thank God for every person who chose values over interests. Some welcomed Ukrainians into their home. Some donated to noble causes. Whole towns gave up their "quaintness" and became refugee/volunteer hubs. Entire nations were ready to endure higher gas prices not to finance the bloodthirsty killer. I praise God for every heart that chose solidarity over indifference and stands in prayer for Ukraine. I praise God that we see the world choosing values over interest, which means there's still hope.

Day 57 · April 21

There are numerous stories where Ukrainian people call the special phone line to report the location of Russian troops. An interesting twist is added to the story when these people are ready to sacrifice their property to make sure the enemy is stopped. For example, one man asked to destroy his business on the temporarily occupied territory as it was used as an ammunition warehouse by the Russian army. Another man had surveillance cameras installed on his property. He had evacuated to a safe location but was regularly checking on his property. When he saw that the Russians chose his home as their headquarters, he immediately reported it to the Ukrainian army and asked them to do what had to be done without thinking about the property.

Day 58 · April 22

In the past couple of days, I received a few messages from different praying friends, all of them pointing out Psalm 94.ᵛ As I meditated on it, I realized it reflects my prayer in response to this pain:

  ❧ O Lord, God of vengeance,
  O God of vengeance, shine forth!

  ❧ Rise up, O judge of the earth;
  repay to the proud what they deserve!

  ❧ They crush your people, O Lord,
  and afflict your heritage.

  ❧ The Lord will not forsake his people;
  he will not abandon his heritage;
  for justice will return to the righteous,
  and all the upright in heart will follow it.

  ❧ When I thought, "My foot slips,"
  your steadfast love, O Lord, held me up.

  ❧ When the cares of my heart are many,
  your consolations cheer my soul.

❧ But the Lord has become my stronghold,
and my God the rock of my refuge.

❧ He will bring back on them their iniquity
and wipe them out for their wickedness.

Day 63 · April 27

Today, our air-defense system shot down ten Russian UAVs, each costing an average of $100,000. When I think of these numbers, I remember the looted homes in the Kyiv suburbs. The Russian soldiers were packing away underwear, kitchen appliances, washing machines, and even toilet bowls! And when I see the astronomical sums wasted on this war, I can't understand why that money couldn't be spent on improving the lives of people in Russia. Many Russian people join the army because they live below the poverty line, and the army would at least provide them with food, clothes, and housing. It explains why they were so surprised and angry to see people living decent lives in Ukraine. It's another proof of the inhumane nature of the Russian government, so I pray for its defeat and liberation of people (both in Ukraine and in Russia) from this evil.

Day 67 · May 1

As we approach Victory in Europe Day, the Victory Day over Nazism in World War II, I can't help but draw parallels. There wasn't a family in Ukraine that remained untouched by WWII. We grew up listening to stories of our grandparents. I could never imagine that I would have to experience war first-hand.

During the early weeks of the war, my son asked me why this was happening. What caused the war. We had a long conversation with him about our decisions and their long-term consequences. An 8-year-old could understand it at his level, but I kept thinking about it long after we were done talking.

Wars don't start overnight. People don't turn into beasts overnight. It is a gradual, sometimes barely noticeable process that takes you further and further away from the Light. If you think about it, even night rarely comes suddenly – there's sunset and lingering twilight before everything is swallowed up by darkness. However big or small, every decision we make will either bring us closer or distance us from God. It is up to us to choose, but we must remember that small steps make up long distances, and we need to make sure we are aware of which direction we are moving in.

The war Ukraine is fighting today is a war of worldviews. The worldview adopted and promoted by the Russian Federation stems from the communist worldview of the Soviet Union. The losses of the Soviet army in WWII were colossal, but the army generals believed a soldier's life is of no value. They said the women would give birth to more soldiers, so there was no need to feel sorry for the dead. Russia has already lost over 25,000 soldiers in the past two months of this war. I'm not even talking about the number of people they killed. The Red Army heavily relied on barrier troops, anti-retreat forces called to prevent the flight of servicemen from the battlefield and capture saboteurs and deserters. Often, they would shoot the "cowards" to make sure no one left the battle. There are many reports about Russia using barrier troops to execute deserters seeking to escape the combat zone. In the intercepted conversations, the Russian army soldiers and those forcefully mobilized from the occupied Donetsk and Luhansk regions complain that they don't want to fight but are afraid to surrender because they would be shot in the back by the anti-retreat detachments.

Like any totalitarian government, the Soviet Union used propaganda to brainwash people. We know about the Soviet occupation of Poland under Molotov-Ribbentrop Pact, but the USSR took advantage of WWII to also occupy Latvia, Lithuania, Estonia, and Finland. The Red Army that was praised for the victory over Nazism (and they did deserve praise for that) is the same army that invaded these independent states. The soldiers were told they were defending and liberating ethnic Ukrainians and Belarusians. Eighty years have passed, and they use the same pretext to send brainwashed Russian troops to invade Ukraine. The Russian soldiers expect to be welcomed as liberators, and they are raging in search of the "Ukrainian Nazis" but are utterly confused when they see the reality.

Why did I share this long "history lesson"? It's just my reflection on the danger of ideas circulating in our world. We must be careful and thorough in examining what we believe in and take responsibility for our decisions. Otherwise, in a few decades, we may find ourselves not that different from what we call evil today.

Every day in my prayers, I ask God to guard our minds and help us discern truth from lies. Our mind is one more battlefield the enemy is launching its attacks on.

"For the weapons of our warfare are not of the flesh but have divine power to destroy strongholds. We destroy arguments and every lofty opinion raised against the knowledge of God, and take every thought captive to obey Christ" (2 Corinthians 10: 4-5).

Day 72 • May 6

As you can see, WWIII is only a matter of time if the bully is not stopped soon. Please, pray for deliverance and divine intervention.

Please, keep praying for Mariupol. Today, Azovstal suffered 34 air-raids. It is bombed and shelled using all possible weapons from the land, sea, and air. There are over 1,000 Ukrainian defenders there, and hundreds of them are wounded without access to the medical care they need. May God's mercy and power be with them.

And I will keep praising God and waiting for His vengeance:

> ⚜ Glorious are you, more majestic than the mountains full of prey. The stouthearted were stripped of their spoil; they sank into sleep; all the men of war were unable to use their hands. At your rebuke, O God of Jacob, both rider and horse lay stunned. But you, you are to be feared! Who can stand before you when once your anger is roused? From the heavens you uttered judgment; the earth feared and was still, when God arose to establish judgment, to save all the humble of the earth.
> (Psalm 76:4-9)

Day 76 • May 10

Resilience seems to be my theme word of the day.

The last few days, I felt overwhelmed with the news from Mariupol, and the situation with the Azovstal Steel Plant remains serious, so keep praying, please. As if in response to this, today, God kept sending my way beautiful stories of hope as if reassuring me that He is with us and He is working.

While digging trenches in the Odesa region, the Territorial Defense group discovered ancient ceramic amphoras. The findings are dated around 4-5th century BC and will be added to the collection of the National Archaeological Museum.

Every day, a 20-year-old man bakes 300 loaves of bread for the defenders of Kharkiv and cooks 200 hot meals for the elderly. When the explosions get close, he turns up the music.

A girl who evacuated from Borodyanka (one of the small suburban towns that were leveled with the ground) in early March remembers their way in-between shelling and says, "I will remember this day forever. That's when I truly saw the power of God and believed." Another girl from Makariv (Kyiv region) whose home was burned down by the Russians remembers all the precious memories and family photos destroyed there. Still, she ends with a phrase, "If we could take four bare walls and turn them into a home, we'll be able to do it again, even if it takes years."

A man and his two brothers were taken captive by the Russians in the Chernihiv region when their village came under occupation in mid-March. The men were interrogated and tortured for three days. Then they were shot in the head and thrown into a grave. One of the men regained consciousness in a few hours, got out of the grave even though his hands and feet were tied, and managed to get to a nearby village, somehow getting past the Russian positions! The bullet went through his cheek and came out just below his ear without damaging any vital organs.

I saw a photo taken in one of the liberated villages. The Russian bombs destroyed the house, but the wood-fired oven remains standing. The woman is cooking the traditional Ukrainian borscht. This photo, along with other stories, gives me hope as it so beautifully reflects the spirit of our nation. They may be trying to kill us, but we refuse to die. We will not give up, and every day each one of us does everything to bring us one day closer to our victory, even if it means cooking borscht.

"We are afflicted in every way, but not crushed; perplexed, but not driven to despair; persecuted, but not forsaken; struck down, but not destroyed" (2 Corinthians 4:8-9).

Day 78 · May 12

At the same time, the Ukrainian Army has pushed the enemy further away from Kharkiv, cutting one of the roads used by Russians to send supplies to Izum (Kharkiv region). Many experts say that in many locations, Ukraine is starting counterattacks while Russia switches to defense mode. Even though it is too early to celebrate any military victory, I will praise God for every inch of our land liberated from the occupiers.

More and more intercepted conversations reveal the desperation of Russian soldiers. Most of them hope to get an injury to come back home alive. Even their relatives start wondering what they are fighting for and why the government is silent about the losses. Please, keep praying for the Russian people – for the veil of propaganda to be lifted from their eyes, for them to embrace the truth, and for Russian soldiers to surrender or flee in fear.

Tonight my good friend shared a verse that came to her mind when she prayed for Ukraine. I pray we see it fulfilled in Mariupol and all of Ukraine:

"Give us aid against the enemy, for human help is worthless. With God we will gain the victory, and he will trample down our enemies" (Psalm 108:12-13 NIV).

Day 80 · May 14

We often hear the phrase that history repeats itself. Today, I pray with all of my might that it wouldn't. I pray that Russia will be stopped and that this vicious circle of oppression will be broken. I pray that we would never forget the price our defenders are paying for us to be able to live in peace, and there is no greater love than this.[vi]

Day 81 · May 15

This morning, my son shared his dream with me. He said he saw a lonely man at home by himself during this war. And then God sent His angel with a sword to be next to this man to protect him and make sure he didn't feel lonely. I kept thinking about this dream throughout the day. I am sure that what my son saw in a dream is real and happens every day. I thought about my friends from YWAM Kyiv who evacuate people and bring aid to the liberated villages – they not only bring care packages but come with open hearts, listening ears, and the Good News. I thought about stories I heard during the first month of the war from different people I know – a few of them shared how they needed help and someone (a neighbor, a colleague from years ago, or even a stranger) would come "out of nowhere" bringing them what they needed. I've heard from many people that as they were praying at the beginning of the war, they saw visions of legions of angles coming from Heaven to fight the evil that came to Ukraine. I praise God for His angels, and I encourage you to persevere in prayer because prayer is a powerful weapon that we have the privilege to use.

Day 86 · May 20

Please, keep praying for the temporarily occupied territories, for people trying to evacuate, for the cities experiencing artillery shelling and missile strikes. Pray there would be no new attacks, especially using the armed forces of Belarus and "Transnistria." Pray for the light of truth to shine brightly and expose the lies of the Russian propaganda that have spread far beyond the territory of Russia. Pray that God would guard the hearts of our people, and especially our soldiers, that they would not grow bitter but would draw near to Jesus.

Day 96 · May 30

Celebration,
While Aware of the Costs

A season to bloom: *The crowning season for the tulips arrives as their flowers reach to the sky. But celebration is vulnerable – the tulip has used huge amounts of the bulb's resources in the hope of future goodness.*

As I read stories of survivors, I can't help but see God's miracles and angels at work. Three women left Bucha on foot to get to Irpin. They called it "the road of death" because many died on that road, so they were praying the whole time. When they got to a checkpoint, the soldiers asked where did the fourth one go because they saw a man leading their way.

A lady was peacefully sleeping in her bed on the second floor of her house. She woke up because she heard a noise downstairs and decided to check on it. She didn't have the time to reach the first floor when her house was shelled – a rocket broke the roof and the bed she was sleeping on but did not explode. She wasn't even scratched.

A man in an occupied town left his bomb shelter to go across the street to get water. His wife heard gunshots, saw him fall to the ground and Russian soldiers pass him by. After the soldiers left, he got up unharmed. He explained that he didn't see them coming but he heard a voice "drop to the ground" and did it just in time to dodge the bullet. It saved his life.

A family was sheltering in their garage basement in Mariupol for weeks. They were praying and reciting Psalm 91, especially during shelling. Their building was one of the very few that remained untouched during heavy shelling. By God's grace, their friend was able to get into the city, find them, and bring them out of Mariupol. Later that day they found out that their garage was bombed during an airstrike.

A man showing the reporters a missile rocket that did not explode said, "Do you know what this is? It's an answer to someone's prayer, and we see lots of rockets that did not explode, so please, keep praying."

May these stories encourage us and help us pray with even more fervor. The following days and weeks will be very hard and very important as the enemy will concentrate on crushing Mariupol and completely occupying Donetsk and Luhansk regions. The spirit of our army is strong, yet the enemy has powerful weapons and lots of personnel. Please, pray for this "David and Goliath" battle to bring glory to God and victory for Ukraine.

Day 43 · April 7

I know I've said this before, but I'll repeat it. This war has taught us to appreciate and value what we have. And I'm not talking just about things in our personal lives. It has taught me to love my Ukraine, its every town, every village, every person. While we used to dream about vacations overseas or in Europe, I now dream of the day when the war is over, and we can visit all the regions of our country that are racked with pain at the moment but will become glorious again. This love that I feel for my country now is very deep and personal; it's a very intimate kind of love. That's what makes the pain more excruciating. That's why I can't pretend the war is over just because the front has moved away from Kyiv.

Day 44 · April 8

That is why I rejoice whenever I hear about the way our people respond to this destruction. I rejoice when I see pictures of volunteers cleaning the streets of Irpin from rubble for life to triumph over death. I have tears of joy when I read about a lady from a town in the west of Ukraine sending young trees to Kharkiv to be planted in the destroyed park. I rejoice when I see pictures of our soldiers with pets they find and rescue in the war zone because it shows their values and the condition of their hearts. I am glad that there's this enormous gap between us and "them" because it unmistakably shows what we are fighting for.

Please, keep praying for Ukraine. There were a lot of missile strikes on Dnipro, Mykolaiv, and Kharkiv yesterday and today. Russian troops are regrouping in preparation for an attack – pray for their utter defeat. Pray for Mariupol – may it be invincible under God's protection. Pray for the values and light to prevail over emptiness and darkness.

"Whoever is righteous has regard for the life of his beast, but the mercy of the wicked is cruel" (Proverbs 12:10).

Day 46 · April 10

In Korolivka, Kyiv region, Ukrainian forces discovered a Russian warehouse with ammunition (about 100 boxes of shells). The invaders abandoned it in their flight.

A twenty-year-old Ukrainian soldier along with his two friends was taken captive by the Russians in one of the villages in Kyiv region in early March. They were interrogated and released, but the Russians started shooting at them as soon as they got in the car. He was the only one who survived but he was severely wounded. He walked through the woods for two days to get to the positions of the Ukrainian army. When they took him to the hospital, the doctors realized he was wounded in the heart and the bullet was stuck in the posterior wall of the heart. They performed a highly risky surgery but it went so well that the next day he was back on his feet.

In the first days of the war, a Russian warship attacked the Ukrainian border guard on the Snake Island (you may have heard that story). Today, this warship, which happens to be the flagship of the Russian fleet, missile cruiser *Moskva*, was hit by Ukrainian missiles. Once again, it became possible because of the weather – heavy rain prevented the Russian air-defense system from recognizing those missiles, and the stormy weather makes it hard to send rescue teams to the warship. Many compare that missile cruiser to Goliath, something that was deemed invincible. But with God, everything is possible.

"For the Lord will vindicate his people and have compassion on his servants" (Psalm 135:14).

Please, be encouraged to pray with even more fervor.

Day 49 · April 13

As the fighting intensifies, we're subconsciously looking for something "big" to report, but the situation is changing every hour, and I have to remind myself that sometimes "Nothing big to report" is also God's answer to our prayers.

I must admit, last night, as I was going to bed, with air-raid warnings in all regions of Ukraine, I was wondering what the night would bring. Just like in the first weeks of war, I hesitated before opening my phone in the morning and let out a sigh of relief when I discovered that the enemy attacks weren't successful.

Day 55 · April 19

A secret warehouse with ammunition and components for military equipment worth $200 million was found in Kharkiv region. This ammunition had been stolen from the military arsenals of Ukraine with the intention of handing it over to the invaders. The warehouse contained 60 complete tank engines, a large number (10 railway cars) of spare parts for armored vehicles, and 26 guided air-to-air missiles for standard military aircraft and helicopters.

Russian soldiers have started rebelling against their commanders (recent reports came from Zaporizhzhia region). They are demoralized, and one of the main reasons for rebellion is that they are not paid the promised money. Conflict Intelligence Team said that up to 40% of Russian soldiers who were used in Ukraine refuse to return to fight.

According to military experts, over 9,000 artillery shells of different caliber did not explode when they reached the intended target, 400 of them are aviation bombs! One of them was successfully neutralized in Irpin today – a 500 kg bomb that could have detonated any moment after it was thrown on the city over three weeks ago!

Day 56 · April 20

Today, there were more missile strikes (on Odesa airport and the Dnipropetrovsk region), but it looks like there are no casualties.

There was a successful POW exchange today – Ukraine was able to get seven civilians and seven soldiers (including one pregnant woman) from captivity. We know that our people are kept in inhumane conditions and are often tortured by Russians while in captivity. There's proof that the Russians execute Ukrainian soldiers who chose to surrender. I praise God these people were rescued. Please, keep praying for the hundreds that remain in Russian captivity.

Twenty civilians were evacuated from Azovstal (Mariupol) during a short ceasefire! Hundreds still remain under the rubble, hundreds are wounded, but let's pray there are more safe evacuations both for the civilians and servicemen in Mariupol.

"I will remember the deeds of the Lord; yes, I will remember your wonders of old. I will ponder all your work, and meditate on your mighty deeds" (Psalm 77:11-12).

Day 66 · April 30

Honestly, I didn't expect a response right away; I was just pouring out my heart before Him. But God is always good and faithful, and He showed me an article from a popular online news media. The report[vii] tells about fishermen who saved 2,000 people in the Kyiv region from starvation during the Russian occupation in March. Strakholissia (literally: Scary Woods) is a village with about 700 residents in the Kyiv Reservoir area. The fishermen organized an evacuation and supply of humanitarian aid by crossing the vast "Kyiv Sea" on their boats. A woman was in her last month of pregnancy with a scheduled c-section and no way of getting to the hospital. The fishermen brought her from the occupied Vyshhorod region to the left bank of the Dnipro River and helped her get to Kyiv. The whole time she was praying the Lord's prayer as they were navigating the stormy, icy waters of the river. She gave birth to a healthy boy and named him, in honor of one of the disciples of Jesus who was a fisherman from Galilee.

Another woman jokes that Jesus needed only five loaves of bread and two fishes to feed thousands, but they needed a lot more food. She and her friends were fishing and distributing the catch among the villagers. She said they never planned to become volunteers, but they knew it was their responsibility when the time came. A man and his friends evacuated people on their boats in broad daylight in front of the Russian invaders. Some villages seemed to be hidden from the eyes of the invaders, and the locals could easily navigate all the water meadows, swamps, and islands. He was surprised they were never shot at, they weren't attacked from the air (with numerous UAVs, helicopters, and planes flying above them), and they were safe even during storms.

Most of these heroes happened to be in Strakholissia "by accident." They were drawn to this village in-the-middle-of-nowhere a few years before the invasion, and they could never really explain it to their friends. Now, they realize they were brought there to organize the river crossing to the "Kingdom of the Living."

Day 69 · May 3

Praise the Lord, all the women, children, and elderly have been successfully evacuated from the Azovstal plant in Mariupol. The plan is to evacuate the wounded and medical workers as part of the second stage. Please, keep praying for the servicemen still bravely fighting in Mariupol.

The story that really lifted my spirit today was shared by people from Irpin. That family evacuated early with a bare minimum of belongings. When they returned home this week, they saw that most of their expensive things were missing. They were sad but thankful that at least they were alive. When they looked around, they realized that their items were not stolen. In fact, someone got into their apartment through a broken window and hid their valuables (took a TV off the wall and hid it behind couch cushions, hid small appliances in a children's bed, hid their cash, and didn't take a thing, even from the fridge!) This person also boarded and sealed their window afterward. I praise God for He sends His angels in unexpected forms to unexpected places.

Please, pray for the abundance of His angels in Ukraine, especially on May 8-10.

Day 73 · May 7

Praise God, today was rather ordinary for a country at war. We were anxious about what Russia may do on the "Victory Day" when they celebrate their military might. Thankfully, Putin did not initiate a nuclear strike, did not declare general mobilization, and didn't announce the annexation of temporarily occupied regions of Ukraine, and it's good.

Day 75 · May 9

Today, Ukraine celebrates its victory in the Eurovision Song Contest. While the song contest in itself is not so important, this victory is very symbolic for us. First of all, it shows the unity of the European nations against the brutal war waged by Russia on different fronts. Many participants called for peace in Ukraine. The participants from Ukraine (Kalush Orchestra) risked disqualification and ended their performance with a call, "Save Mariupol! Save Azovstal now!" I praise God that He allows us to use different platforms to cry out to nations and world leaders.

Day 79 · May 13

Even though I felt overwhelmed today, I saw a beautiful story in the reported news. A 28-year-old soldier was brought to a field hospital with an abdominal wound. It was during the surgery that the doctors discovered that the wounds were a lot more severe – the shell tore through the liver, diaphragm, lung, and heart. This type of wound is considered deadly. But the miracle was that a vascular surgeon was available in that hospital and was able to remove shell shards and piece everything back together. This soldier is now undergoing further treatment in Kyiv. The doctors say he lives only because someone who could perform this unique surgery was there to do it immediately. I praise God for His providence.

Day 91 · May 25

My glimpse of hope for today came from the intercepted conversation between a Russian soldier and his wife:

You are invaders and murderers. I don't know how I can live knowing you are murdering people. You should have refused to go on February 23. You are killing people!

No, I'm killing enemies. There are no people in war.

You invaded their country. You attacked them, not the other way around. If they had attacked us, you would have been a defender of your country. But now, you are an invader and a fascist.

I praise God for every person in Russia who is willing to see the truth and is not afraid to act upon it. I pray for God to send prophets to Russia who would be able to speak boldly and bring the nation to repentance because repentance is vital for their (and our) future.

Day 96 · May 20

Loss and Lament

A season to regenerate: *Far too quickly are the days of the beautiful flowers gone. The tulip begins to replenish its stores under the ground. This stage is not lovely to look at, but if the stage is cut short, tulips are at risk of dying.*

Tonight, they reported that all of Kyiv region has been freed from Russian troops (with a high chance of numerous undercover groups staying behind though). As soon as you hear it, you naturally want to rejoice. But you are surprised to discover that you can't be joyful. You look at the pictures from Bucha, Hostomel and Irpin – once beautiful suburbs of Kyiv. You hear about the cruel unspeakable things that people had to go through. I don't even want to mention them here on my page as if it would somehow make it go away even though I know it's not true. I hope that all of these war crimes are properly recorded for the court not so much for the guilty to be punished but for the world to know how cruel and inhumane people can be. There are people who try to justify Russian soldiers by saying that they didn't want to come to Ukraine but didn't have a choice because they were given an order. Well, here we see things that are done not by orders but by choice. Shooting unarmed civilians in the back of the head, raping women and children, looting homes – these things sound horrible on their own and I omit unspeakable details on purpose. And we know only a tiny little bit. How would we feel after we learn about things that happened in Chernihiv, Sumy, and Kharkiv regions? Which stories from Mariupol will forever remain unspoken? I'm afraid to even think about it.

I'm often asked these days if I ever feel hateful. Well, I hate what I see. I hate what my people are going through. I hate that our children had to mature overnight. I hate the pain we experience every day. I hate that so many of us will never see our loved ones again because their lives had been taken. I hate that someone decided that they have the right to take our peaceful life away. I hate the evil that has come to our land. I know the root of this evil and I know that it can only be overcome by God's power. Do I hate these people? I don't think so, I just want them gone from my land and I want them to stop terrorizing Ukraine and stop being a threat to the civilized world.

That's why I pray for them to repent and turn from their wicked ways. And I choose to trust God, trust in His character, and rely on His justice. I know that He has already defeated death on the cross, and I am looking forward to the day when He will defeat all evil.

Day 38 · April 2

The 39th day of war was still filled with shock and grief over the war crimes discovered in the small towns surrounding Kyiv. Your mind seems to be developing a sort of defense mechanism to keep you from going insane from all the horror movie scenes you see in the news reports and about which you hear from your friends. But just as you thought that the shock of the war was wearing off, it hits you with a new strength leaving you at a loss for words.

At first, you try to accept that "the unthinkable" happened, and Russia decided to start a full-scale war in Ukraine, attacking from all possible directions. You convince yourself that soon it will be over, and you and everyone else will be able to come home. You know that lives will be lost, but you want to believe that those will be mostly "military losses," which are as bad and as painful but at least expected during any war. And you try to live with this thought.

Then you hear about Mariupol, Kharkiv, Chernihiv, Okhtyrka, Volnovakha... Bombs being purposefully dropped on hospitals to maximize casualties... Shelling of residential areas. Random missile strikes throughout Ukraine. You find out that family members of your friends are in those dangerous locations, and they've been out of touch for days. You know that war is cruel; you fervently pray for each town in occupation and in the line of fire; you realize that hundreds of civilians have died, but you want to believe that most of Ukraine will be spared and even those who are in immediate danger today will somehow be delivered. And you try to live with this thought.

Then you hear about the Bucha massacre (which stands not only for Bucha but also for other suburban towns in Kyiv area that experienced hell)... You want to believe it's something that belongs in history books and cannot be taking place in the XXI century. No, we are civilized people! We are humans, for heaven's sake! That can't be true! Tell me it's not true! Tell me it's fake news and someone's cruel joke! But you know what it truly is. It is genocide taking place in the heart of Europe. You know it didn't come to Kyiv and wasn't repeated there on a bigger scale only because these towns took the hit and stopped the enemy. You don't understand how anyone can find justification for it, especially when everything is so easily documented with the use of modern technology. And then you wonder if you'll ever be able to live with this thought.

Day 39 · April 3

Forty-four days of full-scale war on Ukraine.

In my mind, it's still February, and only the change of landscape outside the window reminds me that the spring is coming. I am surprised every time I look at the calendar, and I swear there was no March this year.

I tried to work a little bit, and I even tried listening to online lectures on non-fiction translation. I see messages from my neighbors who are slowly returning to Kyiv. It is so tempting to pretend that the war is over. You can simply shove it away, squeeze it out of your mind and your routine. Forget it ever happened – what matters is that you are safe, and you can "go back to normal." But if you do it, will you ever be at peace with yourself?

The world is still trying to get over the shock of #BuchaMassacre, but every day we learn more horrible accounts from towns in Kyiv region. Yesterday, they destroyed another portion of the railroad blocking the only route of evacuation trains bringing people from Donetsk and Luhansk regions. They keep blocking evacuation busses coming to get people out of Mariupol, Melitopol, Berdiansk, Kherson...

The cynicism of Russia is beyond what one can comprehend.

This morning, Russian missiles landed on Kramatorsk railway station just as thousands of people were trying to evacuate. It was a deliberate terrorist attack that took the lives of over 55 people (including five children) and left hundreds wounded. It was done on purpose knowing that hundreds of people were trying to evacuate. The words on the rocket say, "for the children". In their mind, that's a fitting inscription for a missile that killed at least 39 people (including four children) and wounded over 100.

꙾ There are six things that the Lord hates, seven that are an abomination to him: haughty eyes, a lying tongue, and hands that shed innocent blood, a heart that devises wicked plans, feet that make haste to run to evil, a false witness who breathes out lies, and one who sows discord among brothers.
(Proverbs 6:16-19)

Day 44 · April 8

On Monday night (April 11), Russian occupation forces used chemical weapon, a poisonous substance of unknown origin, against Ukrainian military and civilians in the city of Mariupol. It was dropped from an enemy UAV. The victims have respiratory failure, vestibulo-atactic syndrome. The consequences are being clarified.

Please, pray for God's deliverance! Pray for His miracle. Pray for protection of everyone in Mariupol. May God show His power and mercy there!

Pray for protection over the rest of Ukraine (and the world). This evil must be stopped!!!

"Woe to the wicked! It shall be ill with him, for what his hands have dealt out shall be done to him" (Isaiah 3:11).

Day 47 · April 11

Please, pray for people who are forcefully deported from the occupied territories. It's been reported that over 600,000 people have been taken to Russia (including over 120,000 children). They go through filtration camps there, and oftentimes men, women, and children are separated. There were reports that some families were sent to the remote economically depressed regions of Russia. Today, they announced "language camps" to force abducted Ukrainian children to learn Russian. They're also promoting a "simplified adoption program" for Russian families to take in Ukrainian children. Please, pray for the protection of everyone, especially the most vulnerable ones!

Day 49 · April 13

Fifty days of war. Over 1,540 missiles launched at Ukraine. 5,794 air-raid alerts (an average of 118 alerts a day). A total of over 700 hours (the equivalent of 30 days) that Ukrainians had to spend in bomb shelters. One hundred and

The hat of a child killed in war - Day 56, April 20, 2022

ninety-seven children killed (and 351 wounded). How much longer? I don't know. How will it end? I don't know. But I know that God knows and He cares. I know that today we are one day closer to the day when He will restore justice, wipe our tears, and bring peace to our land.

Day 50 · April 14

On Friday, when Jesus was crucified, it looked like the enemy had won. It was so sudden. The disciples were confused, scared, and desperate. They felt hopeless, all of their expectations had been betrayed. They couldn't make sense of it all. They didn't know how they should then live. Their world had come to an end.

We, Ukrainians, have been living in this "Friday" mood for 51 days. The paragraph above describes how we feel. We see death and destruction. We have put our lives "on hold" indefinitely. We don't know when or if we'll return to our homes. We are aware that any day could be our last one.

The only difference is that, unlike the disciples of Jesus, we know how His story unfolds. We know that He has won. We know that the present darkness is just for a little bit, but the Light is coming. We know we have hope in Him.

Day 51 · April 15

I talked to a friend whose family used to live in a village not far from Brovary. Even though they evacuated ahead of time and their village itself was not occupied, they can't imagine going back there as it would mean passing familiar places that lie in ruins now. I can only imagine how much pain is inside their hearts.

I remember friends who considered moving to Irpin, and the chills go down my spine as I thank God they never did.

Last night, there was a missile strike on Kyiv, the rocket hitting an object in the district where we live. I remembered that I passed that location several times last year while taking our car to a service station. I'm wondering if I'll ever be able to drive down that road again without thinking about war.

You can imagine the whirlwind of emotions we go through every day. It is so easy to fall into despair. It is so easy to start blaming God. It is so easy not to notice His miracles. It is so easy to become paralyzed by fear. Which is why I am incredibly thankful to all of you, our prayer warriors, the knights of God's spiritual army. Please, keep lifting up Ukraine in prayer.

"Be gracious to me, O God, I put my trust in you. In God, whose word I praise, in God I trust; I shall not be afraid. What can flesh do to me?" (Psalm 56:1-4).[viii]

Here is a picture of a 13-year-old's hat. The boy was killed by Russian occupiers when he and his mother and three-year-old brother tried to get out of the occupied Peremoha village in Baryshivka district.

Today, the media reported Putin ordered his Minister of Defense not to attack the Azovstal plant (the last citadel for Ukrainian forces and shelter for hundreds of civilians in Mariupol). A mere couple of hours later, the plant was bombed and heavily shelled while Kadyrov troops happily reported that they had successfully destroyed the city. This shows what Russian words are worth. Thankfully, the Azovstal shelter proves to be stronger than enemy weaponry. "The salvation of the righteous is from the Lord; he is their stronghold in the time of trouble. The Lord helps them and delivers them; he delivers them from the wicked and saves them, because they take refuge in him" (Psalm 37:39-40).

"Mom, when will this war be over?" This was my son's question as he was going to bed tonight. I wish I knew the answer. It would have been easier to wait then. Many people have returned to Kyiv, and as I read messages from our neighbors, I long to be back as well. We're just a couple of hours away from Kyiv, so it's hard to remain reasonable and resist this temptation.

Day 64 · April 28

Going for a walk when you feel like it.
Choosing what you would like for lunch.
Getting coffee from a local coffee shop.
Visiting family and returning home.

All these things are so trivial and could be something you did today. For me (and for millions of Ukrainians) these little things mean freedom. There's very little freedom in the temporarily occupied territories. Freedom is virtually nonexistent in the active fighting zones. Those of us who are not in immediate danger (who evacuated abroad, found a temporary home within Ukraine, or live in a relatively safe place) may seem fine and comfortable on the outside but we are deeply affected by this loss of freedom.

Day 66 · April 30

Russia is known for its pompous Victory Day on the 9th of May. Over the years, this holiday has turned into an aggressive celebration of their military might. That's why they desperately need something to present as their big victory on that day. They've decided to use Mariupol as their victorious symbol, so they're cleaning the streets and disposing of dead bodies. They're planning on having a military parade there. I can't imagine their level of cynicism even though we see proof of it every day. Just thinking about it makes me sick.

There were more missile strikes today. One of the rockets damaged a railroad bridge in the city of Dnipro. We heard airplanes flying over our place during the evening air-raid warning. We knew it was our armed forces, so we prayed a blessing over them and asked for God's protection and guidance for them. It also reminded us that even though the frontline is hundreds of kilometers away from us, the war is still very near.

Russia keeps forcefully deporting people from temporarily occupied territories. Our authorities have been able to locate 300 people from

Mariupol. They were taken to Vladivostok (a town in the far East, close to the Russian border with China and North Korea!). They have no money and no means of communication. They have no documents and are offered only unqualified low-paid jobs. The USSR used the same region and a similar strategy to punish those who dared to think differently from what the Party allowed. And how is it different from the Nazi labor camps? Please, pray for these people. Also, pray for the thousands whose location is still unknown.

As Russian troops seem unable to succeed, more and more experts start talking about the nuclear threat, and Russian propagandists actively entertain this idea. Even though the use of a nuclear weapon seems suicidal, we've seen enough of Putin's suicidal decisions to know this threat can't be dismissed or taken lightly. I want to believe that God would interfere and prevent this disaster from happening. Please, pray, as this is the only weapon that's much stronger than nuclear strikes.

Russia keeps looting Ukraine. They have stolen over 100 tons of wheat from Luhansk region (and destroyed 30 tons of grain in Rubizhne, Luhansk region). This supply could have kept the region fed for almost three years. This cannibalistic government wants to starve Ukrainians just as they did less than 100 years ago during the Holodomor (1932-1933). The farmers aren't allowed to start the planting season in the occupied territories; their farming equipment is confiscated. Please, pray for God's provision and protection.

Day 70 · May 4

We may read a short statement, "The enemy launched an attack on [insert a city name] but did not succeed," and it may seem small, but hundreds (if not thousands) of our soldiers made this statement possible. Many of them sacrificed their lives and health to make it happen. Mariupol defenders continue their resistance for over 70 days against all odds – it's a short line representing pain and heroism mixed together. Even when we don't speak about Mariupol, we keep lamenting over it, begging for a miracle.

Day 72 · May 6

Today is May 8, the Day of Remembrance and Reconciliation, when we celebrate the end of WWII in Europe, remember all the victims, and honor those who defended their homeland and the world from Nazism.

Today, I think about my relatives whose lives were marred by that war. I remember Iakiv Ikonnikov (1902-1941) – my great-grandfather. He was killed in a battle not far from Kakhovka, Kherson region. Today, his hometown is under Russian occupation. I remember Dmytro Hryb (1913-1995) – my great-grandfather. He was mobilized and sent to fight barehand. He was wounded in 1941 in his first battle about 100 miles from his native village. He was captured by the Nazis and put in the prisoner camp near the city of Uman. The doctors amputated his wounded leg. Somehow his wife (my great-grandmother) found out where he was kept, hired a horse wagon, and brought him home. Since he was discharged so soon, the Soviet government never recognized him as a war veteran, so he couldn't receive any social benefits. I remember him and his pegleg.

I remember Tetiana Hohulia (1919-2004) – my great-grandmother. As a young girl, she was sent to Germany to work in a labor camp in an underground aviation plant (Mittelwerk) from 1942 to 1945. She shared many of the stories from those years, but I guess the most important thing that I heard from her was that not all the Germans were evil, and there were people who tried to support the "ostarbeiters" (labor camp slaves) and treated them as people, not as dirt. I guess her stories about people who chose to be kind despite the given orders help me pray for the Russian people today.

I remember Olena Ikonnikova (1929-2003) – my grandmother. She finished elementary school when WWII broke out, and that was all the education she had. After the war, she had to work, so there was no time to study. I guess that's why she loved to read and had lots of books and newspapers at home as if trying to make up for all the lost time. By God's grace, she and her siblings were spared during the war by what can be described as no less than God's intervention. I never understood why my grandma would always stock up on food and why she would always say, "We'll make do as long as there is no war."

There are many other war-related stories that shaped the life of my family. Many of my relatives had to live under the Nazi occupation in the war zone. They were changed by the war.

On this day, I can't help but wonder about the (future) children and grandchildren of the soldiers who defend Ukraine today. Will they get a chance to meet their parents and grandparents? Will they live long enough to make happy memories together? How many kids will have grandparents with "peglegs" and prosthetic arms? Will all of those forcefully deported to Russia find their way back home? We've been saying #lestweforget and #neveragain for decades, but the world is witnessing the horrors of war #again in the XXI century. Will we learn the lessons this time to make sure this never happens again?

As we celebrate Mother's Day and thank God for our moms (or mother figures in our lives), let's also pray for mothers in Ukraine: Pray for mothers who lost their children (of all ages) in this war; pray for mothers separated from their children because they are fighting the enemy; pray for those who lost their mothers in this war; pray for mothers and children who won't see each other today because they are separated by the Russian occupation, line of fire, or state borders and refugee status.

Day 74 · May 8

The couple in this picture was married for three days when the husband was killed. They both were in Azovstal, and their military commander officiated the wedding. The rings were made out of aluminum foil. They hurried to live because they knew they could die at any moment.

This war has taught us to treasure what we have and to find a balance between living in the moment while making necessary decisions to ensure your tomorrow.

Day 77 · May 11

My grandma Olena was nine years old when she saw her father for the last time. Stepan was arrested and accused of anti-Soviet activity. We may never know whether he was actually guilty or not, but his case files have clear signs of being fabricated. His wife and five children were labeled the "family of the enemy of the state" and had to leave their house and everything they owned (the state confiscated it). Years later, in 1962, after Stepan's children wrote numerous letters to the authorities to find out any information about their father, they received a note stating that their father died of pneumonia in a prison camp in 1942. The note also said that he was rehabilitated post-mortem due to a lack of corpus delicti. That's all my dad knew about his grandfather.

After Ukraine declassified Soviet KGB archives in 2015, we learned that the reality was different. After being arrested on July 16, 1938, Stepan Somenko was executed on November 1, 1938. The cruelty of the Soviet regime knows no limits – it was not enough to ruin a person's life and torment his family; they also had to feed them lies about the death of their loved one.

How did we find out about it? My husband, Ivan, was going to search archives to learn what happened to his great-grandfather Levko (who was arrested around the same time as Stepan) and offered to look up my family member as well. We were shocked to discover that both of our great-grandfathers had their execution warrants signed by the same people, the "NKVD group of three" of Mykolaiv region.

It took us over 80 years to find out the truth. They were trying to hide it; they were giving false information, they kept the archives classified for decades, fearing the truth might leak out, but it still came to light, just as Jesus said, "nothing is hidden that will not be made manifest, nor is anything secret that will not be known and come to light" (Luke 8:17). I take comfort in this promise and pray for the truth about today's crimes to be revealed to the whole world.

Today, I think about my great-grandfather Stepan. His homeland, Kherson region, is occupied by the Russians. Pro-Ukrainian activists (as well as pastors, teachers, government workers, or anyone who refuses to cooperate) are kidnapped, interrogated, and tortured. Some of them are killed. Some of them are missing for weeks. The occupational forces think they can intimidate people into submission. What we see there today paints a very clear picture of what could happen if all of Ukraine fell into the hands of Russia. All 38 million of our population would become victims of political repressions (except those who would choose to side with the enemy).

Day 81 · May 15

Sometimes I feel bad about writing these updates. I don't want them to be so grim because life goes on, and every day there are reasons to laugh and rejoice. Yet, at the same time, I can't get superficially lighthearted knowing that hundreds of thousands of Ukrainians are going through hell. That is why I come to the Lord every day with my burdens, questions, complaints, and intercessions. He is the source of true joy and peace possible even amid war.

℣ Show us your steadfast love, O Lord,
and grant us your salvation.

℣ Let me hear what God the Lord will speak,
for he will speak peace to his people, to his saints;
but let them not turn back to folly.

℣ Surely his salvation is near to those who fear him,
that glory may dwell in our land.
(Psalm 85:7-9)

Day 85 · May 19

When I was a kid listening to stories about WWII, I had so many questions wondering what it was like to live in times of war. Did people cry all the time? Were there any breaks during the fighting? What did it mean to live under occupation (all of Ukraine was occupied during WWII)?

Unfortunately, today I have a much better understanding of those things, and I thank God that we are in a relatively safe location and I don't have a first-hand experience of many elements of this war.

I often think about people in temporarily occupied territories. Many of them stayed there not by choice but because it wasn't so easy to leave. Recently they reported that Russian forces started blocking all passages from Kherson region to the territories under Ukraine's control, so people are forced to go through Crimea or other occupied territories to Russia. They are also banning all humanitarian aid coming from Ukraine. The stores are running out of food and medicines, and people have to buy things in the street.

My heart breaks for the Kherson region because that's where my dad is from. That's where he was born. That's where my grandmother lived through WWII. That's where my grandparents worked on the construction of a hydropower station. That's where I spent the first year of my life, as my parents were assigned jobs there.

Kherson region is the birthplace of the tastiest tomatoes and sweetest watermelons. It is a region with a rich winery tradition. The unique nature of Kherson region is best known for the Oleshky Desert and the Askania-Nova National Park. Its seashores are the locations of many resorts. This region is intended for leisure and adventure, not bombing and occupation. I know that God will restore it to its true purpose.

It's been three whole months since the beginning of the full-scale war on Ukraine. It's hard to believe how different our lives used to be, and I am sure the changes inside us are much more significant than we can see now.

I've often said it before, but it feels like the time froze, yet the seasons somehow keep changing. I still get confused about which day of the week it is (it always feels like Thursday, the day of the invasion), and it takes me a while to count which month of the year it is. I remember plans I made going to bed on February 23:

I was going to call my hairdresser and make an appointment for a haircut. And I was going to get my nails done on Friday – as we were leaving Kyiv, I was joking if I should call and cancel my appointment because of the war or if that part was obvious.

I was going to do laundry. In the weeks before the invasion, I tried to do laundry every other day to make sure we had clean clothes if (when?) the war escalated. It's funny, but I remember most items in the laundry bin back home.

I was going to volunteer at my son's school. I was helping them with organizing the school library, and I couldn't wait for the project to be accomplished for the kids to be able to enjoy books. In fact, this is one of the things I'm really looking forward to doing once the war is over and everyone is back in Kyiv.

I was going to start preparing for the School of Biblical Studies (SBS), where I had been translating for the past five years. I was looking forward to the new school season. I was going to find out which books I would be teaching and start researching them. I can say that SBS was my dream job because I was doing what I loved in a company of amazing people who inspire me in my walk with God. Even though they had to cancel SBS this year, I believe that God is going to do some amazing things through this school in the years to come, and I'm praying I can still be a part of it.

I was going to step out in faith and try literary translation as a profession. I mostly read Christian literature in English as it's hard to find a good-quality Ukrainian translation, so I'm often disappointed that I can't recommend a good book to someone who doesn't speak the language. Last fall, I dreamed (it felt like my first grown-up dream) of helping make good Christian books available in Ukrainian. I was going to take the first practical steps at the end of February. Unfortunately, this dream has been put on hold by the war, but I hope I'll be able to return to it after Ukraine's victory.

The war canceled or postponed all of these plans, and I have bittersweet feelings about it. Strangely, this list gives me the determination to persevere and do everything I can to make sure these plans are fulfilled.

Day 89 · May 23

What did you feel when
you killed my husband?

Fear

Are you sorry for the
crime you committed?

Yes. I admit my guilt.
I understand you will never be
able to forgive me, but I ask
for your forgiveness.

Why did you come to our land?
What were you going to do here?

There was an order for us to go...
and for me to shoot

Do you know about the "duty to disobey"
(permission to disobey palpably
illegal orders)?

*Yes. I admit my guilt and am
ready to bear the punishment.*

You would think this dialogue is from a movie. I wish. This was a conversation at a court hearing. The first Russian soldier to be on trial for the war crimes committed in Ukraine is only 21 years old. He killed an unarmed civilian in Sumy region. He was sentenced to life in prison.

What a tragedy! My heart breaks. I weep for the family of the killed man. His wife is devastated. I weep for over 4,000 Ukrainian civilians killed by the Russian army (the number doesn't include those killed in Mariupol and other temporarily occupied territories). I weep for this Russian soldier who had his whole life ahead of him, yet he's already wasted it. We can get into a lengthy debate on whose fault all of this is. Does Putin bear sole responsibility for the war? Is this soldier's commander to blame for the death of this civilian? Is this young soldier simply a hostage to the circumstances?

I'd say no to all these questions. Freedom of choice is one of the greatest responsibilities entrusted to us by God. It is up to us to choose what to do with our lives, whom to follow, and which values to uphold. We are called to exercise this right wisely. And we must remember that all our choices have consequences – it is one of the first truths we taught our son.

Did this young soldier act in fear? Did Russian propaganda blind him? Is he genuinely repentant? I don't know. Honestly, I don't know what I would do if I were put in his shoes. I feel deep sorrow for this soldier's life, and my heart breaks for his family. But I know that he must face the consequences of his choices, and I pray he finds Jesus and true repentance in the process.

We may live under the illusion that our choices don't matter, that it is not up to us to solve "big" problems, that someone else is to blame for our circumstances. I understand that situations may differ, but I know that ultimately, we make the choice. Millions of Russians (or people from any other nation, for that matter) are also making a choice today, even if they choose to be "neutral" or passive. Even the ordinary and least significant ones, our words and actions have the power to build up and give life or kill and destroy. It is up to us to choose, so may we choose wisely.

This war takes all of us for a ride on the rollercoaster of emotions. My "rollercoaster" has been going downhill lately. The initial shock has long since worn off, and the weariness has set in.

Today, the hardest thing for me is seeing how some people from democratic countries, some of whom claim to be Christian and even profess the right values, try to justify Russia. This sort of betrayal (or blindness, ignorance, indifference, I don't know the right name for it) pains me the most. I am not blaming anyone, I am thankful for all the help we get (both on personal and government levels), but I am grieved for the state of humanity. After 2014, we all knew that Russia would start a full-scale war; there was no illusion, so it was not unexpected, even though it is still horrific and brutal. But we didn't expect we would also have to fight for the hearts of people we expected support from.

One of the popular statements I saw in comments online (and it is also one of the cliches of Russian propaganda) was, "Why were you silent about (insert any nation or conflict here), and why are you so concerned over Ukraine now?" Well, I'll respond to this one. I must confess that I was silent about many conflicts in the past. I remember reading reports about the war in Syria. I remember talking to my friends during the escalation between Azerbaijan and Armenia a few years ago. I briefly followed the situation in Afghanistan last year. These are recent examples, and I admit, I was too busy with things going on in my life to get to the bottom of what was going on there, even though I did pray as I came across news reports or received specific prayer requests from my friends. That is why when I pray about the situation in Ukraine today, I thank God for every caring heart and ask Him to make the hearts of Ukrainian people sensitive to the sufferings of others. With that being said, I'll also argue that two wrongs don't make it right. It may have been wrong of some person or government to be silent about bad things in the past, but it doesn't justify doing the same today. You may recognize that something was wrong in the past, and that can't be undone, but you still have the power to change your present and future actions.

Day 93 · May 27

According to the official reports, 242 children have been killed in the war, and over 440 have been wounded. Please, keep praying.

Day 94 · May 28

Resilience and the Seeds of Future Hope

A season to multiply: *The tulips begin to multiply and prepare for the following year. This invisible work of resilience is crucial. The commitment to goodness brings life into the world.*

Day 38, another day with mixed feelings.

We often talk about the things we will do after the victory. We may even plan how we will celebrate our victory. I don't know when it will happen but I know that that day will never turn into a festive celebration because of the price we pay for it now.

Day 38 · April 2

I am desperately searching for God in every account that I read.

Where was God? He was with a 13-year-old girl from a small village in the southern part of Ukraine. She was wounded during shelling, and a metal piece got stuck in her skull but didn't even cause bleeding. The doctors were able to stabilize her condition until three weeks later (!) she could be transported to Kyiv and underwent complex neurosurgery. Don't you see God's hand in this?

Where was God? He was with a family sheltering in Vorzel (a small town to the northwest of Kyiv, next to Bucha). One day, as they decided to evacuate and drove out of their gates, a man came running to their car. He knelt before the vehicle and started begging them not to leave otherwise they would be killed. They decided to listen to him for some reason, and it saved their lives as many cars were shot on that route that day. Twenty people, including two pregnant women, many children, and the elderly, stayed back and were able to evacuate the next day through the state-organized evacuation line. Don't you see how God sends His messengers to protect His children?

Where was God? He was with a group of students in Mariupol. As the city was left with no gas and no electricity, the only way to make food was over an open fire. To their great surprise, they discovered that old wooden window frames replaced with plastic windows in their dorm before the war hadn't been taken away but were carefully stacked by the building. Don't you see God providing in unexpected ways?

Where was God? He was in many other "coincidences," big and small. He is with us as long as we care to notice Him.

> ❧ By day the Lord commands his steadfast love,
> and at night his song is with me,
> a prayer to the God of my life.

> ❧ I say to God, my rock:
> "Why have you forgotten me?
> Why do I go mourning
> because of the oppression of the enemy?"

> ❧ As with a deadly wound in my bones,
> my adversaries taunt me,
> while they say to me all the day long,
> "Where is your God?"

> ❧ Why are you cast down, O my soul,
> and why are you in turmoil within me?

> ❧ Hope in God; for I shall again praise him,
> my salvation and my God.
> (Psalm 42:8-11)

Day 39 • April 3

I see light and hope in the stories of my friends from YWAM Kyiv. Friends of mine share personal stories of people they meet as they serve in Kyiv amidst war. Follow them to discover faces that stand behind the statistics. They do not consider themselves heroes; they simply do what they can where they are.

I see light and hope when I hear about a family doctor who stayed in Bucha and was saving lives in occupation. She helped several wounded, including a mother and her 1-year-old kid whose car was shelled as they tried to leave the town. When there was no water, electricity, or heat, she helped deliver a baby. She does not consider herself a hero; she was simply doing what she could right where she was.

I see light and hope when I hear about a woman who is mayor of a united territorial community of Ivankiv (located about halfway between Kyiv and the Russian border). She refused to evacuate to stay with her community even though she knew the invaders would be after her. It was her joy that they managed to keep the local hospital and bakery working throughout the occupation. At night, she would wear a mask and black coat and go around bringing food to the sick and elderly. One night, she saw a girl in the street just as the Russian soldiers were going wild, shooting at any moving target. She grabbed the girl and covered her with her black coat as they both fell to the ground – it saved their lives. She does not consider herself a hero; she was simply doing what she could right where she was.

I see light and hope in a picture I saw today. In it, a boy in the liberated Bucha reads a children's Bible while his mom stands in line for humanitarian aid. He is not a hero, but he lived through hell, and we can only pray there is room for light in his heart.

Day 42 · April 6

This morning, as I went outside, I heard the bees busily buzzing over the blooming apricot tree that was still in hibernation yesterday. To me, it was a message of hope.

"The Lord is good to those who wait for him, to the soul who seeks him. It is good that one should wait quietly for the salvation of the Lord" (Lamentations 3:25-26).

Day 51 · April 15

Yesterday, I read an interview with one of the church leaders in Ukraine. He said that perhaps God allowed this war to happen to draw people's attention back to Him. As the world watches Ukraine defend itself, they also witness Ukrainians calling on the name of the Lord, Ukrainian soldiers praying before battles, Bible verses and encouraging statements (such as "God is with us", "God didn't flee from Ukraine", "If our God is for us then who can stand against?", etc.) on billboards. He thinks this could bring awakening to the world and traditionally Christian nations that are slowly drifting away from

God without even noticing it. He believes that as the world watches Ukraine call out to God, they will also see His mighty hand as a testimony to all.

These thoughts from this church leader reminded me of the verses God pointed out to me in the first days of the war – Zechariah 4:6 "Not by might, nor by power, but by my Spirit, says the Lord of hosts."

I'm praying we see it fulfilled soon!

Day 55 – 19 April

As I read Easter greetings from our President, the Head of Ukraine's Intelligence Agency, the Commander-in-Chief of the Armed Forces of Ukraine, I was amazed because all of those addresses could be mistaken for sermons. I know that they all have speechwriters, and these messages are used as publicity tools; nevertheless, I praise God that He is reaching out to our nation even through these greetings. Those who do not believe in God but believe in our Armed Forces and have great respect for our military leadership heard the Gospel proclaimed! What other proof do we need to recognize that God can use any circumstances for His good purposes?

Day 61 · April 25

Today, I spent most of the day outside – we were planting trees in my grandma's garden. It was our way of defying the war and the destruction it brings. It was our life-asserting act. We did the same thing two years ago, during the first COVID lockdown when life was full of uncertainty as well. Maybe one day, when our grandchildren play in this garden, we'll be able to walk them to each tree and tell the story behind it. I was joking that hopefully, there won't be another disaster to commemorate in a couple of years, but Ivan Kapitonov said that even in case of an alien invasion, our Armed Forces would be ready to protect us. It felt good to be outside and laugh together.

Day 62 · April 26

This evening we went for a family walk. As Ivan and I were discussing my Facebook posts, our son asked me to include him in my post tonight. He wanted to ask people to pray the Lord's prayer over Ukraine and tell everyone that God is with us, so we will soon have our victory. Amen! May it be so!

Day 67 · May 1

Today, we started planting my grandma's vegetable garden. Even though I usually enjoy it as it enables us to partake in this mystery of the planting and harvesting cycle, I felt some special awe this time. Our life is filled with more uncertainty than ever before. We don't know how long the war will last. Thankfully, we are blessed with having more than enough food and having the rest of our needs covered today, but we don't know what the fall or winter may bring. That's why I was praying as we were planting – praying for a good harvest and abundance (not only for us but for all of Ukraine), praying for those who starve today and may lack food in the future, praying for us to be aware of the needs of others and be ready to share what we have. Please, keep praying for good crops and wisdom in handling them.

Day 70 · May 4

Today I saw a picture of a bird's nest in a ruined house in Irpin.[ix] Life will win.

Day 71 · May 5

Perhaps it's because I am now so close to the soil that all the agricultural metaphors from the Bible become so vivid to me. We plant something, and then I anxiously check the land plot every day to see if anything is sprouting to reward us for our efforts. Sometimes the only thing we see is weeds. Sometimes the newly planted tree looks dead for weeks only to surprise us with tiny buds when we are ready to give up hope. Most of the time, there's very little we can do after planting, and that (in my opinion) is the most powerful tool in teaching us to rely on God. We do our share in proper preparation, planting, and care, but only God knows how the seeds will grow, what the weather will be like, and what harvest He will bless us with.

Day 79 · May 13

I am also praying for everyone who was forced to leave their homes because of this full-scale war (whether they were forcefully deported to Russia, had to relocate within Ukraine, or had to seek refuge internationally). I am looking forward to the day when God will restore justice.

"Woe to those who call evil good and good evil, who put darkness for light and light for darkness, who put bitter for sweet and sweet for bitter!" (Isaiah 5:20).

Day 81 · May 18

A bird's nest in a ruined house - Day 71, May 5, 2022

I am a "night person," so it takes me a while to get to bed. Last night I was up until almost dawn. I heard the multitude of birds singing their different tunes. I know that's how the birds welcome the sunrise and the new day. However, I was surprised to realize that they start singing while it's still dark. They start singing before the first rays of sun peek through the horizon. They sing in anticipation of sunrise with complete assurance that it will come. Last night, I realized that we must learn from the birds. That's why, even though the war still rages in Ukraine, today, I will sing to God in anticipation and in full faith that He is going to bring deliverance and victory to Ukraine.

Day 89 · May 23

My gardening experience comes in helpful when I get impatient. You plant seeds, and then you wait. You hope for the rain, or you water it yourself, but there is very little you can do to make the seed grow. You just wait. This waiting may be excruciating, and it takes a lot of faith and hope. I remind myself about it when I eagerly check the news.

Day 96 · May 30

Chapter Four

Winter's Cold Breath in Summer

June 1 - July 30, 2022

Tonight, as I was getting ready to write my daily post, I felt like I didn't have words. After all, what new can you say after 117 days of brutal violence?

Day 117 • June 20

I saw a daisy in our yard today. I remembered a childhood game when you pick off petal after petal saying, "He loves me... He loves me not", and the last petal determines your "fate." It is such a blessing to know that we don't need a daisy to determine God's love. He is good. Praise the Lord!

Day 146 • July 19

Hope Based in Past Memories

A season to plant: *Planting tulips is an expression of hope, based on past experience. After a bulb is placed in the ground, half a year passes before the gardener knows whether their hope is realized.*

100 days of full-scale war on Ukraine.

After the first month of the war, one of my fears was that the count of days of war would go into the hundreds...

Today, I was reflecting on these 100 days. When we woke up to the sounds of explosions at 5:00 am on February 24, in a way, I felt relief. No longer living in fear. No longer second-guessing. The inevitable had come. We knew that the only thing we could do was trust God.

I remember that sticky exhausting anxiety in the weeks before the invasion. I remember the hushed conversations on what people would do if "it" happened. Ivan and I discussed the things we needed to pack. We talked through what we would do if there were no cell phone reception. We checked with the school to see their plan in case of an emergency. Every day, I would take a deep breath, drop off my son at school, go to work, and keep checking my phone for news to make sure I was up-to-date on everything, and I would exhale only after all of us were home together in the evening. I remember putting together a grocery list and wondering if we'd actually get to cook and eat that food. There was an important doctor's appointment for our son, and we had to postpone it due to sickness, so I was constantly wondering if we'd actually make it. We saw the doctor late in the evening on February 23. It was on the other end of the city. I remember driving home that night and thinking, "We must make it home before it starts."

These 100 days changed us. They have changed the world. Even though Ukraine has suffered dramatically and still has much suffering ahead, I believe we have already won. We've gained a moral victory in this war. Our children and grandchildren will not be ashamed of our decisions. We didn't compromise. We didn't run in fear. We stood up for what we valued and did it with dignity.

We've seen God's faithfulness. It was evident in big and small things. And I pray we'll see many more of His miracles. I pray we'll remain faithful to Him. I praise God for all the support we've had and pray the support for Ukraine will continue.

Tonight, once again, there was an air-raid warning for all regions of Ukraine. And tonight, I will stand firm on what I know about God and His character. I will stand on the promises of Psalm 34:[x]

> ❧ I will bless the Lord at all times;
> his praise shall continually be in my mouth.

> ❧ I sought the Lord, and he answered me
> and delivered me from all my fears.
> Those who look to him are radiant,
> and their faces shall never be ashamed.

> ❧ The angel of the Lord encamps
> around those who fear him, and delivers them.
> When the righteous cry for help, the Lord hears
> and delivers them out of all their troubles.

> ❧ The Lord is near to the brokenhearted
> and saves the crushed in spirit.
> Many are the afflictions of the righteous,
> but the Lord delivers him out of them all.

> ❧ Affliction will slay the wicked,
> and those who hate the righteous will be condemned.
> The Lord redeems the life of his servants;
> none of those who take refuge in him will be condemned.

Day 100 · June 3

When I get overwhelmed, I remind myself that the Lord is in control. We may not know what awaits us, but we can be sure He will not let us down.

℣ I lift up my eyes to the hills.
From where does my help come?

℣ My help comes from the Lord,
who made heaven and earth.
He will not let your foot be moved;
he who keeps you will not slumber.

℣ Behold, he who keeps Israel
will neither slumber nor sleep.
The Lord is your keeper;
the Lord is your shade on your right hand.

℣ The sun shall not strike you by day,
nor the moon by night.
The Lord will keep you from all evil;
he will keep your life.

℣ The Lord will keep
your going out and your coming in
from this time forth and forevermore.
(Psalm 121)

Day 122 · June 25

I believe in the God who practices steadfast love, justice, and righteousness in the earth. I know that we see God bringing His justice every day, and I am waiting for the day when His justice will be restored completely.

Day 127 · June 30

They often say that war brings out the best and the worst in people. As I read life stories of different people, I praise God for the goodness I see in them. I don't know if any of them are Christian, but as I read stories of care, compassion, and self-sacrifice, I am reminded of Matthew 5:16, "Let your light shine before others, so that they may see your good works and give glory to your Father who is in heaven." What a great responsibility we are given, and how evident it becomes in hard times.

Day 138 · July 11

After the sorrowful few days, I'm searching for strength in simple things, and I'm coming to the Lord for comfort and counsel.

> ✣ Blessed be the Lord, my rock,
> who trains my hands for war,
> and my fingers for battle;
> he is my steadfast love and my fortress,
> my stronghold and my deliverer,
> my shield and he in whom I take refuge
> (Psalm 144:1-2)

I believe that God has a role for each one of us in this war. And He is faithful to train and strengthen us. And I know this war goes far beyond the state borders of Ukraine. Every day, many people face a choice to pick up their "swords" and "shields" and fight for the truth or to surrender to the circumstances or accept the bribe of a comfortable and seemingly safe life and not think about the long-term consequences.

I praise God for the people who choose to stand against evil, defend the oppressed, care for the wounded, and intercede for the broken. I praise God for the people ready to sacrifice their immediate comfort to share the burden of those in pain.

I praise God that He never leaves us. I shared about a woman who was recently released from Russian captivity. She gave a few interviews about her time in a Russian prison. She said she was under constant pressure there, and they wanted to break her spirit. To resist it, she was praying through Psalm 91, which she had memorized, and it kept her going.

God prepared her for that experience, was present with her throughout it, and gracefully delivered her. I believe God is doing the same with each one of us as long as we are faithful in seeking Him.

Day 144 · July 17

It's lamentable to see the scale of destruction brought by this war, but I believe in the power of God's justice and restoration.

Day 149 · July 22

Every day I remind myself that salvation and victory belong to the Lord. I know that He's already received victory on the cross. I know that even though it may seem to some that God is only passively waiting out this war, but in fact, He (once again!) has done the impossible. All military experts expected Ukraine to fall in a couple of days, but we keep resisting.

Day 153 · July 26

Indeed, this full-scale war serves as a magnifying glass. God's power is undeniably evident every day, mainly because of our weakness (both personal and on the national scale). He is the One who leads us out of hopeless situations, He is the One who finds ways to provide, and He is the One who promises to be with us and never forsake us. Yet, we beg for His mercy and the complete defeat of our enemies.

Day 158 · July 31

The Experience of Survival

A season to make roots: *Having planted our tulip bulbs, we move forward into the busyness of preparing for winter. This is a practical time, built around survival.*

Tonight, there was an air-raid warning for all the regions of Ukraine. The air-defense forces shot down a missile about 100 kilometers from Kyiv, but four missiles hit Lviv region. I guess it was a Children's Day greeting from Russia (which, ironically, also celebrates it today). Intense fighting continues in the East. Again and again, we hear about the Russian army mercilessly destroying our cities to avoid street fighting with our military. They don't care for the civilians and infrastructure, they don't even care for their own army men, so there's very little influence on someone with absolutely no morals. Please, pray for divine revelation to the Russian soldiers, for fear of God to set upon their hearts, for a miraculous and complete change of heart.

Day 98 · June 1

Russia keeps launching missiles all over our country and shelling villages and cities along the Ukrainian border. The fighting in the east is really intense – the Russian army is more numerous and more equipped. However, even this doesn't serve to their advantage – they can't proceed fast, they have communication problems, and are completely demoralized.

Day 101 · June 4

It's so easy to forget about the war when it is hundreds of miles away. However, when I woke up and checked the news this morning, for a moment, I was paralyzed with that sticky fear I felt every day in March when the Russian army was close to Kyiv. I read about a missile strike on Kyiv (we are still in a relatively safe location away from the city). I also learned from our Kyiv neighbors that many of them saw and heard the missiles early in the morning. It looks like the rockets hit a train repair factory. It was the first airstrike in Kyiv after five quiet weeks. Moreover, at least one of these missiles went low over the Pivdennoukrainsk Nuclear Power Station, which could have caused a nuclear disaster if it (or its fragments) had hit the nuclear plant.

Day 102 · June 5

There was a report about the first cholera cases in the occupied Mariupol, so the city is going to be locked down for quarantine. It seems surreal in the 21st century, yet Russia makes it possible. The conditions in Mariupol are far from sanitary. People can get water from a water carrier once every two or three days. Still, the occupational forces don't mind wasting water as they demonstrate the watering of flowerbeds for the Russian propaganda channels.

The world is concerned over the looming food crisis. Many African countries depend on Ukraine's grain supply, which Russia has blocked. World leaders are trying to come up with ways to resolve this problem. Meanwhile, Russia steals grain from Ukraine, burns up grain storage facilities on the territories under Ukraine's control, and tries to sell the stolen grain. Once again, it seems surreal and overly wicked, yet it's true.

Leaving the temporarily occupied territory was hard enough, yet it's getting harder. According to the intercepted conversations, Russian soldiers were permitted to kill any suspicious person crossing their checkpoints. However, people in Kherson region are very resilient – most teachers and doctors applied for vacations, took sick leaves, or simply quit their jobs to avoid collaborating with the enemy. According to some sources, Russian soldiers abandoned checkpoints close to Melitopol (Zaporizhzhia region) in fear and anticipation of the Ukrainian counter-attack.

Day 103 · June 6

"I can do all things through him who strengthens me" is a very popular (and often misused) Bible verse. People usually quote it when talking about their plans and achievements. However, I believe this verse is much more profound. Paul writes that because of Christ, he could survive hunger, need, and having very little, especially knowing what it's like to live in abundance. Jesus is the One who sustained him in those times and provided for him.

I thought about this verse because the war changed the everyday lives of Ukrainians. Of course, not everyone lived in abundance, but many people had decent lives. Before the invasion, many people had respectable jobs or owned businesses that has had to close down now. Most of them have a good education, some with master's diplomas from a university. Many families owned a car. They could afford to eat out (even if it's a fast-food restaurant) at least a couple of times a month. A family could afford a week-long vacation in Ukraine or abroad. They could buy fruit and vegetables on a regular basis and not consider it a luxury. All of these are not necessities, and you can do without them, but it's something that used to be a normal part of life. It's not easy for many people in Ukraine now. Some of my friends are in Europe, and it's not easy for them to live as refugees as well because they had their lives figured out in Ukraine, yet they are grateful for what they've been given now.

I'm writing this not because our family is in need. Praise God, we are doing fine. But just like everyone else, we had to adjust our lives to this new reality we are living in. We walk instead of driving when it's possible to conserve gas (we're still experiencing fuel shortage, and the prices have doubled). We rely on fruits and vegetables from our grandma's garden, even if it means waiting an extra month. Our meals are simple, but they are tasty, and we have more than enough. I traded my laptop for a watering can and weeding tools to keep myself busy while I don't have my regular job. These are small things, and it's even hard to call them inconveniences, especially when thinking about millions of Ukrainians who lost everything they had.

We are enduring these new circumstances with grateful hearts, in complete confidence that we will be able to endure whatever comes as long as we rely on Christ who strengthens us. We also know why we are doing it. All of these "inconveniences" are not a high price to pay for the chance to live in a beautiful democratic, peaceful Ukraine free from Russian bondage.

Day 104 · June 7

Speaking of Mariupol, according to recent information, the city's current population is around 100-120 thousand. People live in half-destroyed buildings, cook meals over a fire, and have no electricity or running water. About 47 thousand residents of Mariupol were forcefully deported to Russia. Another 50-70 thousand moved from Mariupol but remained in the temporarily occupied territories. Over 22 thousand were killed. About half of the pre-war population (200 thousand) were able to get to the part under Ukraine's control. This is the sad aftermath of the "peace" brought by the

A preschool in Kyiv - Day 106, June 9, 2022

Russian army. Let's continue praying for Mariupol – all who remain there, all who were uprooted from their homes, and all who lost their loved ones there.

Today's photo is of a preschool in Kyiv. Only preschools with bomb shelters are allowed to work now. They have made the bomb shelters cozy for the children as sometimes they spend a few hours a day there during the air-raid threats. The children also nap in the shelter to make sure their sleep is not interrupted by danger.

Day 106 · June 9

The war continues. Every evening, we hear the sounds of airplanes or missiles. Sometimes we see them, and sometimes we understand they are further away from us. Tonight there was a missile strike in Ternopil region, heavy shelling of villages in Dnipropetrovsk region, and bombing of villages in Sumy region. All of these are outside of the "active combat" zone. At the same time, the Ukrainian army has advanced some in Kherson region, that's been under Russian occupation since the first days of March.

Day 108 · June 11

One of our greatest needs (the one we usually don't notice until it's gone) is the need for privacy. The luxury of having a room to yourself and just enjoying yourself in quiet surroundings – I remember what a rare treasure it was in my university days when I lived in a dorm. This basic need becomes a rare thing during the war.

Most of us are used to having some alone time in one form or another. We are used to at least having privacy in a bathroom or while taking a shower. We can take a walk in solitude or find a quiet corner to spend time with God. None of that is available to our soldiers or the people in heavily shelled cities.

Last week I had a chance to talk to a woman who evacuated from Mariupol at the beginning of May, having lost her home and spent two months in a bomb shelter. When I carefully asked her about her life during those two months and if they had enough food or other essentials, she paused for a moment as if my question took her by surprise and made her think. She said she realized they must have had enough food because she didn't remember seriously lacking it. However, she said her greatest need was to take a shower and to be alone. None of that was possible as they shared a small bomb shelter room with 20 people, and everyone going outside risked being shot. Thankfully, now this woman and her family are in a relatively safe place with the help of Dmytro Bereza, who serves with the World Without Orphans group. This family doesn't have much, but they have the luxury of seclusion and appreciate even these small blessings.

Privacy is a struggle for many Ukrainian refugees. Living in refugee homes and having communal meals cooked by volunteers are a generous blessing to those who had to flee from the war. Not wanting to be considered ungrateful, many Ukrainians are afraid to say they miss having their own rooms or being able to cook their own food. Those displaced within Ukraine often move to safer regions and stay with their relatives or family friends. And even though they don't complain, choosing safety over privacy does take its toll on their wellbeing.

Needless to say, there is no privacy at the front lines. Our defenders sleep cramped up in trenches in-between enemy attacks to give us the privilege of sleeping safely in our beds. And that's the least of the discomforts they experience.

Day 112 · June 15

Over the past 24 hours, Russia has launched over 50 missiles from the territory of Belarus, the Black Sea, and the occupied territories. Most of them were launched in the wee hours of the morning when people were sound asleep in their beds. That's the favorite time for their air strikes as people are caught off-guard and are more vulnerable. Our air-defense forces took down quite a few missiles, but some still hit objects in the Zhytomyr, Kyiv, Chernihiv, Khmelnytskyi, Lviv, Mykolaiv, Dnipropetrovsk, Kharkiv, and Rivne regions. At the same time, this air attack accomplished nothing. Its sole purpose was to send Ukrainians into panic and demonstrate Russia's power to the world. It's pathetic. In my opinion, it only proves Russia's helplessness and agony.

It was the first time that an air-raid was performed from the territory of Belarus. Russia keeps trying to get Belarus to join the war on Ukraine openly. They are conducting joint army training at the Ukrainian border now, so we should expect any sort of provocations.

Day 122 · June 25

Picking cherries from a tree, savoring your first vegetables from your garden, canning for the winter season. The kids riding their bikes and getting wet in water gun fights. Enjoying cooler evenings after a hot summer day. That's what summer should be about. And we are blessed with these glimpses of a careless peaceful life when the word "war" seems to be a concept from a history book, not the reality we are living in. However, this bliss doesn't last long, and our thoughts go back to the front lines and the occupied territories.

Even life in the relatively safe regions of Ukraine is filled with many questions and uncertainties. Many people have lost their jobs due to war and are struggling to find a way to earn their living. The prices keep going up – the fuel prices have almost doubled since the beginning of the war and come to about 1.7 euros per liter ($6.5 per gallon).

While the Ministry of Education of Ukraine promised that the schools would return to offline mode in September, there are many questions regarding if it would actually be possible. Schools are required to have bomb shelters within a reasonable distance, and many parents doubt that it's safe to send their kids to school when Russia has been known to attack public places, schools, and hospitals. Our son's school is still deciding what they will do in September – please, pray for wisdom and the Lord's guidance. There are concerns about the upcoming winter season. Most cities use centralized heating systems, and the utility bills might get astronomical as Russia is set to destroy Ukraine's energy industry.

Add to it not being able to return home (because it's in the occupied territories or was destroyed by the Russian army), not seeing your loved ones for a while (being separated by hundreds of kilometers or because they serve in the armed forces of Ukraine now), constantly monitoring air-raid warnings, and trying to deal with PTSD we all are suffering from. You get a glimpse of what it's like for those who are blessed not to be directly touched by the war.

One of the things I've learned over these past four months is that we are more interconnected than we may think. And the world is tiny; in fact, what seemed distant yesterday can turn into your reality today. That's why it is so important to keep our hearts and minds open to each other, especially when your own problems weigh heavy upon you.

Day 131 · July 4

It was late at night, but I wasn't asleep when I heard the loud noise of airplanes. I didn't need to check my phone app to see if there was an air-raid warning. Even though I knew it was Ukraine's aviation (Russian planes wouldn't dare to go that far thanks to our air-defense forces), I still got tense. I immediately prayed for the safety of the pilots, other soldiers, and all those who might suffer a missile attack. The morning report said two Russian missiles aimed at the Mykolaiv region were fired from a submarine in the Black Sea but were shot down by our air forces.

Day 133 · July 6

Last night, we had a big thunderstorm. I can't imagine how people who had experienced bombing survive a thunderstorm. I had to pause and listen every time to make sure it was thunder, not the sound of the airplanes. And it was an uneasy experience even though we live hundreds of kilometers away from the active hostilities.

Day 136 · July 9

Back in March, I saw a post on Facebook – a woman from Mariupol was looking for a young soldier who saved her life in Mariupol. I remembered that post because there was an unusual twist – the woman said that a young soldier stopped her from committing suicide. Today, I read an article[xi] about that serviceman. He is only 19 years old. On March 12, the woman's apartment building was shelled, killing her 16-year-old son and brother-in-law. Her mom, niece, and sister were severely wounded, and she had a concussion and some minor injuries. Her neighbor took them to the hospital, and that's where they met the soldier – he noticed that one of the tourniquets wasn't tight enough and fixed it, thus saving the life of her mom. She herself was in shock and was considering suicide. The soldier asked her what happened, listened to her story, then looked her in the eye and said, "Look at all the wounded. They need help. You can't do something to yourself. You are needed here. Let's go help." She hadn't told him about her intentions, but he must have felt it in the air. She said she was ready to ignore him, but he reminded her of her son (killed earlier that day). She stayed and helped at the hospital and later evacuated to a safer location within Ukraine. When she tried to find the soldier, his mom told her he had been taken captive.

I'm impressed with this story on so many levels. This young guy cared not only about his immediate responsibilities but also looked beyond them and cared to notice, listen, and encourage. I am so grateful for the kindness in his heart and for all others like him who go out of their ways to serve those in need.

This article also highlights a problem that may not be that obvious. Many people in Ukraine now live with post-traumatic stress disorder. Many people who had alcohol or substance abuse issues in the past can't cope with their current circumstances and return to their old ways. Many people who have lost their loved ones or witnessed the unspeakable are on the verge of a nervous breakdown and may be contemplating suicide. May we be sensitive to these problems. May we be slow to judge and quick to listen. May we care to notice. May God use us to bring healing, just as he used the soldier in her life.

I follow a Facebook group where you can ask a health-related question, and the moderators connect you to a doctor who can give you medical advice if it's something that can be addressed over a distance. In the past few months, there have been way too many questions from parents whose children had a first-hand experience with this war. A two-year-old child who stopped speaking after spending two weeks in a bomb shelter in Mariupol. A five-year-old child who started wetting the bed at night after a recent missile strike in their city (they were a couple of blocks away from the site when it happened). Kids who started stuttering after evacuating from the war zone. Teenagers with signs of depression and ten-year-olds with suicidal thoughts because of the experienced stress. A nine-year-old child who is afraid to stay in the room by herself and panics every time she has to be separated from her mom, even for a few hours – her father serves in the army, and she and her mom had to leave their home in search for safety. If you were a parent of these children, would you ever agree to any "peace treaty" and the rule of someone who inflicted this upon your child?

Day 132 · July 16

Living at this pace is draining. The days blur together and make you wonder if you ever had a "normal" life.

Praise God, there's hope for the export of Ukraine's grain.[xii] Over 400 million people, especially in African countries, depend on it. The food crisis there can cause new migration waves into Europe, so it's one more proof of how interconnected we all are. Please, pray for Russia not to be able to weaponize food.

Please, pray for the cities terrorized by daily shelling and missile strikes. Mykolaiv, Kharkiv, and Nikopol seem to be affected the most. Also, pray for the towns in the active fighting zone.

There are six things that the Lord hates, seven that are an abomination to him: haughty eyes, a lying tongue, and hands that shed innocent blood, a heart that devises wicked plans, feet that make haste to run to evil, a false witness who breathes out lies, and one who sows discord among brothers.
(Proverbs 6:16-19)

Day 148 · July 21

I woke up at around 6 am because of the loud airplane sound. It usually means that there's an air-raid warning. Later in the morning, we learned about a missile attack in Vyshhorod district (north of Kyiv) and Chernihiv region. A few hours later, there was a missile strike on Kropyvnytskyi. These are agonizing attempts by the terrorist state to break our spirit. By the way, the US Senate unanimously voted for the resolution to recognize Russia as a state sponsor of terrorism, so now it is up to the State Department.

We are no longer surprised by any of the Russian attacks. Often, I can hardly find words for it, so, as always, I turn to Psalms:

> ᚷ Lead me, O Lord, in your righteousness because of my enemies;
> make your way straight before me.
> For there is no truth in their mouth;
> their inmost self is destruction;
> their throat is an open grave;
> they flatter with their tongue.
>
> ᚷ Make them bear their guilt, O God;
> let them fall by their own counsels;
> because of the abundance of their transgressions cast them out,
> for they have rebelled against you.
>
> ᚷ But let all who take refuge in you rejoice;
> let them ever sing for joy, and spread your protection over them,
> that those who love your name may exult in you.
> (Psalm 5:8-11)

Day 155 · July 28

Russia has destroyed most of the infrastructure of the Donetsk region. The government published an announcement about the mandatory evacuation from the Donetsk region because the government won't be able to provide utilities in the area, especially in the cold winter months. People already don't have gas, electricity, and running water in most towns there. The Russians claim they came to "liberate Donetsk." Apparently, they meant getting rid of any of the goods of civilization.

The situation is pretty difficult in Mykolaiv as well. The city doesn't have the supply of safe drinking water (which used to come from the now-occupied Kherson). People need to stand in lines to get drinking water. The city is also shelled daily.

Day 157 · July 30

When Hope Felt Distant

A season to cool: *Winter buries the memory of the hopes that we had planted with our tulip bulbs.*

June 1 is traditionally celebrated as Children's Day (Day for Protection of the Children) in Ukraine. This day has a much deeper meaning today. According to the UN statistics, every day in Ukraine, two children die, and four are wounded. At least 262 children died, and 415 were injured since the invasion
on February 24 (the numbers do not include children from temporarily occupied territories). Two out of three Ukrainian children had to leave their homes due to the war. I'm crying as I read these statistics, especially since I realize that it doesn't translate all the pains our children are going through.

Usually, June 1 is also the first day of the summer break. Today, I would like to acknowledge the great work of Ukrainian teachers and other educational workers. You might have seen pictures of teachers conducting their lessons (or university lectures) from the bomb shelters or trenches, organizing schools in subway stations, and ministering to the needs of children despite the circumstances. Our schools kept functioning (mostly in online format) throughout these three months of the war. People were willing to stay and keep working or ready to step in and substitute for those who left. Our teachers did their best to support children, welcome new students from displaced families, and teach the required curriculum. They did it with a gentle smile while their hearts were breaking for their loved ones in the occupied or heavily shelled cities. I praise God for their dedication and care.

Day 98 · June 1

I remember how we rejoiced over even the most minor good things in the early days of this invasion. As the war goes on, we get weary and overwhelmed, and our vision of our blessings gets blurry. Lord, please, help us be grateful and never take your blessings for granted!

Day 114 · June 17

We enter the fifth month of the full-scale war on Ukraine. There are days when I wake up, and it feels like this war was just a terrible dream. Sometimes I feel like asking someone to pinch me because I still refuse to believe that such a brutal, barbaric war is possible in the 21st century in the heart of Europe. It's unfathomable that someone would revel in unprovoked violence and genocide. It seems so vividly wicked, as if it's a scene taken out of a dystopian movie. And it's so hard, almost impossible, to comprehend that it's happening for real in my country, even after 122 days...

Day 122 · June 25

I will always be amazed by how God speaks into our lives just at the right time. In the past week, I felt weary and, at times, overwhelmed. I suddenly realized that it is July already; the summer would be over soon, and more and more experts say this war may take many more months, if not years.

As my spirit was getting low with these heavy thoughts, God started showering me with messages from long-time friends and strangers from all over the world sharing stories of how they see support for Ukraine in their countries.

Day 124 · July 7

Today, I read Psalm 140, and it resonates with our daily prayers so much so that I feel like there is very little for me to add.

> ℣ Deliver me, O Lord, from evil men; preserve me from violent men, who plan evil things in their heart and stir up wars continually. They make their tongue sharp as a serpent's, and under their lips is the venom of asps.

> ℣ Guard me, O Lord, from the hands of the wicked; preserve me from violent men, who have planned to trip up my feet. The arrogant have hidden a trap for me, and with cords they have spread a net; beside the way they have set snares for me.

✣ I say to the Lord, You are my God; give ear to the voice of my pleas for mercy, O Lord! O Lord, my Lord, the strength of my salvation, you have covered my head in the day of battle. Grant not, O Lord, the desires of the wicked; do not further their evil plot, or they will be exalted!

✣ As for the head of those who surround me, let the mischief of their lips overwhelm them! Let burning coals fall upon them! Let them be cast into fire, into miry pits, no more to rise! Let not the slanderer be established in the land; let evil hunt down the violent man speedily!

✣ I know that the Lord will maintain the cause of the afflicted, and will execute justice for the needy. Surely the righteous shall give thanks to your name; the upright shall dwell in your presence. (Psalm 140)

Day 140 · July 13

There have been a few days during this war when I choke for words, when I feel physically sick and numb at the same time. When I don't feel capable of mercy and forgiveness and cry out for God's wrath on those who started and support this war. Today is such a day.

10:45 am. A missile strike on Vinnytsia, a city hundreds of kilometers away from the front line that's become a shelter for many internally displaced people. I've gone through that city many times and have friends who live there. This morning, Russia launched four high-precision Kalibr missiles (allowed deviation from the target is only three-four meters / ten feet) at Vinnytsia. Two of them were shot down by the air-defense forces, and two hit the city center, one of the busiest intersections. They hit an office center, a diagnostic clinic, and a parking lot. As of now, 23 people (including three children) have been found dead, but only six of them have been identified – the heat from the fire and the explosion wave tore bodies to pieces leaving them unrecognizable. Sixty-six people (including three children) were hospitalized, 34 of them are in serious condition, and five are in critical condition. Thirty-nine people are missing.

Today I saw a picture of a four-year-old girl. Her mom really wanted to have kids. During one of the prenatal screenings, the doctors discovered that the child has Down's Syndrome and recommended her mom terminate the pregnancy to avoid "unnecessary torture." But her mom kept the baby, loved her, and was doing her best to help her child's development. They went to another town, hoping to escape the war. This morning, they went to a speech therapy class. An hour later, the girl was killed by the Russian missile. You may have seen a picture from today with a lifeless child's body next to a stroller – that was her. Her mom lost a foot and was taken to a hospital in critical condition without regaining consciousness and unaware of her baby's passing.

As one of the missiles hit a neurological diagnostics clinic, the most seriously injured people are the doctors and patients of that clinic.

Such terrorist attacks are meant to cause panic, fear, and despair. Instead, they cause anger and resolve. We grieve the losses, but that makes us long for justice even more.

Day 141 · July 14

Five months of the full-scale war. Five months stolen from our lives. Thousands of lives lost forever...

Today, I asked God what we are doing and if it makes any difference. As I kept struggling with this question throughout the day, I felt that the answer to this question is that we wait upon the Lord. We are waiting for the manifestation of His power and justice. However, this waiting is not (at least, should not be!) passive. It's the type of waiting when you do everything in your power to speed up the anticipated result. It's what apostle Paul referred to in 1 Thessalonians 1:3 (NIV) when he praised them for their "work produced by faith, labor prompted by love, and endurance inspired by hope in our Lord Jesus Christ."

Day 151 · July 24

❧ I am weary with my moaning;
every night I flood my bed with tears;
I drench my couch with my weeping.

❧ My eye wastes away because of grief;

it grows weak because of all my foes.
(Psalm 6:6-7)

Well, apparently, the Russians saw that their missiles didn't have the desired effect, so they started bombarding us with their atrocities. Today was filled with news reports that you refuse to believe.

This morning, the Russians shelled a bus stop in Mykolaiv. At least five people were killed. The street was covered in blood.

They also published a cruel video of the mutilation of a Ukrainian POW (I am intentional about not including the gruesome details, but the full report is available).[xiii] This cruelty is not something new – similar maiming has been practiced since 2014, so you can only imagine the level of physical and mental pressure our soldiers have to endure. Please, pray for every POW.

As if that wasn't enough, today, the Russians committed another war crime. Many captive soldiers from Mariupol (especially the Azov regimen and marines) were kept in the temporarily occupied Olenivka (Donetsk region). The Russians carried out a false-flag operation and blew up the building the POWs were held in but tried to present it as if it was attacked by the Ukrainians using western weaponry (namely HIMARS). There is evidence that they are lying, and the intelligence services are already getting a picture of who is behind it.[xiv] According to the preliminary information, over 50 soldiers were killed and over 100 wounded. "Miraculously," none of the Russian guards were affected in this incident. I'm just sick of their blatant cynicism. To some, it may be just statistics of war losses, but during this full-scale war, we've become like one nationwide family, and the pain I feel now can be compared to the pain of a loss of a brother, even a brother you've never met.

So, all of these events didn't happen today by accident. It's another terrorist attack, a provocation to either get Ukrainians to surrender or to make Ukrainian soldiers bloodthirsty with revenge and show the world that "both sides are to blame" (which goes in line with the Russian propaganda so readily accepted by some). So, we keep fervently praying for the hearts of our soldiers, for the love and justice to prevail.

Today, I was watering our plants (this summer has been unusually dry) and talking to God. We came here on February 24 and saw this land still covered in snow. I remembered how the first warm spring days were the only encouragement in the gloom of the news reports. I remembered planting this vegetable garden and praying for a good harvest. Today it hit me that two months of summer are already over, our vegetable garden is finally yielding fruit, some plants are already dying, having fulfilled their mission, and this war is still going on. I asked God, "How long, Lord? We were praying and hoping for this war to be over by Easter, by the beginning of summer. Will it be over by the start of the school year? How much longer, Lord?" Almost immediately, a Bible verse came to my mind, but it wasn't the answer I wanted to get.

"My grace is sufficient for you, for my power is made perfect in weakness" (2 Corinthians 12:9).

Defiance in the Face of Aggression

A season to grow: *In spite of the sometimes-returning onslaughts of fading winter, tulips start growing below the surface. This is a time of defiance and hope.*

"Russia must not be humiliated in Ukraine," said French President Emmanuel Macron. A corrupt official must not be humiliated in his office. An abuser must not be humiliated in his family. A murderer must not be humiliated in court. Hitler shouldn't have been humiliated, so it was a mistake for Nazi Germany to capitulate. Do you see how absurd these statements are? Unfortunately, not everyone does.

Russia has already humiliated itself by invading Ukraine, killing thousands of people (and hundreds of children), and ruining millions of lives. Those who started it, who support it, and those who justify it should be ashamed of themselves, for their choices have humiliated themselves and their dignity.

"No one who put hope in you will ever be put to shame, but shame will come on those who are treacherous without cause" (Psalm 25:3 NIV).

I get frustrated when I see statements such as Macron's. I get disappointed. I want to grab those people by their collars and bring them to the children who lost their limbs, to the kids orphaned by the war, to devastated parents. Many world leaders and ambassadors visit Ukraine and go to Bucha, Irpin, or Borodyanka to see destroyed buildings, but I wish they would instead look into people's eyes. See young kids run to shelters at the sound of the siren. See the weeping families as they say goodbye to each other for who-knows-how-long. I want them to see those whose homes and lives were utterly destroyed by Russian bombs and missiles. Would they still be talking about "allowing Putin to keep the face" then?

Day 101 · June 4

In an interview on Russian TV, a Russian officer talked about captive Ukrainian soldiers. He unwittingly praised the resilience and dignity of our warriors but also admitted that the POWs are tortured in captivity. Please pray for all captive soldiers, especially the Azovstal group from Mariupol.

Day 106 · June 9

In Mykolaiv region, the village mayor would receive phone calls as soon as the artillery fire was over with questions about how long people should wait before getting rid of the shell craters and replanting what's been destroyed by Russian bombs. Ukrainian people can't wait for this war to be over. We want to live and love. Ukrainians will keep fighting for it.

Day 107 · June 10

Tonight, I came across an article about life in occupied Kherson.[xv]

On March 1, the Russian troops entered the city and killed about 70 members of the territorial defense. That really shook the city, and even though Kherson was never known for great patriotic rallies, on March 5, up to 10,000 city residents came to the central square chanting, "Kherson is Ukraine!" They were persecuted, arrested, threatened, and shot at. Still, they kept coming together for pro-Ukrainian rallies until May 9, when only about 20 people showed up, and all of them were arrested. Over the past three months, over 1,000 people were abducted during or after these rallies. The whereabouts of most of them are still unknown. Many other people were also arrested and tortured to coerce them into cooperation.

A Father of the Orthodox Church of Ukraine is one of them. He has been volunteering as a military priest since 2014, so he was ready for the invasion and evacuated his family on the first day. On February 25, he organized a humanitarian headquarters at his church. People would bring the food they had to share. They also set up a hairdresser station and coffee machines in the church building to give people an opportunity to come together, talk, and find some peace. He was also finding ways to pass by Russian checkpoints – he would dress up as a Russian Orthodox priest to find and bring medication and hygiene products to people. On the first Sunday after the occupation, the church was flooded with people – they needed communication and comfort. And God was caring for his parish, providing everything at the right time. Once, someone donated lactose-free milk, and moments later, a lactose intolerant person showed up asking if they had any. Another time, they needed a printer to print announcement posters, and it was donated in seven minutes! "God was giving us everything I was asking for!" he said.

Day 108 · June 11

Today, as I was thinking about all of this, I remembered a passage from the book of Daniel. I heard it for the first time at a youth group event many-many years ago, but this verse has stuck with me.

This is a story of Daniel's friends, Shadrach, Meshach, and Abednego, who refused to bow down and worship the golden image of Nebuchadnezzar. The king threatened to throw them into the fiery furnace if they didn't worship him, to which they replied, "If we are thrown into the blazing furnace, the God we serve is able to deliver us from it, and he will deliver us from Your Majesty's hand. But even if he does not, we want you to know, Your Majesty, that we will not serve your gods or worship the image of gold you have set up." (Daniel 3:17-18). As you know, they were thrown into the fire, but they came out unharmed and even with no smell of fire. This caused Nebuchadnezzar to praise God and recognize His power.

"But even if He doesn't." I believe this is the greatest kind of faith. They didn't doubt God's power when they said it, yet they recognized His sovereignty and trusted His judgment. When we look at the list of heroes of faith in Hebrews chapter 11, I think we can add this "but even if He doesn't" to each one of them. Noah didn't know for sure if the ark would survive the flood. Abraham didn't know for sure that God would provide a sacrifice when he was commanded to offer Isaac. Moses didn't know what getting out of Egypt and to the Promised Land would look like. They didn't know it, but they were going to trust God with whatever was to come. They were taking steps into the unknown, admitting that it is better to walk with God, even when we are not sure when or if He will give us what we are asking Him for.

I pray that God will graciously let us see our victory soon. But even if He doesn't do it soon or in the way I want it to be, I will still worship Him, and we'll keep fighting for the truth.

Day 109 · June 12

Today my friend shared a story witnessed by her husband. As he was in line to cross the border from Poland to Ukraine, a family knocked on his car window and asked if they could cross the border with him – there were two women and their disabled parents. The elderly parents lived in the Kharkiv region, close to the Russian border. On February 24, their village was occupied. Cattle were taken away, communication was cut off, and there was no electricity and gas. All exits from the village were blocked. It was possible to leave only through Russia. They didn't want to leave their home, so they stayed despite the trials. On May 31, they were thrown into a car and taken to Russia. Their relatives found volunteers who helped the elderly travel to Estonia, where their daughters met them. From there, they went through Latvia, Lithuania, and Poland. The trip took seven days. After crossing the border, the old man took a deep breath and said he was finally sensing the smell of true freedom. Where were they going? They are heading back to Kharkiv to live with their relatives until our armed forces liberate their village.

I am in tears when I read stories like this.

Please, pray for all the displaced families to be able to find healing and new (temporary?) homes. Pray for the safety of all who stay in the occupied territories because they have no place to go or because leaving their life behind feels worse than dying. Pray for the volunteers in Russia who help people get to the border and safety – for protection from persecution or any other mean plans devised by the Russian government.

Day 110 · June 13

According to the Melitopol mayor (Zaporizhzhia region), the occupational forces do not have the support of the city residents and are afraid of the resistance movement, so they threatened to implement public executions. They simply add new means of genocide, but I believe God will restore justice.

Day 118 · June 21

Today, I'll start with a brighter report. UN's cultural agency (UNESCO) added Ukrainian borsch (a beetroot soup) to its endangered intangible cultural heritage list. What's so special about this?

As any nation has the special dishes it is known for, Ukrainians have borsch (among other foods), whose history dates back to as early as the 16th century. In 1584, Martin Gruneweg, a German merchant from Gdansk, was traveling across Eastern Europe to Moscow and taking extensive notes from that trip.

Describing his time in Kyiv, he mentioned borsch as something cooked in every home and a daily meal for the local people.[xvi] That was the first written mentioning of borsch (as known so far). Little has changed over the past four hundred years.

When Russia invaded Ukraine, when they tried to wipe Ukraine out from the face of the earth, when they were trying to exterminate Ukrainians along with their culture and traditions, Ukrainians were cooking borsch. It seemed to be an act of national resilience or something that was calling from deep within. My friend's mom was cooking borsch in-between air-raids in a bombed city. Another friend was leaving a bomb shelter to go upstairs and cook borsch for their neighbors. This hearty soup is missed at the front lines, so volunteers prepare dry borsch mixes that can be quickly cooked in a trench. It sounds silly, but it is something that resonates with Ukrainian hearts, and seeing it recognized on the world level is an encouragement amid devastating news.

Day 128 · July 1

The resistance is also very active in the occupied territories, especially Kherson and Zaporizhzhia regions. Last night someone blew up a bridge in the Zaporizhzhia region that was used to bring supplies and ammunition to the Russian forces. According to Ukraine's intelligence service reports, few Russians are willing to go to those regions to serve as newly appointed officials. They are afraid, so I pray for more fear to come into the hearts of Russians so that they can repent and stop this bloodshed.

Day 130 · July 3

And the same feeling of being connected to my people causes my heart to tighten with pain as I learn about the sufferings and hardships in war-torn Ukraine. Today, there were missile and artillery attacks on Kramatorsk, Sloviansk, and Kharkiv, with many people wounded and killed. There are sad reports from the occupied territories – according to the Head of Luhansk Military Administration, Russian occupational forces shoot people in the streets of Kreminna (Luhansk region) if they refuse to collaborate.

My heart breaks from these reports, yet I will not let them crush my spirit. I will call upon the Lord and praise Him for His faithfulness and love that we experience wherever we go. And I will praise Him for He never leaves us in our weaknesses but sends His messengers of hope just at the right time. May we all be sensitive to His calling to become this kind of messenger to those in need.

Day 134 · July 7

This week, swarms of locusts came over one of the districts of Krasnodar Krai in Russia. [xvii] While the Russians set Ukrainian fields on fire, the crops in their fields are being devoured by locusts. The interesting fact is that the city suffering from locusts the most is the city whose airfield is used for the air strikes on the east of Ukraine (the plane that bombed the drama theater in Mariupol took off from that airfield). Even though this probably will not have a significant impact on the well-being of Russia, I believe it is a clear sign of God's judgment.

We've already won because the Lord will restore justice and punish the wicked.

Day 139 · July 12

These days, everyone is feeling tense. I can't say that we've ever felt relaxed since February 24, but with the recent missile strikes and threats of a new invasion from the territory of Belarus, you can't take your mind off the war.

As I've said many times, Russia is using terror in an attempt to subdue Ukrainians and break their spirit. However, they achieve the opposite. With every missile strike, there's more pain and anger and less room for forgiveness in the foreseeable future. Because it is not the amorphous force that's killing Ukrainian people. Behind every missile, there are very specific people who give orders, who execute the order, there are people who joyfully support this wickedness, there are people who gladly ignore this wickedness (not because of the lack of knowledge, which is virtually impossible in the age of the internet, but because of lack of responsibility), there are people who pay for this wickedness (through taxes and business transactions with Russia). I'm taking comfort in trusting that God will restore justice, even if not in our lifetime, and I pray for our enemy's repentance, even though I start to lack faith in it ever happening.

Day 143 · July 16

I went outside tonight after dark and was amazed by the beauty and depth of the starry summer sky. It's hard to believe that a few hundred kilometers away, there's no room for this quiet contemplation. Instead, there are explosions from the Russian bombs. As I'm writing this, the firefighters are rescuing people after a missile strike on the Odesa region. A couple of hours before, there was a report on heavy shelling of Nikopol (Dnipropetrovsk region). Mykolaiv and Kharkiv are under attack every day. Lots of towns remain under occupation. What does their sky look like?

Earlier today, I read Psalm 145 and was meditating on it throughout the day. Honestly, I had mixed feelings. I wanted to praise God as David does in this Psalm, yet I was having a hard time because the war continues, and many of our prayers remain unanswered (for now).

However, it all fell into place when I saw the photo accompanying today's post. A young guy stands with a Ukrainian flag in front of the destroyed drama theater in the occupied Mariupol.[xviii] He dared to do it despite harsh persecutions for as much as the Ukrainian language or Ukrainian colors. For example, a 23-year-old girl was arrested today for wearing a yellow-and-blue ribbon in her hair.

Seeing this resilience and courage reassured me of Ukraine's victory, even if it will not happen for a while. The Old Testament prophets sometimes wrote about future events using the past tense, as if they had already happened because they were so confident that these events would happen. It's the anticipation with certainty that gives you the foretaste of the expected and this almost tangible confidence.

Day 145 · July 18

Today I saw pictures showing a vegetable garden in Velyka Dymerka, Kyiv region. A cabbage patch and flowers next to the burned-down Russian tank. To me, this image is not just about resilience; it is also symbolic of our future – the war will leave its ugly scars, but life will prevail.

Day 150 · July 23

Will it crush our spirit? It does shake us, but Ukraine will resist anyway. However, with every such incident, there's less room for forgiveness in the foreseeable future. I can't understand what's going on in the heart and mind of an "average" Russian citizen, and I pray for their repentance if it's still possible. I'm not buying excuses such as "we didn't know" or "we didn't have a choice." We always have a choice – even two criminals crucified next to Jesus had a choice in the last minutes of their lives. The question is, are we ready to make this choice?

I thank God for each person who chooses to stand with Ukraine and pray for Ukraine. Please, don't grow weary. Call your government representatives, participate in rallies or organize an event supporting Ukraine. Don't let the world forget about us.

Celebration,
While Aware of the Costs

A season to bloom: *The crowning season for the tulips arrives as their flowers reach to the sky. But celebration is vulnerable – the tulip has used huge amounts of the bulb's resources in the hope of future goodness.*

"If God is for us, who can be against us?" (Romans 8:31). I love it when God shows His power and uses nature against our enemy. We've seen enemy troops blown away by the strong wind when they attempted aerial deployment. We've seen their boats swallowed up by the stormy sea. We've had wild geese take down an enemy airplane, and hungry bees attack a camp of Russian soldiers. Some would call these stories magical; others would say it was a happy coincidence, but I know it is God's hand above all creation.

A few days ago, a similar incident took place in a temporarily occupied village in Zaporizhzhia region. About 40 Russian soldiers stationed themselves in a local hospital building. They mined and booby-trapped the territory around and felt safe in their camp. That's when a heroic goat came in. It was randomly walking around the territory and hit a few booby-traps. The chain reaction caused a massive explosion which severely wounded a few Russian soldiers. This story was shared by the Main Directorate of Intelligence of the Ministry of Defence of Ukraine.

Day 119 • June 22

One hundred forty-four Ukrainian soldiers (95 of them were defending Azovstal Steel Plant in Mariupol) returned home today. The oldest is 65, and the youngest is only nineteen years old. Most of the exchanged prisoners are seriously wounded and need medical care. We rejoice and praise God for this miracle, but at the same time, we remember that about 2,000 Ukrainian warriors were taken captive only in Mariupol, so we need to keep praying for them and all the civilians abducted by Russia in filtration camps as well as forcefully taken to Russia. May God be with them and bring each of them home safely.

Even though there was a lot of devastating news today, I will rejoice in this one and use it as a reminder of God's faithfulness.

There is a small Snake Island in the Black Sea, about 35 kilometers from the Ukrainian coast. It delimits Ukrainian territorial waters. On February 24, 2022, two Russian navy warships attacked Snake Island and took Ukrainian coast guards captive. We saw justice restored on April 14, when the Ukrainian army destroyed one of the attacking warships, the flagship of the Russian navy, *Moskva*. However, the island was still under Russian control and was used for radio (electronic) reconnaissance and served as a stronghold in the possible attack from the sea on Odesa. Today, Ukraine finally pushed Russian forces from the island, having performed several high-precision airstrikes and artillery attacks on Russian bases there. As a joke, Russia announced that it had withdrawn troops from the island in a "gesture of goodwill" after military objectives were complete. Well, we would greatly appreciate the same "gesture of goodwill" with Russia completely withdrawing its forces from the rest of the territory of Ukraine.

There have been quite a few military successes lately. Most likely, the promised western weapons are finally reaching the front lines (and we continue to plea #armUkraine, please). Today, the air forces of Ukraine destroyed two enemy command posts, up to 20 armored vehicles, 10 tanks, and two field ammunition warehouses. I know that these destroyed enemy positions mean more Ukrainian lives spared, so I will keep praying for all the enemy ammunition to malfunction, blow up, and never reach the target. Please, pray especially for the places with the fiercest fighting – the Sumy and Kharkiv regions (daily heavy shelling from the territory of Russia), Luhansk region (Lysychansk), Donetsk region (Bakhmut, Sloviansk), Mykolaiv region (suffers from daily missile attacks), Kherson region (expected Ukrainian counterattacks there), and for the protection of the borders of Ukraine, especially parts bordering with Belarus and "Transnistria" (occupied territory of Moldova).

As we wait upon God's deliverance, we notice answers to our prayers. This morning, Russia launched four Kalibr missiles at the Khmelnytskyi region, all four of which were shot down by our air-defense forces. Such 100% efficiency can only be granted by the Lord!

Day 151 · July 24

Today was my birthday. I hope it was my only birthday during this full-scale war.

Today, I was showered with birthday wishes from my friends, old and new. I was surrounded by my loved ones. I could rejoice in all of God's blessings. It felt right and wrong, all at the same time. It was something from my "pre-war" life and made me painfully aware of how the enemy is trying to take the life out of our existence.

So today, I will allow myself not to write about war, not to look for words, but instead focus on being thankful. Thankful for all of God's blessings. Thankful to our defenders who risk their lives for our nation. Thankful to all the people who support, pray, and donate. I am blessed beyond measure.

"Every good gift and every perfect gift is from above, coming down from the Father of lights, with whom there is no variation or shadow due to change" (James 1:17).

Back in April, when my son had his birthday, his friend told him to make a wish before blowing out the candles on a cake. He looked at her and said, "It's just a superstition. If you really wish for something, you need to pray. I pray for Ukraine's victory." I remembered his words today, and I simply couldn't agree more.

Day 152 · July 25

Perhaps one of the things that astound and inspire me during this full-scale war is the sense of unity and communion with people from across the world. This support is something that's truly cherished and will not be forgotten.

I will not list all the countries that support Ukraine or the list of people who have shown their support on a personal level. I won't be able to name everyone, and I don't want to miss anyone, but I'll share what touched me the most (please, know that I'm not trying to compare anyone's aid or efforts).

I'm especially encouraged by the support of Poland and the Baltic states. They also went through the Soviet occupation, so we have a lot in common, but they were more successful in breaking away from the communist heritage in the 1980s-1990s. It's inspiring to see their support now because they are not big, rich, or influential. After all, they themselves are at the risk of escalated conflict with Russia, yet they join us in this fight on all possible fronts:

Poland stated that they would not participate in any events where Russia and Belarus are participating. I appreciate their boldness. Estonia has provided military aid that amounts to almost 1% of their GDP even though they also have Russia as their neighbor. I appreciate their faith. Lithuania was not afraid to follow through with the European Commission decision on sanctions against Russia and closed passage through its territory to Kaliningrad, which resulted in threats from Russia. I appreciate their uncompromising support. Latvia has provided 100% of the promised military aid, closed all Russian TV channels, and plans to eliminate the Russian gas by the next year. I appreciate their practical ways of showing support.

These are just bits of big decisions, but I can continue with things that won't be reported in the media. Stories of ordinary people showing extraordinary love and care. A couple of days ago, I got a message from a friend in Latvia who said she'd seen lots of sunflowers planted in their area this year (and that's not a usual flower for them), and that to them, it's a daily reminder to pray for Ukraine. I was moved to tears and literally had goosebumps just trying to comprehend this act of solidarity. I am amazed how God can use something so simple to be such a powerful message!

Day 154 • July 27

Loss and Lament

A season to regenerate: *Far too quickly are the days of the beautiful flowers gone. The tulip begins to replenish its stores under the ground. This stage is not lovely to look at, but if the stage is cut short, tulips are at risk of dying.*

Our day today was hot but windy. It was the kind of wind you hear rather than feel. I was sitting outside and could hear its strong gushes up in the treetops, and the branches were bending and crackling. What I could feel on my level, though, was a gentle breeze. It made me think about our present situation. The war still rages, people are dying and suffering, and the wickedness seems to be on its spree, yet it's a "gentle breeze" compared to what's going on "up top" in the spiritual realm in the heavens. The spiritual war is still raging, and the evil tries to prevail, yet it stands no chance, for the victory has been won on the cross once and for all. This true victory can empower us to endure our circumstances and fight the good fight.

Reading news from Russia has never been easy. The level of lies and cynicism is unbearable for me. Sometimes a report would come up in my newsfeed on Facebook, and it's so ridiculous that I think someone posted fake news, but it turns out to be true. For example, a few days ago Russian parliament suggested canceling the independence of Lithuania since it "contradicted the Constitution of the USSR." It sounds absurd, yet it is clear evidence that if Putin is not stopped in Ukraine, Lithuania and the Baltic countries will become new objects for coercion to brotherhood.

My heart has been heavy for the people in the temporarily occupied territories. Every day I pray for their safety, Lord's provision, and speedy liberation from the Russians. Much healing is needed for all of us, but especially for those who experience hell on earth.

Day 107 · June 10

A volunteer who works with children in Poland shared a warning on the doors of all playrooms at volunteer centers. "No balloons allowed." What a great tragedy behind these three words. How much pain...

My niece woke up this morning asking, "Is the battle/[war] over?" I guess that's what she dreamed about. Her question moved me to tears because this is the question we all wake up with and search for answers to in the newsfeed. And that's what we pray for every day.

Day 108 · June 11

My heart has been heavy lately. Not because I don't believe that God will grant us victory. I am confident He will. But my heart breaks as I think about how much suffering our nation will have to endure until it happens. My heart breaks as I realize that we start growing numb from the casualty reports. My heart breaks as I see people who live thousands of miles away from Russia yet have been poisoned by the Russian propaganda.

Day 109 · June 12

Today, there was a funeral of a young activist. He actively joined the Revolution of Dignity (Euromaidan) in 2013-2014 when he was only 16 years old. In 2018, he led an initiative against an attempt to build skyscrapers in a park zone in Kyiv. After the beginning of the full-scale war, he joined the Armed Forces of Ukraine and was killed in the Kharkiv region. He would have been 25 in July. It is painful to know that the war takes away such promising young people, so we pray their sacrifice will not be in vain.

Day 115 · June 18

On this Father's Day, please, pray for:

• all Ukrainian fathers fighting at the front line for the future of their children

• all Ukrainian fathers separated from their children because of the need to get them to a safe place

• all Ukrainian fathers who lost their children in this war

• all Ukrainian fathers in the occupied territories who are doing their best to protect their children

• all Ukrainian fathers who were taken captive by the Russians and can see their children only in their dreams

- all Ukrainian fathers who were severely wounded and are recovering in hospitals waiting for the day to be reunited with their children
- all Ukrainian fathers who are away from their families volunteering and serving those in need
- all Ukrainian fathers who have the responsibility of explaining to their children what their nation is fighting for
- all Ukrainian children who lost their fathers in this war

"Father of the fatherless and protector of widows is God in his holy habitation. God settles the solitary in a home; he leads out the prisoners to prosperity, but the rebellious dwell in a parched land" (Psalm 68:5-6).

Day 116 · June 19

Today, there were more attacks on Kharkiv, five people were killed, and eleven were injured. The enemy army couldn't occupy the city and has been pushed back almost to the border, so they are punishing it for its resilience. It takes about three minutes for a missile launched from the Russian territory to reach Kharkiv, so there's little time to react.

Day 118 · June 22

Today, Ukraine was granted EU candidate status. This is a historical event that seemed almost impossible even four months ago. Of course, we understand that this status is just the first step toward the long road of reforms that must be successfully implemented in Ukraine.

Eight and a half years ago, in November 2013, the pro-Russian president Viktor Yanukovych refused to sign the EU Association agreement and announced tighter relations with Russia. This caused civil protests because people felt cheated and demanded the promised agreement with the EU. President Yanukovych decided to get rid of the protesters by force. On the night of November 30, 2013, about 100 protesters were encircled in Independence Square and brutally beaten by the riot police. They thought this would silence the people, but they were wrong. On December 1, 2013, up to 1 million people came to Independence Square to protest this violence and widespread government corruption, abuse of power, police brutality, and violation of human rights in Ukraine. That was the beginning of the Euromaidan, or the Revolution of Dignity.

Unfortunately, by February 2014, these protests escalated. Ukraine lost over 100 people brutally killed by snipers and special police forces – they are called the "Heavenly Hundred" and can be considered the first victims of this Russian-Ukrainian war. On February 20, 2014, when the pro-Russian president and officials fled the country, the parliament took over and managed to stop the violence. On that same day, Russia started its "special operation" in Crimea, which resulted in its annexation and gave way to the invasion of Donetsk and Luhansk regions.

And here we are eight years later. Russia wasn't satisfied with what it got in 2014. This time, they are after the whole of Ukraine, seeking to destroy it as a country and exterminate Ukrainians as a nation. They want revenge.

Yet we also see God restoring justice. In 2013, the protests started with a refusal to sign the political and economic association with the EU. Today, after eight years of war and thousands of Ukrainians joining the "Heavenly Hundred," we were granted the EU candidate status. And I believe that we will soon witness Ukraine's victory in this war.

Just as President Yanukovych thought violence would make people run in fear, that was the hope of the Russian army during the invasion of 2022. But they both were wrong. Ukrainians will fight for their nation and their dignity.

Day 120 · June 23

I may not wait until the evening to post my daily update.

There was a missile strike on Kyiv this morning. The missiles hit a residential building and a preschool in one of Kyiv's districts.[xix] There were also explosions in Cherkasy. Perhaps, that's a message to the G7 meeting that's taking place today. Or it could be a response to the Ukrainian army hitting a few weapon warehouses and Russian command centers in the occupied territories. Well, Russia is a terrorist state, so there's no surprise here.

How do I feel about it? Honestly, I feel nothing. I force myself to feel nothing, not to be consumed by despair and hatred. I force myself not to think about a seven-year-old rescued from the debris of the destroyed building – her father died as he covered her with his body. Her mother (ironically, a citizen of Russia who has been living in Ukraine for a long time) was trapped under the heavy cement blocks and is being taken care of by the doctors now. I force myself not to think about the complete terror these people experienced. I force myself not to think about the people in the north Kyiv region who were traumatized by the Russian occupation in March and have to hear explosions again and are unwillingly reliving that experience in their minds. I force myself not to think about it because it's too much pain. You could somehow explain and mourn the losses of our soldiers at the front lines and people caught in the line of fire, but there's no explanation for these cruel deaths hundreds of miles away from the battlefield. I force myself to be numb about it now, but I know that I will mourn and process it later when this war is over, and we can finally exhale and openly weep and lament.

As if that wasn't enough, my heart is further broken by the rejoicing on the Russian social media.[xx] They celebrate the deaths of innocent people. They leave comments such as "We are proud of you" and "Good morning ***." Are their hearts made of stone?

The Belarusian activists published a fragment of the intercepted conversation between a Russian dispatcher and a bomber pilot, who fired missiles at Kyiv, "We saw everything. It was beautiful. Good job, guys." So it was not a mistake. It was not a missed target. They intended an attack on a residential building. Do you need any other proof that Russia is a terrorist state?

I'm not always comfortable with imprecatory psalms. However, sometimes I know that instead of suppressing your feelings and letting the bitterness take root in your heart, it is better to honestly pour out your heart before the Lord and trust Him to do justice in His wisdom and steadfast love.

℣ Save me, O God!
For the waters have come up to my neck.
I sink in deep mire,
where there is no foothold;
I have come into deep waters,
and the flood sweeps over me.

℣ I am weary with my crying out;
my throat is parched.
My eyes grow dim
with waiting for my God.

❧ More in number than the hairs of my head
are those who hate me without cause;
mighty are those who would destroy me,
those who attack me with lies.
But as for me, my prayer is to you, O Lord.

❧ At an acceptable time, O God,
in the abundance of your steadfast love answer me in your saving
faithfulness.
❧ Deliver me
from sinking in the mire;
let me be delivered from my enemies
and from the deep waters.
Let not the flood sweep over me,
or the deep swallow me up,
or the pit close its mouth over me.

❧ Answer me, O Lord, for your steadfast love is good;
according to your abundant mercy, turn to me.
Hide not your face from your servant,
for I am in distress; make haste to answer me.
Draw near to my soul, redeem me;
ransom me because of my enemies!

❧ You know my reproach,
and my shame and my dishonor;
my foes are all known to you.
Reproaches have broken my heart,
so that I am in despair.

❧ I looked for pity, but there was none,
and for comforters, but I found none.
They gave me poison for food,
and for my thirst they gave me sour wine to drink.
Let their own table before them become a snare;
and when they are at peace, let it become a trap.

Pour out your indignation upon them,
and let your burning anger overtake them.
Add to them punishment upon punishment;
may they have no acquittal from you.

℣ But I am afflicted and in pain;
let your salvation, O God, set me on high!
I will praise the name of God with a song;
I will magnify him with thanksgiving.
This will please the Lord more than an ox
or a bull with horns and hoofs.
When the humble see it they will be glad;
you who seek God, let your hearts revive.

℣ For the Lord hears the needy
and does not despise his own people who are prisoners.
Let heaven and earth praise him,
the seas and everything that moves in them.

℣ For God will save Zion
and build up the cities of Judah,
and people shall dwell there and possess it;
the offspring of his servants shall inherit it,
and those who love his name shall dwell in it.
(Psalm 69[xxi])

Day 123 · June 26

There are days when I feel like David in Psalm 22, "my strength is dried up like a potsherd, and my tongue sticks to my jaws." I am weary from crying, "My God, my God, why have you forsaken me? Why are you so far from saving me, from the words of my groaning?" Kharkiv is being shelled every day. Today, five people were killed, and 22 were wounded (including five children). Lysychansk (Luhansk region) is under Russian attack. Today, people were standing in line to get some water from a cistern (no running water in the city) when the Russian army intentionally shelled that location.

Eight people were killed (including two children, 14 and 15 years old), and 21 were wounded.

Kremenchuk (Poltava region) became a target of a Russian missile strike. They hit a shopping mall. The estimated number of visitors at the time comes to about 1,000 people. As of now (the numbers are not final as the rescue operation continues), there's information about 15 people killed and 59 injured. Over 40 people contacted the police to report their loved ones missing after the missile strike.

Russia is a terrorist state. Since the first day of this invasion, we've seen them attack hospitals, maternity wards, theatres, schools, kindergartens, Holocaust memorials, residential buildings, grain storage facilities, and shopping malls. But that's not all. Putin's regime started with terrorist attacks in Russia and used the same technique to justify wars in Chechnia. Almost eight years ago, on July 17, 2014, Russian-backed separatists (using a Russian missile launcher) shot down a Malaysia Airlines Flight 17 (MH17) passenger flight from Amsterdam to Kuala Lumpur, killing 283 passengers and 15 crew members. Back then, the world didn't have enough courage to recognize the guilty and hold them responsible. Now, eight years later, we still hear voices who advocate for Russia and are reluctant to face the truth. The only difference is that the victim count has significantly increased since 2014. The blood of innocent victims will keep crying out to the Lord for justice.

I will keep praying for God's justice. I pray that one day soon, our nation will be able to sing Psalm 124 as a testimony of God's mercy and grace:

℣ If it had not been the Lord who was on our side
when people rose up against us,
then they would have swallowed us up alive,
when their anger was kindled against us;

℣ then the flood would have swept us away,
the torrent would have gone over us;
then over us would have gone
the raging waters.

℣ Blessed be the Lord,
who has not given us

as prey to their teeth!

℔ We have escaped like a bird
from the snare of the fowlers;
the snare is broken,
and we have escaped!

℔ Our help is in the name of the Lord,
who made heaven and earth.

I didn't feel like checking the news today. I was dreading new reports about missile strikes. And I was right. Massive missile attacks on Kharkiv, Mykolaiv, Ochakiv, and Dnipro today. News deaths, including children. I have no words.

Walking outside today, I was talking with God and searching my heart. I remembered a "conversation" I had in the comments section of someone's post during the early days of this invasion. Someone responded to my statement about the brutality of this war with the words, "Russia is doing justice. That's what your country deserves." I couldn't understand how someone could say that, so I responded to that person and said I wished they never had to experience something like this; otherwise, they wouldn't wish it to someone else. That person said they were from Kosovo, so they did experience city bombing in the 1990s and knew exactly what they were talking about. That's what left me speechless.

As I was searching my heart today, I knew I was feeling angry and weary. I know that it's not just Putin who started this war. He has the support of many Russian (and not only Russian) people. Yes, some of them have been brainwashed with Russian propaganda, but it doesn't mean they are not to share the blame. Everyone who doesn't protest against this war, everyone who pays taxes to the Russian government or does business with Russia, supports this aggression, whether they realize it or not. Everyone who voted for Putin or was quiet about the crimes of his regime for years (Putin has been in power for 20 years!) and let him strengthen totalitarianism in Russia shares the guilt. I know that we can't always change our circumstances, and I know that life is too complex to give basic answers to complicated questions, yet I think we must understand that the problem is not just Putin. The problem runs a lot deeper.

So today, I asked myself how I feel about Russian people and wondered if I could be like that person from Kosovo who lived through war and didn't feel sorry for others experiencing it now. I realized that I couldn't allow myself to be that way. I don't want Russian children to play the "hiding in a bomb shelter" game like my son and niece did today. I don't want Russian mothers to wake up in terror during a thunderstorm thinking it was an explosion. I can't wish for someone to experience the horrors my nation is experiencing now, especially in the occupied territories. Yet, at the same time, I want justice and trust God with that part. I pray for the Russians to repent and turn from their wicked ways. I know that repentance doesn't always come easy, and some may never come to it, especially if you've been working hard on hardening your heart. I know that sometimes it takes pain to reevaluate your life and choose the right path. I don't wish for our enemies to live through the pain we are experiencing now, but I will keep praying for God to restore His justice and do it in the way He sees fit.

> ❧ Contend, O Lord, with those who contend with me;
> fight against those who fight against me!
>
> ❧ Take hold of shield and buckler
> and rise for my help!
>
> ❧ Vindicate me, O Lord, my God,
> according to your righteousness,
> and let them not rejoice over me!
> (Psalm 35:1-2, 24)

Day 125 · June 28

We are still recovering from the shock of missile strikes on Ukrainian cities earlier this week (even though missiles keep landing on non-military targets). There are some bits of personal stories shared on social media by the witnesses of the missile strike on a shopping mall in Kremenchuk.

A young girl who was in the shopping mall minutes before the attack managed to leave the building because of the air-raid warning. She said there were lots of people in the mall that day, many pregnant women and families with children in the grocery store. After the explosion, when people realized what happened and tried to find a safe place, many young men ran inside to rescue people before the firefighters arrived. People cleaning up the debris say most victims were found in toy stores. I don't want to think further about what stands behind those words.

A firefighter who was part of the rescue operation at this shopping mall for two days straight shares his part of the story. They came to the site about 20 minutes after the explosion. By then, there were many volunteers bringing people out and cleaning the debris. Hundreds of people (authorized and instructed by the authorities) were working alongside the firefighters. Many volunteers brought water, sandwiches, and sorbent medicines to reduce the intoxication from the smoke exposure. I am moved to tears when I think about these acts of love and care.

Please, keep praying for Ukraine, especially for the cities that recently suffered from missile strikes (Kremenchuk, Kyiv, Mykolaiv, Ochakiv). As I was writing this post, they reported a missile attack on the Odesa region; a residential building was hit there, and over ten people were found dead (the number is not final). Pray for our soldiers. Pray for people in the occupied territories. Pray for the Spirit of the Lord to be poured out on all people of Ukraine so that we can stand in the Lord against this evil.

Day 127 · June 30

As I read news reports, sometimes I get lost. Too many missile strikes, too many artillery attacks. How do you remember them all? How do you not grow numb? How can you find the balance between not breaking down entirely yet remembering that those are real people behind the dry statistics?

Last night, Russian missiles hit a resort village in the Odesa region. Over 20 people were killed (the number is not final), including two children and 38 injured. This village is located hundreds of kilometers away from the active fighting. There was no way to know which target the enemy would choose this time. I try not to imagine these people's lives last night, hours from their death. Did they have a bad feeling, or were they enjoying their lives? How are their relatives coping with this pain now? Those who survived, how long will they be afraid to go to bed in case another missile comes? I don't have answers to these questions, and honestly, I'm afraid to ask them because the pain can be unbearable.

Day 128 · July 1

I've noticed myself getting more sensitive to words or phrases that seemed so ordinary before. At the same time, there are so many things we've learned over these months of the full-scale war that I wish we never had to know – for example, I could definitely do without the knowledge of military equipment. I wish we could have our ordinary "boring" lives back, but I don't think we'll ever be able to return to the way we were before February 24, 2022. We have to live in the here and now, not really making plans for the distant future because everything changes so fast, yet our daily lives come down to one question – how can we help bring our victory near?

Day 133 · July 6

For the past couple of weeks, my heart has been especially heavy for those in the occupied territories. Today, I came across a few articles that give glimpses of the life there, so I am reassured of the need to persevere in prayer for their liberation.

A couple of those articles talk about people forcefully deported to Russia. The United States has identified at least 18 "filtration camps" set up by Russia to detain and forcibly deport Ukrainian civilians to Russia.[xxii] All people who want to leave the occupied territories must undergo this humiliating procedure. If they are let go, they are taken to the territory of Russia (Taganrog or Rostov-on-Don) for a follow-up check-up. A Russian volunteer who helps the deported Ukrainians shares some shocking details about how children are taken from their parents.[xxiii] The volunteers try to offer their help before it comes to that. If people didn't have a place to go, the Russian officials would send them to the Far East (Vladivostok, Kareliya, Yakutiya, etc.). The volunteers find miraculous ways to take people to safety in Estonia or other Baltic countries.

In another article, they share an interview with a girl from Mariupol who went through all of this and wondered if it was easier to die than to go through the so-called evacuation.

While many people were able to evacuate before the active hostilities, thousands remain in the occupied territories, and we can only hope to hear their stories one day.

I saw something chilling today. Every time I look at it, I feel like an iron hand is clenched around my throat. The Russian forces intentionally set Ukrainian fields on fire. The weather has been very dry this summer, so the fields quickly catch fire from a spark. However, the Russian army doesn't leave it to chance – they fire special shells that explode mid-air and send the rain of burning shards to the ground. They use hunger as a weapon to dehumanize and subdue not only Ukrainian people but also millions of those who depend on Ukrainian grain. Do you remember when Jesus was being tempted in the wilderness, Satan tried to use hunger as a manipulation tool? It's obvious whose schemes the Russian army uses.

Day 135 · July 8

Reconciliation is a process involving both sides. It's a mutual effort to restore broken relationships. We taught our son from a very young age that if you did something wrong, you must ask for forgiveness and do your best to undo the wrong (clean up your mess, fix what was broken, return what was taken without permission, etc.). And this second part is essential as it is an outward sign of your repentance.

While I believe it is important for us as Christians to be forgiving, I also know that this war has already brought so much pain (and it's not over still!) that recovery will take a while. Some will be ready to forgive sooner than others. But would you blame a mother who lost her only child, a young soldier who lost his limbs, or a lonely elderly lady who is left without a roof over her head? It's so important to be sensitive to the pain of others and remember that there are people and lives behind the statistics. Even though our family has been blessed not to be significantly hurt by the war (especially compared to people living in the war zone or under occupation), there are days when I am swallowed up by bitterness and self-pity. On other days, I am desperate and broken-hearted for the evil inflicted on my friends, relatives, and simply my people. The healing and the road to forgiveness will be the greatest challenge and responsibility of the church in the post-war years.

Day 136 · July 9

There are days when there's nothing much to report, so I can allow myself to post some deeper personal insights and reflections. And there are days like today when I don't know where to begin.

Should I write about Mykolaiv, which suffered severe missile attacks yesterday and today? This morning they destroyed two universities there. My dear friends were in the city at this time. Should I write about that?

Or should I write about Dnipro, my husband's hometown, where my parents-in-law live? Russia launched six missiles, four of them were shot down by the air-defense system, but two rockets hit an industrial object in the city, causing a massive fire and bringing more destruction and death.

Or I could write about Kremenchuk (Poltava region) and Kramatorsk (Donetsk region). These city names sound very similar and, probably, indiscernible to foreigners, but both of them were attacked with Russian missiles tonight.

Perhaps I should write about the de-occupied Sumy region that was shelled 59 times from the territory of Russia today. I could write how people who live in the regions neighboring Russia and Belarus live in constant tension, wondering if or when they will be attacked.

I could write about another Russian missile that a Ukrainian military pilot skillfully shot down in the Kyiv region within 50 miles of our temporary residence. We didn't hear anything, but we are immensely grateful to God for His protection.

Should I write about my conversation with our son as he was going to bed? He was crying and saying that it felt like this war would never end. He felt worried about his grandparents in Dnipro and sad that it was still not safe for us to go home.

Or I could write about my inability to focus, work, read a book or finish a task for my online course. These past few days brought too many flashbacks from February and March, only we are wearier and even more resolved now.

There are so many things I could write about, but instead, I will turn to Psalm 142 and will keep begging God for His justice.

> ❧ I cry to you, O Lord;
> I say, "You are my refuge,
> my portion in the land of the living."

⅍ Attend to my cry,
for I am brought very low!

⅍ Deliver me from my persecutors,
for they are too strong for me!

⅍ Bring me out of prison,
that I may give thanks to your name!

⅍ The righteous will surround me,
for you will deal bountifully with me.
(Psalm 142:5-7)

Day 141 · July 14

Today, I had lots of thoughts on my mind and was struggling with many questions. It was one of those days when you desperately want your old predictable life back. I want to know that my son will have a school to go to and will be safe there. I want to be back in the School of Biblical Studies classroom, getting to know new students, translating, learning, and teaching. I want to have tea with my friends (now scattered across the globe) in my cozy kitchen in Kyiv. I want to dream and make memories with my family. And I wish that not just for myself but for all Ukrainian families.

As I was struggling with these questions, I read Psalm 146, and it felt as if God was giving me the answers I needed. I am amazed at how often the psalm corresponding to the number of the day seems to be the perfect fit for our circumstances. I will keep trusting in the Lord.

Day 146 · July 19

Today's post may be a lengthy read because it's something that's been on my mind for a while.

A couple of days ago, Russian propaganda aired a video clip encouraging mobilization. It was aimed at "simple people" living in remote regions of Russia and was not aired in Moscow. The video clip showed a simple Russian family, the elderly parents of a Russian soldier who was killed in Ukraine. The parents received government compensation for the loss of a son and purchased a car in memory of him.

You may ask how such a story would stimulate mobilization. Well, the logic is simple. The promised compensation for a Russian soldier killed in the war in Ukraine is about $120,000 (that a family may or may not get depending on the bureaucratic procedures). This is an astronomical amount for a family in the remote regions of Russia with a high unemployment rate and extreme poverty. You may remember stories of Russian soldiers retreating from the Kyiv region, looting homes, and packing away anything they could take, from underwear to gadgets, fridges, and washing machines. People in the de-occupied villages tell stories of Russian soldiers surprised that Ukrainian towns have electricity and asphalt roads. Some soldiers saw an indoor toilet for the first time. This extreme poverty and lack of education motivate people to contract with the army.

A few days ago, there was a video of an interview with a captive soldier who said he decided to enlist because he needed expensive dental work and had no money to afford it.

There's no "middle class" in Russia, and those who do fall into this category are primarily clustered in large cities, namely Moscow and St. Petersburg. Most people in Russia have never been abroad, and some have even never left their region. They struggle to make their ends meet, so all the economic sanctions would possibly have very little effect on their day-to-day life as they could never afford these imported goods anyway.

Do I feel sorry for them? Yes, I do. I have friends living in Russia who lost their source of income and whose future looks uncertain. Even though they struggle, they say this is not a high price to pay for what their country is doing to the people of Ukraine. That's why I pray for Russia's healing.

On July 15, Russia launched six missiles at the city of Dnipro (that's where my husband is from). The cost of these missiles comes to 78 million dollars. Just think about it! Spending that much money in one day on one city to bring death and destruction there. Last week, our President said that Russia had launched over 3,000 missiles since the beginning of the full-scale war. Why couldn't they spend this money on the well-being of their population? That's a rhetorical question.

While I feel sorry for the circumstances Russian people are in, I am well aware that their life situations may not be used as justification for their actions. I believe that we always have a choice, even when it seems that there's no way out.

A police officer consoles a grieving father - Day 147, July 20, 2022

I studied International Business at University, and I remember a professor who once told us that business and morals have nothing in common. He said that a true business person should jump at any good opportunity. He then said the most profitable business industries are human trafficking and pornography, so a true businessman would never turn down an offer in those fields. I was outraged and ended up having a half-hour discussion/ argument with him. In the end, he said, "I see that you don't have a spirit of a businessman within you." And I thought to myself, "Praise God, I have the Holy Spirit within me!"

I remembered this conversation today when I was thinking about this sad situation when people are ready to go and kill (or send your loved one to go, kill, and quite possibly be killed) just to get some money. Unfortunately, the situation described by my university professor is no longer hypothetical but plays out on a national scale in the neighboring country. That's why I pray for the Holy Spirit to dwell within me, within every believer, and work in the hearts of the lost to lead us all out of temptations.

"I call heaven and earth to witness against you today that I have set before you life and death, blessing and curse. Therefore choose life, that you and your offspring may live, loving the Lord your God, obeying his voice and holding fast to him, for he is your life and length of days, that you may dwell

in the land that the Lord swore to your fathers, to Abraham, to Isaac, and to
Jacob, to give them" (Deuteronomy 30:19-20).

Today's picture has been shared by so many people today because it speaks
volumes. During an artillery shelling of Kharkiv, a bus stop was hit. Three
people died, including a thirteen-year-old boy. His father sat beside his body
for two hours, holding his hand and praying over him. This whole time the
police lady was sitting next to him, holding the father's hand. How would
you describe this image with one word? Despair? Hope? Faith? Care? Love?
I'm at a loss for words.

Day 147- July 20

The occupied territories have been on my heart a lot. I've shared before that
the Kherson region is especially dear to me because that's where my dad was
born and where I spent my first year of life. Our distant relatives (whom I
never met) still live there. I recently saw a few posts on social media that paint
a pretty grim picture of life in occupation – people live in constant terror, the
activists are abducted and tortured, and the life there is unbearable, so many
people say they don't mind living in the active war zone as long as it means
liberation.

The Ukrainian army is slowly advancing in the Kherson region, and they
make no rushed moves to avoid unnecessary risks and save people's lives
(both military and civilians). Please, keep praying for the complete liberation
of all occupied territories.

As I was thinking about the song of praise, I wanted to share with you the
beauty of the Kherson region. It's known for unique natural landscapes, the
most delicious watermelons, and wine produced by the Prince Trubetskoi
Winery. I want to visit that winery one day when the war is over because of
its history. It has a century-long tradition of wine production, and the first
vineyards were planted at the end of the 1800s.

But I'm drawn to that place not because of wine. My great-grandmother
worked as a cook at the Prince Trubetskoi mansion. My grandma said that
during the Soviet revolution, when the Trubetskoi family had to leave, Mrs.
Trubetskoi gave my great-grandmother a set of silver spoons as a sign of
gratitude for her faithful service. We don't know what happened to the spoons
later. They must have been confiscated along with all the family belongings

years later when my great-grandfather was arrested and proclaimed the "enemy of the people" during Stalin's Great Terror years.

Over the years, the Trubetskoi mansion turned into a ruin, but the winery kept functioning, and the current owners had grand plans for the restoration of the former glory of this place. Unfortunately, that part of Kherson region has been occupied since the first days of the invasion. The winery was turned into a station for the Russian forces, the labs were destroyed, the vineyards were mined, and the unique wine was lost.

Day 149 · July 22

The enemy is trying to crush our spirit, take away our ability to rejoice and ruin our hope. That's the real battle we all face despite our proximity to the front line.

A couple of days ago, I shared a praise report about the possibility of exporting Ukrainian grain and aiding in the world hunger crisis. Writing that news piece as a praise report, I was fighting doubts. I knew Russia couldn't be trusted, so I kept asking myself what evil would come out of this "act of good will." I was upset with my own negativity, yet today it turned out that my concerns were reasonable.

This morning, Russia launched four Kalibr missiles at Odesa seaport, one of the three seaports designated for grain export. Our air-defense shot down two rockets, but the other two hit the port and caused a fire. Praise God, there seem to be no casualties, and the missiles didn't hit the grain storage. However, it makes me wonder how anyone can hope for any sort of negotiations with Russia if they break their promises less than 24 hours after giving them. Turkey and the UN officials also signed the grain export agreement, so it's a slap in their face as well.

Of course, Russia immediately claimed it was a provocation and even came up with a wild story of Ukrainians stealing their missiles and then destroying their own city on purpose. Unfortunately, some people still believe such claims. I won't even try to explain why it's ridiculous.

This morning, Russian missiles also hit Mykolaiv (again!) and Kropyvnytskyi, another city fairly far from the front line. It only proves the agony of the terrorists.

We praise God for the good reports. According to the statistics shared by the President in one of his recent addresses, thanks to the western ammunition, the Ukrainian army significantly reduced its personnel losses. In May, the losses peaked at 100-200 Ukrainian soldiers every day, but now that number went down to 30 killed and up to 200 wounded. Of course, this number is still too high, and there are human lives behind these numbers, but we praise God for His protection.

> ℣ Praise him for his mighty deeds;
> praise him according to his excellent greatness!
> Let everything that has breath
> praise the Lord! Praise the Lord!
> (Psalm 150:2, 6)

It was around day 20 when I started turning to psalms daily. Back then, day 150 seemed too far away. Around day 100, I got worried I would run out of psalms (corresponding to the number of the day) before the war ended. Now, this day has come, yet I will keep trusting in the Lord and His timing, and I will keep turning to His word for comfort and guidance.

Day 150 · July 23

Resilience and the Seeds of Future Hope

A season to multiply: *The tulips begin to multiply and prepare for the following year. This invisible work of resilience is crucial. The commitment to goodness brings life into the world.*

A few days ago, a friend shared this quote from *The Lord of the Rings*, "I do not love the bright sword for its sharpness, nor the arrow for its swiftness, nor the warrior for his glory. I love only that which they defend."

This quote has been on my mind a lot. Perhaps because it's such an accurate description of what we are experiencing today. Ukrainians are peaceful people. Our army today consists of teachers, journalists, scientists, craftsmen, businessmen, musicians, and people from many other professions who would much rather do their job yet felt called to defend their land and their loved ones. So, they continue to write songs in the trenches, take pictures in-between artillery shelling, write articles for foreign publications explaining the complexity of Ukraine's history, all the while longing for the victory and the ability to return to their peaceful everyday life.

Day 99 · June 2

It's so hard not to let despair overcome you when you hear such things, so I am looking for God's encouragement, and it comes through ordinary things. Over a month ago, we planted eggplant seeds in a container to start them into seedlings before they could be transplanted into soil. The first seedlings were nice and rich green, so we left them outside to get used to the sunlight. That's when grandma's chickens decided to feast on them. Almost all seedlings were "trimmed" by the chickens. I was ready to cry but not ready to give up. We kept shielding the seedlings and watering them, and they miraculously recovered! I am still marveling at their strength.

Back in April, when we ordered new trees to plant in grandma's garden, there was a peach tree that came in looking rather withered and dead. Nevertheless, we planted it and kept watering it, even though it was non-responsive. Today we saw tiny leaves peeking through.

A similar story happened to a rose bush we planted early this spring. While other rose bushes started growing and thriving, this one looked dead. I was tempted to pluck it out of and forget about it, yet I chose to give it another chance and kept watering it. Now it has tiny buds that are still too vulnerable, yet testify to its will to live.

As I look at all these plants, I am encouraged. If those eggplant seedlings could recover, if dead-looking trees and bushes are brought to life by such a simple thing as watering, then how much more powerful our prayers are! It is easy for us to give up, to say there's no point in it, and lose. Or we can persevere and see beauty rise from the ashes. I believe it can happen in Ukraine, so I ask you to pray with me.

Day 101 · June 4

As I read these news reports and checked world news, I felt like crying out, "Come, Lord Jesus! The world overflows with wickedness and pain, so come quickly!" I also remembered a passage from Revelations 6 – the vision of the seven seals and four horses bringing disasters. War, famine, sickness, and death were revealed to apostle John, and these seem to be the main characters of today's news. However, they are not unique to our time or our nation. If we look at history, they are present in any age because we live in the fallen world, anticipating a complete deliverance from this present evil that will happen when Jesus returns in His glory. And while life may be challenging today, what matters is that we must be ready for what is to come. Because despite our present circumstances, those who put trust in Him will be comforted and avenged.

Day 103 · June 6

Tonight, at bedtime, our eight-year-old son said, "You know, there was a time when I didn't believe in God because how can you believe in someone you've never seen." "What caused you to change your mind?" Ivan asked. Our son responded, "I noticed that when we pray, God answers our prayers, so He must be real." His answer was so simple and sincere, and it reassured me of the importance of remembering God's faithfulness in our lives and sharing stories of answered prayers to encourage each other. Ivan and I then proceeded to tell our son the story of God's faithfulness in the life of a Ukrainian marine whose story we had heard. Witnessing answers to our prayers is important, yet it is equally important to keep praying in faith and anticipation of those answers.

Day 106 · June 9

During the first weeks of this invasion, I couldn't think about my balcony garden without tears coming to my eyes. I felt sorry for the potted plants left to die slowly without care. We are still away from home, but recently someone came to stay in our apartment. Last week, when they asked me if I wanted to see the picture of my balcony, I hesitated. I didn't think I could handle it. But I was in for a surprise. After three and a half months without watering and sunlight, there were some plants still alive, and one of them even brought forth a beautiful flower. I know that this miracle is an exceptional gift from God, who knows me personally and cherishes the deep desires of my heart. I'm in awe as I think that the Almighty God, who holds the universe in His hands, who daily shows His power at the front lines, also chooses to be so intimate. I believe that this "balcony garden of survivors" is not only an encouragement but also a message of hope. In the Old Testament, when the Israelites were sent into exile, God promised to keep a faithful remnant, bring them back, and turn their mourning into joy. I believe these plants hold the same promise, not only for my balcony garden but also for Ukraine.

Day 126 · June 29

Please, keep praying for all the people in the temporarily occupied territories as they are anxiously waiting for liberation. Pray for all prisoners captured and abducted by Russia, especially those from Mariupol, may they be safe, and may we see them released soon. Pray for miracles upon miracles and the mighty hand of God to be clearly evident in this war.

Day 119 · June 22

This week, I started an online course in literary translation. In the opening greeting, the speaker said she feels that holding this course during war means that we will win. Because despite the war, people read books, buy them, and publishing houses announce projects. We've already won because we refuse to give up.

Day 139 · July 12

The hope for God's justice is what keeps me going. It's so hard not to let your heart be filled with bitterness but long for God's will instead. I know that part of the enemy's plan is to dehumanize us, make us lose our dignity, and give up our values. This is the hope not only of our present enemy (Russia) but the spiritual enemy of God's people. That's why we keep praying and asking God to restore His justice.

Day 157 · July 30

Chapter Five

A Time to Prepare

August 1 - September 30, 2022

There are days when I wonder why there can be no days off from war. We had a rainy day today (the first in a long time!), which meant rest from many daily activities and made me yearn for a day of rest from the war. Unfortunately, it won't happen until our victory, which is the best motivation to persevere in prayer.

Day 160 • August 1

Marigolds are common flowers in Ukraine, traditionally used as a symbol of reminder about home and family. There is a song about a mother planting marigolds by her home, and then wherever you are, every time you see marigolds, you remember your mother and Ukraine.[xxiv]

Day 172 • August 14

Today we went to a local event commemorating the struggle of Ukrainians against Bolsheviks in 1919-1922. One of the slogans of the event was really meaningful and powerful – "Remembrance is a weapon." My son made this bouquet for me in the kids' program. I love that it has already dried-up plants and can be kept as a reminder to remember.

Day 178 • August 20

I was encouraged by our aster and lily flowers blooming in the flowerbeds we created this spring. They brighten up my days even if the news is gloomy.

Day 186 • August 28

Hope Based in Past Memories

A season to plant: *Planting tulips is an expression of hope, based on past experience. After a bulb is placed in the ground, half a year passes before the gardener knows whether their hope is realized.*

I felt outraged and upset. I wanted to be angry with the world and anything "international," but God stopped me. He didn't let my heart nurture bitterness but quietly pointed out how He had shown me His love and faithfulness over the past few days. He pointed out all the encouragements He sent me through my friends, old and new. Messages, pictures, music, support, donations to the causes I shared coming from all parts of the world (and I'm not exaggerating!).

I praise God for His indescribable ways and believe that He will be faithful to the end and will grant us victory. "For the Lord will not cast off forever, but, though he causes grief, he will have compassion according to the abundance of his steadfast love; for he does not afflict from his heart or grieve the children of men." (Lamentations 3:31-33).

Day 162 · August 4

Oh, how I long for the day when all nations will turn to the Lord and worship Him and recognize Him as their true ruler and choose to do His will. For that would mean no more war, pain, and tears.

Day 172 · August 14

Today, I was inspired by recent research published by Zagoriy Foundation. According to it, since the beginning of the full-scale war:
86% of Ukrainians took part in charity events
74% of Ukrainians helped the army
33% of Ukrainians volunteered
65% of Ukrainians donated to charity
59% of Ukrainians donated food, clothes, and medicines

39% of Ukrainians provided their services free of charge
24% of Ukrainians paid for the humanitarian needs of other people
20% of Ukrainians provided a place to stay for free
These numbers are impressive and give me hope because they prove that the whole nation is united against this evil.

Day 174 · August 16

My today's psalm is Psalm 27.[xxv] I remember leaving Kyiv on the morning of February 24, and we joined an online prayer meeting organized by our son's school. Someone shared this psalm, and I remember praying through it with tears streaming down my face as we were driving out of the city, not knowing what awaited us ahead. I returned to this psalm again and again over the past months, and I come back to it today as I wait for the Lord.

℣ The Lord is my light and my salvation;
whom shall I fear?
The Lord is the stronghold of my life;
of whom shall I be afraid?

℣ Though an army encamp against me,
my heart shall not fear;
though war arise against me,
yet I will be confident.

℣ For he will hide me in his shelter
in the day of trouble;
he will conceal me under the cover of his tent;
he will lift me high upon a rock.

℣ Hear, O Lord, when I cry aloud;
be gracious to me and answer me!

℣ Hide not your face from me.
Turn not your servant away in anger,
O you who have been my help.
Cast me not off; forsake me not,

O God of my salvation!

℣ Teach me your way, O Lord,
and lead me on a level path
because of my enemies.

℣ I believe that I shall look upon the goodness of the Lord
in the land of the living!
Wait for the Lord;
be strong, and let your heart take courage;
wait for the Lord!

Day 177 · August 19

As I was pondering difficult situations, I was reminded of the times when God used struggles to accomplish the good He intended. After Pentecost, after the disciples were told to go and spread the Good News to the ends of the earth, they comfortably stayed in Jerusalem. It took persecutions to disperse them and to further the Gospel.

Apostle Paul turned his trip to a trial in Rome into one more missionary journey and preached for two years there while waiting for the trial (Acts chapters 27 and 28). He was able to reach the people he would never have met otherwise.

These examples became a great encouragement to me. None of the people in Ukraine got the future they were hoping for, but we got the one God prepared for us, and He will see us through. With the new locations and teams come new missionary opportunities. Being in new surroundings, we may acquire new skills and knowledge that will be invaluable when we return home. When we are challenged and stretched to our limits, we grow and learn to depend not on our strength.

Day 184 · August 26

Considering the sobering realities faced by Ukraine encouraged me today to trust in the Lord of hosts, the Miracle-worker, the sovereign God. He has done amazing things since the invasion, and I believe it is in His power to bring this war to an end once and for all.

Day 198 · September 9

The Lord's Prayer scribbled on the wall - Day 203, September 14, 2022

Today's picture – you may have already seen it, but I can't omit it. In the newly liberated Balakliya, they found "The Lord's Prayer" scribbled on the wall of a torture chamber of a Russian prison. We don't know what happened to the prisoner who wrote it, but I know that he was freer than those who kept him captive and bound. "The Spirit of the Lord God is upon me, because the Lord has anointed me to bring good news to the poor; he has sent me to bind up the brokenhearted, to proclaim liberty to the captives, and the opening of the prison to those who are bound" (Isaiah 61:1).

Day 203 · September 14

Some of the Russian occupiers' commanders are trying to get in touch with representatives of the Ukrainian Armed Forces to lay down their arms and surrender. This was reported by the Operational Command Pivden (South)

Mankind will say, "Surely there is a reward for the righteous; surely there is a God who judges on earth" (Psalm 58:11).

Day 208 · September 19

I guess everyone has seen the image of the bracelets on the exhumed body in Izium. Somehow connecting that image (which is horrifying in itself) to a real person with a family and personal story made it so much more horrifying. Today, we learned that this man's name. He was 36 years old and lived in Nikopol (Dnipropetrovsk region). His son is fourteen years old, and his daughter is nine. The bracelets were given to him by his children when he first left for the front lines in 2014. We've started getting numb to the number of victims (which means that our defense mechanism helps us cope with this insanity). Still, I hope and pray that every soldier and civilian who lost their lives to this horde of wickedness will never be forgotten or left nameless.

Day 209 · September 20

❧ For God alone my soul waits in silence;
from him comes my salvation.
He alone is my rock and my salvation, my fortress;

❧ I shall not be greatly shaken.
Trust in him at all times, O people;
pour out your heart before him;
God is a refuge for us.
(Psalm 62:1-2, 8)

Over the past seven months, my greatest comfort was in knowing that I can always pour out my heart before God. He can take my questions. He can handle my frustration. He is not afraid of my anger. He will not confront me for my tears. That's one of the elements of freedom in Christ – freedom to be who you are and come to the Lord just as you are. Our son is a good example of that – yesterday at bedtime, he wanted to pray for Putin's death, and this morning, he prayed for him to repent and become our friend.

Day 212 · September 23

The Experience of Survival

A season to make roots: *Having planted our tulip bulbs, we move forward into the busyness of preparing for winter. This is a practical time, built around survival.*

Today Russian troops shelled the area near Zaporizhzhia Nuclear Power Plant (NPP) twice. They seriously damaged a high-voltage power line, nitrogen-oxygen station, and the combined auxiliary building. There are risks of hydrogen leakage and sputtering of radioactive substances. Fire danger is serious. It means a nuclear disaster can happen anytime if the Russian troops are not careful enough.

Is it something new? No. The city of Enerhodar (and Zaporizhzhia Nuclear Power Plant) has been under Russian occupation since March 4, 2022. Over the past few months, they have turned the NPP facility into their ammunition depot (which means a high risk of detonation and explosion), and they were interfering with the management and staff of the NPP. A few times, Russian missiles aimed at Kyiv or another region of Ukraine flew really low over the NPP, putting it in danger. It is one more weapon of terrorism, a nuclear one this time. We are literally sitting on a powder keg, and we are fully aware that the risks of Russia using a nuclear weapon or causing a nuclear disaster are not negligible.

What should we then do? I believe we should pray, trust God (for His interference and protection is vital in this situation), and keep on living.

The enemy (both our immediate physical enemy, Russia, and the spiritual enemy) wants us to be paralyzed by fear or anxiety. The enemy wants to steal our joy. He wants us to feel dead while we are still alive. And we must resist it.

Day 163 · August 5

I know that God can use any situation for His glory. I pray that He would use this war and millions of refugees from Ukraine to change the hearts of people, make them more open to each other, and also encourage refugees to be a responsible and worthy representative of their nation.

However, being a refugee or an internally displaced person also means dealing with daily questions of where to stay or what to eat. Some people were welcomed by host families for six months, and that period is nearing its end, which means a new search for a place to stay. In the safer parts of Ukraine, some school gyms or auditoriums were turned into hubs for the people left without homes, but with the beginning of the school year approaching, they will need to find a new location. No one thought this war would be going this long, but unfortunately, it is far from over.

Day 165 · August 7

There are some random things I remember from the first weeks of the invasion. Those are not important things, but they speak volumes to me. For example, because of many supply chains being broken, in those first weeks of the war, you had to hunt for bread because it was hard to come by. Ironically, that was our biggest craving, so I remember how happy we were when we could finally find yeast in the store. It was a true treasure. We smile at this memory now, but I know that, unfortunately, for many people it is still their reality.

And I know that after our victory, many years later, there will be things or words that pull at the strings of our hearts and trigger the memories we weren't even aware of. Who could have thought that we would be the generation to live in times of war? And who knows how many generations will it would take to heal from this trauma?

Day 167 · August 9

Every day, I need to remind myself that time does not stand still, that we cannot just wait until the war is over, but we must make good use of the time we are given.

Ukraine is preparing for winter. As they say here, fix your sleigh in summer. People in the villages buy wood to use wood furnaces in case of gas/electricity outages. In the city, people are heatproofing their apartments and purchasing heaters and warm blankets before the prices go up even more. If the hot phase of the war is not over by winter, Russia will most definitely attack the civil infrastructure to keep Ukrainians freezing, so we'd better be ready.

However, being ready is not easy for those who lived through occupation or had their homes destroyed by the Russian bombs. Over 3.5 million Ukrainians have had their homes destroyed (over 15 thousand apartment buildings and 115 thousand private homes) – that's about the population of Berlin or Los Angeles, just to give you a scale. Many people don't have a place to go, but many refuse to leave even if rubble is all they have left because leaving would mean cutting their roots.

Please, pray for those left without a roof over their heads to have a home by winter. Pray for those in homes to be able to keep them warm. Pray for Ukraine's victory soon and the complete restoration of everything destroyed.

Day 168 · August 10

As I'm writing this, a thunderstorm is raging outside. Flashes of lightning, thunder, and rattling of windows make me freeze for a moment even though I know we are a safe distance away from the front line. Please, pray for the people who don't have this advantage and fall asleep to the sounds of explosions and not thunder.

Day 173 · August 15

Another unsettling report came from Ukraine's intelligence services. Russia may be planning a terrorist attack on Zaporizhzhia Nuclear Power Plant tomorrow. According to the report, most licensed staff of the NPP were asked to stay home, and only a limited number of the operating team will be admitted to the facility. Also, the representatives of the Russian nuclear company Rosatom seem to have left the city even though they had usually been present at all NPP meetings since the occupation. Taking into consideration this information and the amount of weapons stored at the station, a nuclear terrorist attack is highly probable. Please, pray for God's protection. The Zaporizhzhia NPP is the largest nuclear power plant in Europe (almost ten times more powerful than Chernobyl). The consequences of such an attack would be terrifying to the whole world, not just in Ukraine.

Day 176 · August 18

Even though it sounds absurd, the war teaches us to find balance. You learn to balance between panic and passivity, between careless hope and utter despair. It pushes you to extremes while the reason is somewhere in the middle, and you grow as you learn how to find it.

Day 178 · August 20

Please, keep praying for Ukraine, especially as we approach Independence Day (August 24). All kinds of precautions are taken. People are warned to pay special attention to air-raid warnings and stay away from crowded places. New alerts are introduced to inform about chemical and nuclear threats. We need your prayers and God's deliverance.

Day 179 · August 21

Today I saw pictures that captured my heart. They show empty supermarket shelves with a sign that says that we are waiting for the goods produced in the temporarily occupied territories of Ukraine (tomato paste from Kherson region, salt from Donetsk region, and wines from Crimea). They are not forgotten and cannot be replaced.

Day 180 · August 22

It's way past midnight here, and I'm slowly exhaling. Today, Ukraine celebrated the 31st anniversary of its regained independence. It also marked six months since the beginning of the full-scale war.

Today, there was a total of 189 air-raid warnings for all regions of Ukraine. The previous maximum (109 alerts) was on Easter. There were missile strikes (hit critical infrastructure objects in the Khmelnytskyi region, a military airfield in the Poltava region, and a railroad station and passenger cars in the Dnipropetrovsk regions), and top-notch performance of our air-defense forces. There were bomb threats in public places in various cities and lots of fake information online.

However, it wasn't extraordinary for most people in Ukraine. Over the past six months, we've gotten used to Russia's cruelty and terror. Our neighbors started bidding in our messenger chat on the number of air-raids we would get by morning.

This ability to joke in horrible situations, to mock death in its face, seems to be part of Ukrainian nature, a component of our resilience.

Day 182 · August 24

Since we are staying in the village, we are entering the busiest time of the year – the harvest season. For me, it means less time checking the news and more time for reflection (while picking vegetables or canning). I've always enjoyed this season when we can enjoy the abundance of God's creation. This year it's even more special.

We came here at the end of February; I was there for planting and tending, I remember praying for God's blessing on our harvest, and now it feels like a reward for our faithfulness in spring. It reminds me that our faithfulness in the present will be rewarded by the abundance of eternity.

Day 186 · August 28

Today is the last day of summer, which still feels like February. It's as if we are in hibernation mode, going through motions but, in fact, waiting for the time when we'll be able to live and breathe freely.

When I was a kid, we had a tradition for the potato harvesting season. We would usually exchange the first couple of sacks of potatoes for the sweet watermelons and enjoy the treat right there with sticky juice dripping all over the place. The watermelons were brought on a huge truck from Mykolaiv and were sold or exchanged. Later in the fall, the same truck would again bring onions, sweet peppers, and tomatoes in exchange for potatoes. This natural exchange was an excellent solution for the villagers who couldn't afford to buy the vegetables. It was also an ideal solution for the people in the Mykolaiv region – grow what yields a great harvest and exchange it for something that can't be produced locally. This tradition has been ongoing for over 20 years, and the truck drivers knew their regular customers.

Needless to say, this year, there were no trucks from the Mykolaiv region, which makes me wonder where they are today, if their families are safe, and if they will have enough potatoes for the winter season.

Day 189 · August 31

Please, keep praying for our defenders. The days are getting cooler, and the nights are chilly. May the Lord keep them warm and safe.

Day 191 · September 2

The Russian missiles hit a large oil depot in the Dnipropetrovsk region today. It may lead to a new fuel crisis (we had a fuel shortage until mid-summer with things slowly improving).

Day 194 · September 5

As we keep rejoicing over the newly liberated territories, Russia is raging. Interestingly, there are at least two Ukrainian words for raging that derive from the word Satan or demon. I never thought of it, but they are very fitting in this context.

Feeling defeated on the battlefield (the Ukrainian army is approaching the Russian border in the Kharkiv region, and the occupational authorities are running away even from the cities in the Luhansk region occupied since 2014), Russia resorts to its good old strategy of terrorizing civilians. Have they learned nothing? Don't they understand it won't make us give up, so they are doing it for the pure satisfaction of their hunger for wickedness?

It was to be expected, so most of us are especially tense at the air-raid warnings now. Last night, Russian missiles hit the downtown part of Dnipro city and residential quarters of Mykolaiv, and they heavily shelled more towns in the Dnipropetrovsk region. Tonight, they attacked objects of critical infrastructure. Out of eleven missiles, nine were shot down by our air-defense forces. However, missiles did hit a heat and power station in the Kharkiv region, which caused a power outage in all of the Kharkiv and Donetsk regions and most of the Sumy, Zaporizhzhia, Poltava, and Dnipropetrovsk regions. Ironically, it also led to a power outage in Russia's own Belgorod region. A power outage means no electricity, no running water, no heat, and no cell phone or internet connection. Today was a foreshadowing of what our winter could look like – dark and cold.

In tonight's address, our President said that we would rather be hungry, cold, and in the dark than "with Russia," and it's true. We've endured so much already, and we've seen so many miracles and signs of God's mercy that there's no turning back now. Our people are calmly and methodically preparing for all contingencies.

It's symbolic that Russia carried out this massive attack on civil infrastructure today, on September 11, when we remember the terrorist attack on the World Trade Center in New York in 2001. The location is different, and the number of casualties is different, but the general intention is the same – to rob people of their joy, to make them drown in fear, to break their spirit. Russia is a terrorist state, so any negotiations will only lead to more blackmail and terrorism. We pray for the day when Russia will stop being a threat to Ukraine or any other nation and trust in God's ways and His timing.

Day 200 · September 11

Today, Russians fired eight missiles at Kryvyi Rih, hitting hydraulic infrastructure (the Inhulets river dam) and attempting to flood the city. They must have chosen the city because it is the hometown of our President, so they view it as some sort of revenge. Just another day of terrorist attacks.

Day 203 · September 14

There was another missile strike on Kryvyi Rih today. After the previous strikes on critical infrastructure, our officials said it's something they had been preparing for since February, so they were ready to react and adjust.

Day 204 · September 15

We had a violent storm today (not just us, most of Ukraine did), which caused low voltage and power outages. I think everyone has experienced a power outage at some point. Back in the 1990s, we had regular blackouts every evening to conserve electricity and cut expenses, so it's not something completely new. However, it's uncomfortable. You immediately start wondering when the power will be back, if you will be able to finish your work on the computer, and if there are perishables in the fridge (if the power is gone for a long time). You wonder if your candle will last long enough and check your phone battery and the power bank. Thankfully, we are in the village, so we can get water from a well if there is no running water due to a power outage, but we made a mental note to have a few buckets of water stashed somewhere for an emergency. In a way, I marveled at how calmly and reasonably we pointed out our preparation flaws because we know that the absence of electricity is a real possibility for this winter. Thankfully the power came back tonight, but I couldn't help but think about the people in the occupied territories and severely shelled cities. In the recently de-occupied Izium, people spent six months without electricity, running water, heat, cell phone, or an internet connection.

Day 207 · September 18

The UK Defense Intelligence warned that Russia has increased its targeting of civilian infrastructure (strikes against the electricity grid and a dam on the Inhulets River at Kryvyi Rih).[xxvi] As it faces setbacks on the front lines, Russia has likely extended the locations it is prepared to strike in an attempt to undermine the morale of the Ukrainian people and government directly. We've learned that Russia will stop at nothing, so we wouldn't be surprised by anything. Some Russian propagandists talked about missile strikes on the chain of dams on the Dnipro River to flood left-bank Ukraine and drown thousands of civilians. It's a rather unlikely scenario, but we trust in God's protection and His guidance for our air-defense forces. Russia is accumulating airplanes and fighter helicopters along the border. They still have plenty of missiles, and we have river dams, hydropower stations, and nuclear power plants, but we trust in our Deliverer.

Day 207 · September 18

I'll cut my post short today as we have power outage again (most likely, it's the consequence of yesterday's storm).

Early this morning, the Russians launched a rocket attack on the South Ukrainian NPP in the Mykolayiv region. The missile fell 300 meters from the nuclear reactors. The Zaporizhzhia NPP is still under Russian control.

Day 208 · September 19

The Russian army keeps targeting Ukrainian civil infrastructure – over 10 missiles hit Zaporizhzhia tonight, not counting the attacks on other cities earlier in the day.

Day 211 · September 22

Back in January, we were mentally preparing for the invasion – we discussed our emergency plans, stocked up on supplies, and ensured we kept the gas tank full. Now, seven months later, we are mentally preparing for a nuclear strike (and earnestly pray for God's deliverance). Yes, the enemy may be bluffing, but it's better to be prepared. We live in times of insanity....

One of Azovstal defenders, shared that he read the whole Bible during his captivity and that he would secretly pray the Lord's prayer and talk to God. He said that he understood now why his mother had taught it to them. What a testimony amid the despair!

Day 213 · September 24

When I checked the news this morning, I saw that one of the paramedics freed from the Russian activity four days ago, gave birth to a healthy baby girl early this morning. Both the baby and the mom are feeling fine. I spent the rest of the day with this thought – God knows the perfect timing for everything. She spent four months as a prisoner of war. On some days, she had only a couple of apples to eat, and her cellmates made sure she was sleeping on a cell bed every night (they had to take turns as there weren't enough beds). God was with her throughout this time. Had she given birth while in captivity, her child would have most likely been taken away from her under the pretense of proper care (and possibly set up for adoption). Had she gone into labor right before the prisoner swap, she wouldn't have been exchanged and would have had to remain in captivity. But everything happened according to God's perfect plan.

I know that this is only one person's example, but I hope it encourages us to trust God with His timing, even when it doesn't make sense.

Please, keep praying for over 2.5 thousand POWs remaining in Russian captivity.

Day 214 · September 25

Everyone keeps thinking about the possibility of a nuclear strike. It feels good to read optimistic analyses saying that Putin is bluffing, but I remind myself that about seven months ago, most of us didn't believe in the possibility of a full-scale invasion. We keep praying for a miracle. Someone recently pointed out that believing and praying for a miracle is important, but it's not a fool-proof guarantee that something bad won't happen. Jesus had to bear his cross in submission to God's will, not because Mary's prayers weren't fervent enough. May we be obedient to God's will at all times, and may we see His mercy and justice.

Do you need a doctor?

I'm fine. I'm going to visit my neighbors. Here are my documents. Check them. Take my documents, check them...

What are you saying? Don't you see our flag? We are "yours". We are Ukrainian.

That's when the woman started crying; her hands were shaking. She is over 80 years old. She didn't leave her home for days and didn't know her village had been liberated.

❧ Sing aloud, O daughter of Zion; shout, O Israel! Rejoice and exult with all your heart, O daughter of Jerusalem!

❧ The Lord has taken away the judgments against you; he has cleared away your enemies. The King of Israel, the Lord, is in your midst; you shall never again fear evil.
(Zephaniah 3:14-15)

Day 216 • September 27

When Hope Felt Distant

A season to cool: *Winter buries the memory of the hopes that we had planted with our tulip bulbs.*

There is a question asked in Psalm 11 that can either encourage or bring you to despair. What can you do when your homeland is destroyed,when the enemy spreads lies about you, when your identity is challenged, when your values are questioned, when the truth is redefined?

In times like that, we are forced to be brutally honest with ourselves and either seek the Lord and His presence or, as Job's wife put it, "Curse God and die!" (Job 2:9). When your foundation is shaken and your future is uncertain, root yourself in the never-changing Rock.

Oh Lord, search our hearts and cleanse us from our unrighteousness. Help us see the truth, do justice, and love mercy. We pray for your justice and your righteous wrath on our enemies who commit abominable wickedness. May they repent, may this bloodshed be brought to an end. We ask for your miracles. May your hand end this war so the whole world will be in awe and glorify your name. Protect us from the use of chemical, biological, and nuclear weapons. Fill us with faith and wash us with Your Spirit so that you would count us worthy to see your face.

Day 161 · August 3

Mykolaiv, Kharkiv, and Nikopol are shelled every day. About an hour ago, a Russian missile hit an apartment building in downtown Kharkiv. How long, o Lord?

Day 188 · August 30

September 1 is traditionally the first day of school, the Day of Knowledge as we call it. My parents are teachers, so this day always had a special festive mood and anticipation. I've always felt nostalgic and emotional on this day. That's why I feel overwhelmed today and choking with emotions. Because children shouldn't experience war, they shouldn't have their classes interrupted to go to their bomb shelter because of the air-raid. They shouldn't bring an emergency backpack to school (a recommendation from the police in big cities) and have a three-day stash of supplies in case the school is under rubble, and they must wait for the rescue team. They shouldn't be separated from their friends and teachers seeking refuge abroad. They should be reading adventure stories instead of learning to discern different land mines and acquiring the "life in times of war" skills (new recommended school subjects).

Those are only the obvious "wrongs" of this war, but there are so many more deep emotional wounds that will take a while to heal – the fear, anxiety, sense of loss, identity crises, separation from family and home... Only God can heal those.

Day 190 · September 1

Growing up, I heard many stories from WWII because it had taken place in our territory only 50 years before. What always shocked me the most were the stories of people (usually young boys) finding something that turned out to be a land mine from the war. Unfortunately, often those stories didn't have a happy ending.

This present war is no exception. We'll keep coming across its echo long after it's over. For example, today, during a weapon exhibition in Chernihiv, something detonated, wounding five people (four children), one of which is in critical condition. The war keeps killing even those who are hundreds of kilometers away from the front line.

Last night, Russia fired five high-precision Kalibr missiles at Dnipro. Praise God, all five were shot down by our air-defense forces. There's a possibility of a new wave of people leaving Mariupol. The parents living in Mariupol were informed that their children must attend Russian schools in person. No distance learning (with a Ukrainian school program) is allowed. If they fail to do so, they will receive a notice, be issued a fine, and after the third warning, their children will be taken away. This became the last straw for many families, especially since the local schools are not ready for the school year and the city is heavily mined.

You know, they say that not a tear is wasted by God, so I'm looking forward to the day when all the pieces of the puzzle will fall into place, and we will understand why we had to endure this pain.

Day 192 · September 3

❧ Great is the Lord and greatly to be praised
in the city of our God!
(Psalm 48:1)

Every night, when I write the number of the day, my heart sinks for a moment. How long, o Lord? I remember being afraid of the day when the numbers go into the hundreds. Now, I am mentally preparing myself for the day we enter the second year of this full-scale war...

Day 198 · September 9

Today's news reports are heavy. After a week of uplifting reports from the front lines, we must come to terms with the reality of the de-occupied territories.

According to estimations, over 70% of buildings in Izum (Kharkiv region) are destroyed, and most parts of the city don't have electricity or running water. They also found a mass burial site in Izum with over 440 graves, most without names, just numbers. According to some estimations, the number of civilians killed in Izum is over 1,000.

Ukrainian border guard discovered and set free five teenagers kept by the Russians for over a week for "filtration procedures." This is one more confirmation that the Russian is not fighting with the Ukrainian army. It is fighting with civilians, teenagers, and the elderly.

Day 204 · September 15

These past few days, I've been busy with homeschooling and online teaching, so I only had time to check the news in the evening. I think this business was God's way of protecting my heart from despair.

We hear more horrifying stories from the liberated Izum and Kupiansk. The exhumation of bodies continued at the mass burial site in Izum and most bodies have signs of torture and violent death. Sometimes, the whole family is buried together. However, a Ukrainian translator and literary critic, pointed out a morbid yet deep thought that these victims are "lucky" because they were discovered, so they will get a decent burial, and their loved ones will have a chance of closure. At the same time, there is a great number of the "invisible dead" whose remains are gone forever.

My comfort is that "Nothing is covered up that will not be revealed, or hidden that will not be known" (Luke 12:2).

A confirmation of this is the testimony that one of the paramedics we were praying for gave before the U.S. Helsinki Commission.[xxvii] She was taken captive in Mariupol, and her chances for release were slim, but she was exchanged during a POW swap, and now she testifies for the world to hear about the atrocities of the Russian army. She said that one of her guards asked her why she thought they were torturing her, and she said, "Because you can." Everything that Russia is doing now in Ukraine is because they felt they could do it. They were confident they could get away with everything. Ukraine still stands today because of the bravery of our people and the support of our friends from all over the world. But we must make sure that the evil is punished, and the bully is stopped not to return with even greater aggression in a few years.

Day 205 · September 16

More shelling, more missile strikes today... The city names get mixed and lost in the endless list of targets of the Russian army. Kharkiv, Chuhuiv, Kramatorsk, and many more cities along the front line...

Today, I saw a post by a Ukrainian filmmaker and writer, where she shares quotes from Russian officials and propagandists who openly call for the genocide of Ukrainians. After that, I can only put trust in God and wait for His justice.

Day 206 · September 17

In the past 24 hours, the Russian forces have carried out seven missile strikes, 20 air strikes, and fifteen artillery shellings of the military and civil objects in Ukraine. They keep targeting dams and power stations.

The Russian Parliament passed changes to the Criminal Code of the Russian Federation to establish criminal punishment for the avoidance of mobilization or the refusal to perform military duties. Their soldiers are demoralized and demotivated, so now they switch to good old terror, their favorite technique.

Please, keep praying for our soldiers living in trenches and for the people left without a home – there's been a significant drop in air temperature, and we even got a hailstorm today.

Day 209 · September 20

At the same time, more reports come from the liberated territories, and I hesitate to share them because they repeat the horrifying stories we've heard from Bucha and are too cruel even to fathom. Four hundred and thirty-six bodies have been exhumed in Izium. Most of them suffered violent death, and 30 of them were severely tortured. They find bodies with ropes around their necks and arms, with broken bones, and amputated genitals. Most of them were civilians.

People in the liberated villages tell about the invaders mocking them, looting their homes, and raping their women and children (some younger than ten years old).

Meanwhile, Russians are conducting a "referendum" in the temporarily occupied regions of Ukraine to present "evidence" that the people want to join Russia. The "referendum" takes place in the streets, no passport is required, and even minors can vote. They also come to people's homes with armed "guards" and ask people to vote at gunpoint.

A few kids got hurt at a school in Mariupol because of a detonation of the remains of careless demining. I don't understand how people still live there.

The mobilization announced by Putin a couple of days ago is also meant to be extended to the occupied territories. There are reports from the occupied Crimea about Crimean Tatars being the first to receive mobilization summonses, especially in the villages where they are ethnically settled. They are already grabbing men in the streets (especially those who received Russian passports). I've written before that this mobilization is also meant to wipe out non-Russian ethnical groups, and this is one more proof of that.

As you can see, the prayer requests are numerous. As I was reading these reports one after another, I felt fury burning inside of me.

Day 212 · September 23

I was stalling, feeling like I had no energy to write my daily update. I'm weary from the anxiety over the possible nuclear strike, tired from the senseless cruelty, weary from the complexity of the questions we all need to answer. When I made myself open the Bible to the daily psalm, it felt as if God was speaking to me directly:

> ℟ God shall arise, his enemies shall be scattered;
> and those who hate him shall flee before him!
> As smoke is driven away, so you shall drive them away;
> as wax melts before fire, so the wicked shall perish before God!
>
> ℟ But the righteous shall be glad;
> they shall exult before God;
> they shall be jubilant with joy!
> (Psalm 68:1-3)

I choose to trust this promise and cannot wait for its fulfillment.

Many cities suffered missile strikes in the past few days – a residential district of Mykolaiv, Kramatorsk, towns along the front line. Dozens of killed and wounded. My heart is especially heavy because of the attacks on the city of Dnipro (my husband's hometown where my parents-in-law live). For the second night in a row, missiles land in residential areas.

Last night's story is horrifying and makes me want to howl in pain. The Russian missile hits the house, leaving a huge crater. Everything turns to ashes, and the fragments of remains are scattered in the area, making it even harder to identify the victims. Once the details are pieced together, we learn that the victims are the grandmother, mother, two children (12 and 8 years old), and their puppy. The mom decided to take her children from downtown Dnipro to her mom's place, thinking a private house should be safer. When the rescue team came, they found a blinded, shell-shocked dog sitting on the rubble, crying and howling. The dog's name is Krym (Crimea) because that's where he came from as a puppy. The most heart-wrenching part of the story is that the father of the family, who now serves in the Ukrainian Army, came to see it.

Will we ever be able to forgive and heal?

Putin is going to announce "independence" and possible annexation of the temporarily occupied Kherson, Zaporizhzhia, Donetsk, and Luhansk regions. The fake "referendum" will be presented as the "legitimate proof." He plans to intensify attacks on civil infrastructure and continue with the nuclear threats under the pretense that Ukraine is attacking "Russian" (annexed) territories. Does it change anything for Ukraine? Not really, they are already doing it and don't feel any restraints. Will it justify their actions? Only in the eyes of the fools that still believe the Russian government.

Please, pray for God's intervention and vindication.

Pray for the countries that welcomed the Russian men trying to escape mobilization – for these countries to be protected from provocations and any other negative long-term consequences of their act of good will. There are reports of a big pro-Russian rally being planned to be held in Tbilisi (Georgia) with the participation of thousands of "newcomers." Remember, Georgia went through the same aggression and occupation in 1993 and 2008. How would the people who lost their homes and loved ones to Russian aggression react to the display of Russian flags and pro-Russian slogans?

Day 218 · September 29

Another brutal attack this morning. People were standing in line at the checkpoint near Zaporizhzhia going to the temporarily occupied territories – some were going to evacuate their relatives; others were returning home (to the temporarily occupied Melitopol) after picking up supplies in the Zaporizhzhia. Russian rockets landed right there. As of now, 25 killed (including two children), and almost 100 wounded.

Day 219 · September 30

Defiance in the Face of Aggression

A season to grow: *In spite of the sometimes-returning onslaughts of fading winter, tulips start growing below the surface. This is a time of defiance and hope.*

I don't write about it every time, but daily, Kharkiv, Mykolaiv, and dozens of other cities close to the front lines are heavily shelled, especially the residential areas. The Ministry of Foreign Affairs stated that the Russians attack civilian targets 73 times more often than military ones – 22,000 civil compared to 300 military objects. Yet many people refuse to leave their homes, and they even volunteer and serve others in need!

Day 173 · August 15

Today, there were three large explosion sites in the occupied Crimea – a railroad hub, military airfield, and ammunition depot. Some say it was the job of the secret service of Ukraine. Others say kamikaze drones were involved. In any case, this caused panic in Crimea and a massive line of cars (over 38 thousand) trying to leave Crimea and go to Russia across the Kerch Bridge. The first ones to leave were the Russians who came there after the occupation. They flee in fear of justice, but we know they won't be able to run away from God's justice unless they repent.

Day 174 · August 16

Also, the following week or two may be very intense. In a week, on August 24, Ukraine will celebrate its 31st Independence Day. That day will also mark six months since the start of the full-scale war. We know Russia's love for symbolism and know we should be ready for anything. There are reports of large amounts of missiles being accumulated in Belarus, and that's the direction used for attacks on Kyiv. Please, pray for God's deliverance. Pray for the military orders of Russian commanders to be sabotaged on all levels (due to negligence or willful opposition). Pray for their repentance and for Russia to stop being a threat to others once and for all.

Day 175 · August 17

In the past couple of hours, there were a few powerful explosions in the temporarily occupied Crimea – close to Sevastopol (Belbek airfield) and Kerch. These reports come from the locals; no official information yet. There are reports of explosions in the temporarily occupied Kherson region and a fire at an ammunition depot in Belgorod (Russia). However, now the air-raid warning has been issued for most of the territory of Ukraine, which could mean retaliation. Please, pray for God's protection.

Day 176 · August 18

Throughout the day today, there were reports of sounds of explosions in various parts of Crimea (Yevpatoria, Bakhchysarai, Sevastopol). No clear information on details. These reports bring a whole emotional roller-coaster. I feel joy knowing it signals Ukraine's intentions to de-occupy Crimea, which would mean returning home to many Ukrainians, including my close friends. I rejoice in reading about the Russians leaving in panic while they can. At the same time, my heart tightens up for Ukrainian families living in Crimea. Even though the Ukrainian army uses high-precision weapons to attack only military objects, people would still have air-raid warnings and sounds of explosions. It means that the war is spreading over the territory of Ukraine, even if into the temporarily occupied territories.

At the same time, it was reported that the strike on the Saky airbase in occupied Crimea on August 9 "knocked out" more than half of Russia's naval aircraft.[xxviii]

Day 178 · August 20

Today is Ukrainian Flag Day. One could regard it as yet another government holiday or a patriotism feat. However, this day is filled with deep meaning, especially in our war-torn country. Today, my Facebook feed is filled with so many personal stories.

People evacuating from the occupied territories, going through one enemy checkpoint to another, finally can breathe a sigh of relief when they approach a checkpoint with Ukrainian flags. Prisoners of war swapped during the

POW exchange feeling cautious, expecting any insidious set-up, finally put their guard down when they see badges with a Ukrainian flag and hear the greeting, "Slava Ukraini!" ("Glory to Ukraine!")

People returning to their homes and starting life anew in the midst of rubble put up a Ukrainian flag to reaffirm liberation from occupation. People fearlessly putting up Ukrainian flags in their yards and downtown flagpoles as the enemy army surrounds their city as a symbol of resistance.

Our soldiers guarding their flag and keeping it from the enemies. It can be torn, dirty, worn out, and covered in blood but never carelessly left behind. Over the past six months, Ukrainian flags have appeared all over the world as a sign of solidarity and support, and it's a precious encouragement to the millions of Ukrainians who are far away from home yet can see something that represents "home".

I think it's especially beautiful that Ukrainians can see their flag in the beauty of God's creation – the blue sky and yellow fields of wheat or autumn foliage are a gentle reminder of home anywhere you go.

Day 181 · August 23

Also, there were reports that Russia plans to hold a referendum in the occupied territories to "legalize" the occupation (following their Crimea scenario). However, according to the reports of the Institute for the Study of War, it is not likely to happen in September (the initial deadline) because of the active resistance movement, low number of collaborators, and lack of support among the grassroots.

Day 185 · August 27

Today, Ukraine intensified its offense (counter offense) in the Kherson region. This report makes everyone's heart skip a beat as it's something we've been waiting for so long. However, it's important to remember that offensive operations usually bring more casualties than defensive ones, so please, double your prayers for our defenders and the people in the temporarily occupied territories.

One of the reports said that the enemy army fled from the first line positions in the Kherson region. The interesting element is that the infantry consisted of the people drafted in the occupied part of the Donetsk region

Graffiti evidence of the resistance movement - Day 196, September 7, 2022

(Russia's cannon fodder), but it was supposed to have the support of the Russian regular paratroopers brigade. However, the latter fled for safety.

It's been our prayers for months for God to make the enemies flee in terror. Of course, we took encouragement from the numerous Old Testament stories where God put Israel's much stronger opponents to shame with His power, but it's so powerful to see God do the same in our days in response to our prayers.

"Daddy, what does it mean to give up? – I don't know, son. We're Ukrainians." I saw this phrase online today, and while I could have dismissed it as overly dramatic, I'd say it's very fitting to the situation in the temporarily occupied territories. The resistance movement keeps the enemies on their toes. Ukrainian partisans in Mariupol tricked a military patrol in the city, so they hit their own mine – the town is still heavily mined (which is a

constant threat to the civilians), but the occupational forces keep ignoring this problem just as any other problem in the "liberated" territories.

Please, pray for the enemy army to experience despair and confusion, for them to run in terror or surrender, and for the complete liberation and restoration of Ukraine (even though we're fully aware it's going to be a very long process).

Day 187 · August 29

Today soldiers put a Ukrainian flag in the newly liberated Vysokopillia in the Kherson region, and it moved me to tears. There's great power in this significant act – the message to the people who have lived under Russian occupation for the past six months that they are (relatively) safe now. They are home in Ukraine.

Day 193 · September 4

As of September 5, Russians have lost 49,800 soldiers (over 80,000, according to the UK Minister of Defense, if you count the wounded and taken captive). Initially, Russia brought 140,000 soldiers intended for the invasion. The VoxCheck initiative calculated that Russia has lost 154% of the armored vehicles, 172% of the tanks, 86% of helicopters, 72% of airplanes, 72% of artillery systems intended for the invasion, and 20% of the fleet in the Black Sea. These numbers are stunning and serve as undeniable evidence of God's mercy.

Today, Ukrainian artillery forces destroyed a Russian ammunition depot that stored C-300 rockets for strikes on Kharkiv. The city is heavily attacked daily, but we thank God for this relief.

Ukrainian partisans, the resistance movement in the occupied territories is gaining strength and courage, while the occupational authorities are filled with fear. It looks like they have postponed the referendum in the occupied territories "for security reasons," but we pray they never feel safe here and are driven to repentance by the fear of God.

Day 194 · September 5

Today's pictures come from Mariupol. The resistance movement of Mariupol encouraged people to write letters "ï" around the city as a symbol of resistance. There's also a moving poem calling on the people to guard the tiny candle flame of the letter "ï," the unique letter of the Ukrainian alphabet and one of the letters in the Ukrainian spelling of our country's name – Україна.

Day 196 · September 7

The Russian occupational authorities are trying to escape to Russia or at least bring their families out to Crimea. We ask God to send more fear and panic into their hearts to make them repent, surrender, and restore what they had done.

Day 202 · September 13

This morning, Putin announced "partial mobilization" (however, his order has no specifics regarding the region or time it will be limited to). It made Ukrainians smile and ask, "Oh, is he going to invade us now? Hm... What were the previous seven months about?" Ukraine will resist no matter what they decide in the Kremlin. However, this announcement caused panic in Russia – lines at the border crossings, sold-out tickets to the countries that still allow Russians in and don't require a visa, and spiked internet search requests "how to break an arm and escape mobilization." Once again, Putin's decision is meant to bring death and suffering to his compatriots, and now those who were cheering this wickedness while sitting at home will have to follow through with their actions. Our soldiers know what they are fighting for and whom they are defending, but what will the Russians be dying for?

Day 210 · September 21

Tonight, my heart has a whole mixture of bitterness, weariness, anger, despair, and hope. Pictures were released of one of Azovstal's defenders. One with him in the army, one from his time at a makeshift hospital in the Azovstal bunker (that's the picture we all know him from), and of him after he was released from the Russian captivity.

He spent four months in prison. He was beaten and tortured. He received no medical care – as a result, his wounded arm is disfigured. It is missing 4 cm of bone because the external fixation apparatus was removed with rusty pliers in the Russian prison. You can easily find the picture of his arm now, but I didn't want to post it here because this man doesn't need to be pitied. What impressed me the most in this last picture are his eyes. He is full of dignity and some sort of inner peace. I don't know how he managed to do that, but to me, these eyes speak volumes, they show the unbroken spirit, and it's the answer to our daily prayers.

The mobilization in Russia is causing civil unrest. Men ages 18-50 try to leave the country not to be drafted, which causes long lines at the borders and skyrocketing plane ticket prices. Some regional authorities have already announced that only men with special permits will be allowed to leave the country (which may mean martial law being proclaimed in Russia). Anti-mobilization protests are rising (please, note, they are anti-mobilization, not anti-war, because these people were okay with Ukrainians being killed as long as they didn't have to be the ones on the battlefield), especially in the ethnic republics, which may cause further destabilization in Russia. Our Army Head of Staff reported today that Russia sends these recruits straight to the front line without any training.

Please, pray for God's intervention and His timing.

The merciless mobilization in Russia continues. Our Intelligence Services report numerous phone calls from Russia with questions regarding surrender. Protests are raging in the Republic of Dagestan (Russia), blocking roads with lots of people in the streets. According to some sources, the local officials were taken aback by this resistance and ruled to cancel mobilization in that region (but this information still needs to be verified).

Today, I read an article about a teacher from Volnovakha (Donetsk region) who evacuated in spring but who keeps offering online lessons to the children in the occupied territories so that they would be able to receive a Ukrainian school diploma. These online schools work undercover with students connecting through secret links, using code names, and hiding their private information. The occupational authorities have removed any Ukrainian books, and the school books on the history and geography of Ukraine and Ukrainian literature were burned down. However, the children keep joining this online school even at the risk of persecution.

Celebration, While Aware of the Costs

A season to bloom: *The crowning season for the tulips arrives as their flowers reach to the sky. But celebration is vulnerable – the tulip has used huge amounts of the bulb's resources in the hope of future goodness.*

🙵 I will give thanks to the Lord with my whole heart;
I will recount all of your wonderful deeds.
I will be glad and exult in you;
I will sing praise to your name, O Most High.
(Psalm 9:1-2)

Once again, my psalm of the day seems to (accidentally?) reflect what had been on my mind even before I read it!

Today, I was amazed when I reflected on the inspiring responses of our people to this war. Those are stories of resilience and hope. We read about them in the news or hear them from friends.

One of my friends organized an art therapy support group for people dealing with trauma and stress. Another friend had to move to a European country because of the war, but she actively joins public rallies in support of Ukraine because she feels that it's something that she not only can but also should do. A catering company my cousin works for switched to cooking hot meals for the people in need. Quite a few of my friends run fundraisers or hunt down protective gear for our defenders. Most businesses send a share of their profit to the army's needs. It feels like everyone is doing what they can, no matter how big or small it may look.

Day 159 · August 1

One of the sources of encouragement for me these days is the intercepted conversations of the Russian soldiers. They openly talk to their families and friends and convince them not to join the Russian army, tell them that the Ukrainian army seems to be the strongest in the world, tell them about large

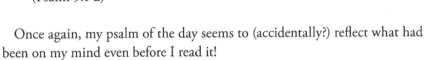

groups of soldiers deserting their positions and running away in fear for their lives. To me, that's an answer to our prayers because we pray for the fear of the Lord to set in the hearts of our enemies and to make them run in fear or surrender.

Our intelligence also reports quite frequent cases of friendly fire or even intentional armed conflicts between the different groups within the Russian army. After each such report, I praise God because this whole time, we have been praying for the enemy army to be confused and disunified, for them to bring evil upon themselves.

Day 160 · August 2

It is in these sad circumstances that we have the chance to experience God's omnipresence. We see Him in good weather for the harvest, we see Him in shot down missiles, we see Him in successful evacuations, we see Him in mercy ministries – He is everywhere as long as you look for Him.

Day 171 · August 13

Today, Ivan and I celebrated our thirteenth wedding anniversary. Usually, on anniversaries we are reminded about what really matters. We had a good time as a family, sharing memories of our married life. Knowing how fleeting it can be, we really cherish the blessing of being together through this storm.

Day 173 · August 15

The Russians keep shelling Ukrainian cities. Tonight, they hit and completely destroyed an apartment building in Kharkiv, leaving seven people dead and seventeen people wounded (as of now). According to some reports, there were deaf and mute people living there, which made rescue operations harder.

The panic in Crimea continues. Ukrainian officials have asked people to stay away from Russian military objects in Crimea for safety reasons. Meanwhile, there were reports of the Kerch Bridge (leading to Russia from Crimea) being closed for traffic because the occupational authorities were evacuating their families and didn't want to be stuck in traffic. Also, every car leaving the peninsula is thoroughly searched. They are looking for Ukraine's special services officers, which may lead to a "witch hunt" in Crimea. Please, pray for special protection for people who openly support Ukraine and for the Crimean Tatars – they have endured lots of persecutions since Crimea's occupation in 2014 and are likely to be presented as the prime suspects.

Day 175 · August 17

On an optimistic note, there is a follow-up to the "People's Bayraktar" story. A couple of months ago (as you may remember), Ukrainians fundraised UAH 600 million (over $16 million) for the purchase of four Bayraktars TB2 (unmanned aerial vehicles) for the needs of the Armed Forces of Ukraine. However, the manufacturing company decided to grant three items for free and free up the funds for other army needs. Today the Prytula Foundation announced that they bought a satellite! To be precise, they signed the deal which gives the Ministry of Defence of Ukraine full access to all the systems and capabilities for one of ICEYE's satellites in orbit over the region. This would provide invaluable information to our army and may be a precious asset.

Day 176 · August 18

Praise God, there were no provocations at the nuclear power plant today. Please, keep praying for protection from any nuclear or chemical threats.

Day 177 · August 19

There are reasons to weep and to rejoice, and as we try to keep our sanity, we cry out to the Lord, "Hear the voice of my pleas for mercy, when I cry to you for help, when I lift up my hands toward your most holy sanctuary" (Psalm 28:2).

Day 178 · August 20

A few thoughts caught my eye today. A Ukrainian writer, wrote today that she learned from the families of our warriors that we need tears to keep our humanity, but we need the joy to win. I think it's a beautiful thought.

Day 179 · August 21

It is through tears and weeping that we celebrate today and praise God. We weep over 22 people killed in a missile strike on the Dnipropetrovsk region, but we praise God for His protection from massive airstrikes. We weep over thousands of POWs in Russian captivity, but we praise God there were no public executions in Mariupol today (even though preparations continue). We weep for the occupied territories but hold steadfast hope for their liberation.

Day 182 · August 24

However, we see more answers to our prayers. We keep praying for the confusion upon the enemy and wisdom upon our defenders. According to the report by the *Washington Post*, Russia has wasted at least ten expensive high-precision Kalibr missiles to hit wooden mockup models of HIMARS MLRS created by the Ukrainian military. The Russians don't have the equipment that would allow them to discern the real ones from the fake. I praise God!

Day 188 · August 30

"Beloved, never avenge yourselves, but leave it to the wrath of God, for it is written, 'Vengeance is mine, I will repay, says the Lord.'" – Romans 12:19. We keep praying for the Russian weapons to malfunction and turn against our enemy. Tonight, during the launch of missiles at Kharkiv from the Russian territory (Belgorod), one rocket flew very low and exploded in the vicinity of the city.

Day 189 · August 31

We keep getting hopeful reports from the front lines. Today, the Russian media was filled with controversial reports – their troops were speedily retreating from Balaklia (the Kharkiv region), leaving behind their ammunition and personnel (who were eager to surrender). Yet, the propagandists kept repeating that everything was going according to plan, and there was no reason to panic. There haven't been any official reports from the Ukrainian authorities, yet we praise God for His faithfulness and pray for the complete liberation of Ukraine.

These days, when we get such exciting reports, it is hard. We want to rejoice, we want things to speed up, but we are painfully aware of the price we are paying for this success. Today, my friend wrote that her father was wounded in combat, and his detachment suffered significant losses. Please, keep covering our defenders with your prayers.

Day 196 · September 7

According to the evening address of the President of Ukraine, since the beginning of September, the Armed Forces of Ukraine have liberated over 1,000 square kilometers (almost 250,000 acres) of the territory of Ukraine.

In the counteroffensive in the Kharkiv region, the Ukrainian army has pushed the front line about 50 km and liberated 20 towns.

I watched a video from the liberated Balaklia – the women coming into the streets, greeting our soldiers, weeping with joy, repeating, "We've been praying for the past six months for you to come and liberate us!" They keep offering, "We made pancakes. Would you like some pancakes. We have pancakes, please, have some," and you realize that those pancakes are meant to communicate the gratitude and love the words can't convey.

At the same time, there are reports about the increased oppression of the people in the temporarily occupied Kherson region. The towns along the front line are almost completely destroyed.

Day 197 · September 8

The recent reports remind me of the news coming at the end of March when our army liberated the north of Ukraine. Now, our military is liberating town after town in the Kharkiv region, and the enemies flee in fear leaving everything behind. However, we shouldn't underestimate the danger of an enraged and desperate enemy. Today, Kharkiv was attacked with heavy artillery. They hit a kindergarten, school, residential building, and other buildings in the area – fourteen people (including three children) were wounded.

Day 198 · September 9

Today, it felt like I was glued to my phone, constantly checking the news and praying. Two days ago, the President of Ukraine said the Ukrainian army had liberated 1,000 square kilometers of our land. In tonight's report, that number doubled.

Over the past two days, our army liberated several towns in the Kharkiv region and successfully conducted offensives in the Donetsk, Luhansk, and Kherson regions. The enemy army is running away in fear, leaving behind their weapons, so our soldiers joke that despite the lend-lease with the US, it looks like Russia is our leading ammunition supplier. The occupational authorities are panicking and trying to escape to Russia.

I can't tell you how many videos from the newly liberated territories I watched today. I was watching and crying. I think everyone has seen pictures of the soldiers being greeted after WWII, with people coming into the streets, throwing flowers, and waving at the soldiers. I remember those scenes from Soviet post-war movies, and I always thought those were staged and scripted. However, when I look at the people greeting our soldiers, I think the emotions were downplayed in the movies.

In one video, the people in the Kherson region stand along the road of a newly liberated town and bring watermelons and fruit to the soldiers passing by.

In the pictures from the newly liberated Shevchenkove (Kharkiv region), people are painting a bus stop in the colors of a Ukrainian flag. I can't help but wonder if they were stocking up on paint in hopes for this day or if it was the urge of the moment.

Kupiansk, one of the larger (and strategically important cities) in the Kharkiv region, is liberated now. The Russians left it in a hurry, but during the raid, our soldiers found Russian teachers who came there to teach the Russian curriculum to our children. They were left behind by the occupational authorities and will have to face charges for the illegal crossing of the border and assistance of the occupational forces.

Encouraging reports also came from the international arena. The Russian propagandists claim that Europe is tired of Ukraine, but recent sociology polls say the opposite: 70% of Germans said they would keep supporting Ukraine despite the increasing fuel prices, and only 21% said the support for Ukraine should be decreased, especially if it meant lower fuel prices.

In this whirlwind of emotions, reports, and pictures, one video stood out. It gave me goosebumps because it's something that could have only been orchestrated by God. Our soldiers pull down a Russian propagandist poster from a billboard in Kupiansk, and underneath it, they find a poster with the portrait of Taras Shevchenko and an excerpt from his poem.[xxix] It felt like a tremendous encouragement and prophetic message:

> And glory, mountains blue, to you,
> In ageless ice encased!
> And glory, freedom's knights, to you,
> Whom God will not forsake.
> Keep fighting – you are sure to win!

God helps you in your fight!
For fame and freedom, march with you,
And right is on your side!

Day 199 · September 10

We rejoice over every liberated village, yet I am also wondering if we are ready to learn what was taking place there during the occupation. I remember how we were numb with pain and disbelief after the Bucha massacre, thinking that humans couldn't have done it. I'm afraid that was only the tip of the iceberg.

Day 201 · September 12

I saw a picture today that is an immense encouragement and reassures me of our victory, for we have already won because we managed to keep our hearts from hardening up. Ukrainian soldiers received this note along with 3 kg of dried fruits from an older man. The note reads, "Dear sons! I bow down to our holy ground for your hard work! I proclaim blessings for your life and our victory." The man is 84 years old.[xxx]

Day 201- September 12

This verse is so fitting today when we learn from the UK Ministry of Defence that elements of the Russian forces that withdrew from the Kharkiv region over the last week were from the 1st Guards Tank Army (1 GTA), one of the most prestigious of Russia's armies, allocated for the defense of Moscow, and intended to lead counter-attacks in the case of a war with NATO. Ukraine's counter-offensive has severely weakened it, and it will likely take years for Russia to rebuild this capability. We praise God and pray for more reports like this.

Day 202 · September 13

Since September 6, our troops have liberated 388 towns and villages in the Kharkiv region. That's about 150,000 people.

Day 203 · September 14

I was going to prepare for my online lessons and finish a written translation before going to bed. Instead, I spent over an hour checking the news, weeping, and having difficulty breathing. And all of that for a good reason.

Tonight, 215 POWs were released from Russian captivity! That's wonderful news! The names of these people make it even more incredible. Among the released, there are people you most likely have heard of, whose faces you've seen, for whom you have been praying: five leaders of Mariupol Azovstal defenders were released, and will be in Turkey under its protection until the end of the war; ten foreigners who were taken captive and even "sentenced to the death penalty" by the self-proclaimed court in Donetsk were also released and are in Saudi Arabia (it was the mediating country); the girl who cheered up Azovstal soldiers with her songs; the photographer whose pictures of Azovstal went viral; the wounded man of Azovstal with external metal fixtures on his arm; Azov soldiers sentenced to the death penalty in captivity; one of the Azov leaders who led a press conference from the bunker in perfect English; three heavily pregnant paramedics (one of them is in her last weeks of pregnancy, and she spent four months in prison): our heroes.

What's even more shocking is that 200 Ukrainians were released in exchange for a citizen of Ukraine and traitor who was arrested a few months ago. Putin happens to be the godfather of his daughter. We see the priorities of Russia. Five Azovstal commanders were exchanged for 55 Russian officers. The irony is that the Russian parliament has just passed a law introducing criminal punishment for "willful surrender" (and how will they prove if someone surrendered willingly?). Stalin had a similar law back during WWII, which is why many Soviet soldiers taken captive by the Nazis were later on trial as "enemies of the people" back home.

I couldn't believe the news. I was weeping with joy and praising God. I wonder how much greater we will rejoice when the war is over and justice is restored!

Day 210 · September 21

Today, we keep rejoicing over the deliverance of our POWs from Russian captivity, but we keep thinking and praying about the thousands that remain in captivity. We also keep praying for the healing and recovery (both physical and emotional) of the prisoners who returned home.

Day 211 · September 22

Loss and Lament

A season to regenerate: *Far too quickly are the days of the beautiful flowers gone. The tulip begins to replenish its stores under the ground. This stage is not lovely to look at, but if the stage is cut short, tulips are at risk of dying.*

I know that this war reveals the true nature of one's heart. When you are stripped of your comfort zone and predictable future, the masks are dropped. But the opposite is also true – living a peaceful life filled with day-to-day activities, it takes a conscious choice to notice the hurting and to love the heartbroken. Having such people in my life is a blessing that keeps me going.

When I read the news, I often feel desperate. Yes, our armed forces do the impossible (and there's no doubt it's God's doing), but the enemy army keeps destroying one town after another. Now, it looks like they plan an attack on Mykolaiv to use it as a base for the attack on Odesa because they draw up troops in the south. They plan to stage a "referendum" in the presently occupied territories to "legalize" the occupation. They keep putting Zaporizhzhia NPP in danger and may disconnect it to leave the south of Ukraine without electricity. These are just a few big items, and I have no energy even to think about what is going on at a personal level for people living there. For example, a recent report said that the teachers in the occupied territories were refusing to cooperate and switch to the Russian curriculum, so there were talks about setting up "correction camps" for them.

Day 164 · August 6

Every night, I put off writing my daily update until late at night because I often don't know what to say. It feels like everything important has already been said dozens of times. Should I highlight the important news? Well, most news is available online anyway (just make sure you are using reliable sources, not the ones feeding off Russian money and propaganda). Should I share personal stories of people? But how do you share over 35 million stories, and how do you hold up when so many of them break your heart? Should I just share my personal reflections? But who am I to do it?

However, I will keep writing these daily updates as long as I can, trusting God to provide the words, for I know it is the burden He has put on my heart. I also hope that this sort of online diary would be something to go to after the war is over to make sure our priorities don't shift.

In today's news, I saw three reports that are good examples of responses to the war on Ukraine.

First, a low-cost airline company from Abu Dhabi is restarting flights to Russia. For almost six months, we've kept trying to communicate to the world about the need to stop sponsoring Russian terrorism. Many companies close their businesses in Russia, understanding their reputation losses, yet this airline chooses money over values. I hope the parent company takes some action or faces reputation losses and is boycotted in Europe. I believe it's essential to take a stand with each company and brand and make them choose their values.

The second report came from Latvia – The Seimas of Latvia recognized Russia as a state sponsor of terrorism. This adds to the decision of Estonia to stop allowing citizens of the Russian federation with Schengen visas to enter its territory (with minor exceptions). Once again, I admire the Baltic states for their boldness and willingness to stand up for what they believe in even though they keep being threatened by Russia all the time. Please, pray for these countries – for the Lord's protection over them and for their zeal for justice to spread.

The third type of response usually comes from international organizations. These institutions are usually "deeply concerned" and usually believe that everyone shares the blame, so everyone should make concessions. It could have worked in a perfect world, but such statements are a joke and a slap in the face of the victim. If you witness a rape, would you ask the victim to be quiet to allow the rapist to finish what has been started and ask the rapist to be gentle to the victim this time and try to refrain from this activity in the future? I'm sorry if this comparison is too brutal, but that's the reality.

I'm writing about this once again because today, the UN Secretary-General issued a statement on the Zaporizhzhia Nuclear Power Plant in which he called on both Russia and Ukraine to stop military activity near the plant and to pull back military personnel and equipment.[xxxi]

It may sound reasonable to an uninformed reader, but it looks like a disgraceful avoidance of responsibility to those who know what's happening. Zaporizhzhia NPP has been under Russian occupation since early March. There have been numerous reports of Russian troops using its facilities as ammunition depots even though it goes against all safety regulations. In the past few days, Russia has been heavily shelling the territory around the NPP, and in our age of technology, everything is easily traced, so there's no doubt on whose doing it is. Yet, the UN still is too shy (even though a stronger word would be more appropriate here) to call it what it is and calls on "both parties" to withdraw forces and equipment even after they know that Russia is the only one doing it.

This third example of "moral supremacy," which in fact is indifference mixed with avoidance of responsibility, reminded me of the words to the church in Laodicea from Revelation 3:15-16, "I know your works: you are neither cold nor hot. Would that you were either cold or hot! So, because you are lukewarm, and neither hot nor cold, I will spit you out of my mouth."

They say that war usually makes you see the world in black and white. And it's true in a way that you would rather have people be honest and openly choose a side rather than look for subtones and hide behind excuses. I am not a fan of absolute statements because I know that life is a lot more complex than we wish to think, but I believe that we must make sure that our actions and words align with the values we profess.

Day 169 · August 11

℣ Some trust in chariots and some in horses,
but we trust in the name of the Lord our God.
They collapse and fall, but we rise and stand upright.
(Psalm 20:7-8)

I often think about these verses from Psalm 20 and trust in their fulfillment in Ukraine.

There isn't a day when our cities are not shelled or attacked with missiles. Sometimes at the end of the day, I don't remember all the names or don't remember if a specific city was attacked on that day. Perhaps it's another sign that the war is no longer something shocking.

The occupational forces in the Donetsk region announced a public trial (and possible execution) of Ukrainian POWs and foreign citizens fighting for Ukraine. It is part of their terrorist agenda. It looks like they would never miss an opportunity to threaten us with mass murder, knowing that human lives are of priority to us. Please, pray for God's intervention.

Today, we went to a local library which organized an activity for the kids. About half of the kids were from families that moved here temporarily in flight from the war. What struck me to the core was the conversation between two girls, about 4 or 5 years old. They were coloring something on paper, and one said completely matter-of-factly,

"When the war ends, I will be starting school. It's sad I won't get to see my friends from kindergarten."

I just froze as if struck by lightning because a million questions ran through my mind,

"Will the war be over by the time she starts school? Are all of her friends safe? Will she remember this part of her childhood when she grows up? How many other children say, 'when the war ends' when making plans?"

These innocent children are the best motivation to persevere and do everything in our power to win this war.

Day 170 · August 12

There is a new art installation in Lviv downtown, "Diplomas that will never be handed over," in memory of students who died defending the country since the beginning of the full-scale invasion.

Day 171 · August 13

I guess one of the hardest things for me has always been saying goodbye to people, even if just for a short time. Because saying goodbye acknowledges that a certain life period is over and you are starting a new page, only God knows where this new page will take you.

On Friday morning, we had an online prayer meeting for the moms of my son's school. As we were catching up on each other's lives, we had to recognize that all of us were in different countries for an uncertain period of time. We had to acknowledge that some of our friends will probably stay in their current country and won't return to Ukraine. We were sending each other virtual hugs knowing that we may not see each other in person to give a hug again for a long time. And it's a painful realization.

It's painful to realize that time does not stand still, and we don't know when we will be able to return to our "ordinary" lives. I dearly miss my "home away from home," the School of Biblical Studies I spent my past five years with, and I keep looking forward to the day when we all return to its classroom.

This "missing out" also has another dimension.

We have friends whose relatives are in the temporarily occupied territories, so they have no way to see them, and even internet or cell phone connections don't work there.

A few months ago, a dear friend from our church passed away, and we couldn't come for the final goodbye because of the fuel shortage and safety reasons.

Thousands of families have been separated as the women and children travel to other countries in pursuit of safety while their husbands or older sons stay in Ukraine.

This war tears us apart, tears apart our hearts and lives, so all I can do is pray for God's restoration and healing. May His will be done in Ukraine and this world.

Day 162 · August 14

Today, there were missile attacks on Kharkiv, Mykolaiv, and Zaporizhzhia, combined with artillery attacks on towns along the front lines and on the border with Russia.

The Russian army seems to be targeting educational institutions on purpose – 216 destroyed and over 2,000 seriously damaged. Of course, an educated new generation of Ukrainians is a serious threat to the evil empire, so their attacks are very logical. Even today, they hit Petro Mohyla Black Sea National University in Mykolaiv and two educational institutions in Kramatorsk (Donetsk region) – Kramatorsk Vocational Design and Technology School and the Donbas State Machine Engineering Academy. Please, pray for the protection of students and staff of all educational institutions in Ukraine, from preschools to universities. The school year in Ukraine traditionally starts on September 1, so the threat may increase in the next couple of weeks.

Day 177 · August 19

Today the Commander-in-Chief of the Armed Forces of Ukraine, shared that 9,000 Ukrainian soldiers have been killed in combat since February 24. We weep and mourn for every person whose life was lost in fighting for our freedom. We need to do our best to make sure their sacrifice was not in vain.

Day 180 · August 22

A couple of days ago, I read that Russia has illegally deported over 5,600 children from the occupied territories. Over 1,000 children from Mariupol have been given up for adoption in Russia. My heart sank as I read it, and I simply couldn't bring myself to think about what these kids had to go through or what their relatives must be feeling now.

Today, I read that Ukraine has tracked down and recovered 53 children who were set up for adoption in Russia. They are safely back home in Ukraine. Yes, it's less than 1% of all abducted children, but it's 53 lives saved and hope for hundreds.

Day 183 · August 25

"I will bless the Lord at all times; his praise shall continually be in my mouth" (Psalm 34:1).

Over the past couple of days, I had a few conversations that left me with mixed feelings. I got a chance to catch up with some friends who are all over the world now. But I realized that all of us, even those who stayed home, must start our lives anew. We are still learning to live in this reality we were thrown into on February 24. Six months have passed, and only God knows how long the war will last, but we are done with the initial shock and must start adjusting our long-term plans. And with this comes a new wave of mourning for what we've lost, the grief for the future we could have had.

Imagine spending time building up your team, dreaming together, sharing a vision for a project, finally seeing this project come to life... But then the war breaks out, leaving your team scattered across the globe.

Imagine finding a perfect school or preschool for your children, getting them adjusted, seeing them make friends... But then the war breaks out, your children are pulled out of their comfort zone, and you start the process from step one.

Imagine living a settled life before February 24, having to move from one place to another because of war, sharing apartments with strangers, and longing for the tiles in your kitchen back home, the home that's under occupation now. So, you are left wondering if you should make a new home with new kitchen tiles or keep hoping. These are just bits of the conversations I had. And my own thoughts are as scattered.

We've decided not to return to Kyiv for now, so we'll have to homeschool our son (thankfully, with the support and guidance of our amazing teachers). If you have kids, you may imagine the questions running through my brain – is this the right decision, will he miss out, will he have enough socialization, will we (Ivan and I) be good enough, and thousands more....

Day 184 · August 26

Today, I am especially praying for the families in the occupied and liberated villages, for those who lost everything because of the invasion, who are facing the uncertainty of the upcoming winter season, and who are struggling to make ends meet.

Day 186 · August 28

I came across a report that reminded me of a scene from a horror movie, not a news report in a civilized world. Remember the Drama Theater in Mariupol? The one that was used as a shelter by hundreds of civilians and was bombed with heavy bombs on March 16. According to the investigation of the Associated Press, over 600 people were killed there. Now, this drama theater is being urgently repaired by the occupational forces. The place is being drenched with chlorine to eliminate the smell of decaying bodies remaining under the rubble and then filled with cement to bury the bodies forever.

It's not the first time that Russia has demonstrated unspeakable disrespect for the dead.

Day 189 · August 31

For some reason, just like it was in the Kyiv region, Russian soldiers left mounds of feces behind – they turned an altar room of the local monastery into a toilet. Who does that? Our troops found beheaded bodies of Ukrainian soldiers and the bodies of the village residents who were killed during the occupation. A 60-year-old and his 93-year-old mother are the only surviving residents. His brother and sister-in-law were killed by the Russians, so he had to bury them in their yard. He and his mother try to treat our soldiers with whatever little food they have and beg them to take a large jar of honey.

When the Russians were escaping, they set the church on fire as it was their ammunition depot. However, for some reason, the fire didn't spread, so our soldiers acquired a large arsenal. Such accounts make me freeze and try to sort through the billions of thoughts rushing through my brain. I feel like rejoicing and crying, praising God and praying imprecatory psalms, worshiping Him and begging Him for answers all at the same time. Would you heal our land and our hearts, Lord?

Day 201 · September 12

The reports from the liberated territories (over 300 towns in the Kharkiv region alone) are horrifying. I will share more in tomorrow's post. Please, pray for the healing and restoration and the protection of all people still living under occupation. It was reported that Russia increased filtration procedures in the Kherson region, and they are terrorizing the locals looking for Ukrainian partisans. God, have mercy!

Day 202 · September 13

I weep and am shaken after reading such reports, but I praise God that these people have been delivered. The pensioners from the occupied territories have already received their pensions for the past four months (they could not get the money because of the occupation), and postal services have already renewed their operations there. Life will return to the Kharkiv region and the rest of the temporarily occupied territories.

Day 203 · September 14

After the liberation of Kupiansk, we learned about seven citizens of Sri Lanka (six men and one woman) who came to the city just weeks before the invasion and were taken captive by the Russians.[xxxii] They were beaten, tortured, and mistreated. Two of them were denailed. They were given small portions of food twice a week and received no medical care. Why? Of course, such treatment is completely inhumane, but if the Russians came to fight the Ukrainians, why take it out on these people? Were they mistaken for Ukrainians? Did they look like dangerous Ukrainian military men? It's yet another proof of the dangers of Russian prejudice.

Day 207 · September 18

There are plenty of videos of the bizarre Russian "mobilization" ("burialization" as many Ukrainians call it, for Putin sends his fellow citizens to their sure death). The saddest part is that people of non-Russian nationalities (indigenous nations of the Russian Federation) are the first to be drafted. There are reports that in some remote settlements, no men are left. Putin managed to create a double genocide – against Ukrainians and against the non-Russian population of his country. May God deal with him according to His justice.

Day 211 · September 22

I usually get to check the news late in the evening (unless something outstanding happens during the day). Trying to make sense of the news in Ukraine, I am caught in the whirlwind of international news. My heart breaks for the protesters in Iran. I know it's unlikely to get any reliable official news from there, so I pray for God's mercy and His will there. Before my son was born, I worked in a ministry organization in Kyiv. We got to know quite a few people from Iran because an Iranian church used our facility for their Bible study. Most of them couldn't go back home because of the risk of religious persecution. May the Lord bring peace and justice to Iran.

Day 216 · September 27

Resilience and the Seeds of Future Hope

A season to multiply: *The tulips begin to multiply and prepare for the following year. This invisible work of resilience is crucial. The commitment to goodness brings life into the world.*

I was contrasting pictures from the city of Makariv (Kyiv region) before the Russian invasion, immediately after the liberation, and now, four months later. I rejoice at the determination to rebuild and restore, because I believe that the desire to make things orderly and beautiful is an element of God's nature in us. He is the creator, He brought order out of chaos, and He made this world a diverse and beautiful place to live in. So, I believe that as long as our people are ready to keep restoring what was destroyed, there is hope. "The thief comes only to steal and kill and destroy. I came that they may have life and have it abundantly" (John 10:10).

Day 179 · August 21

"For his anger is but for a moment, and his favor is for a lifetime. Weeping may tarry for the night, but joy comes with the morning" (Psalm 30:5).

I've been taking comfort in this verse. It's such a good reminder that these hardships are not forever, and the morning will come, and there will be joy dancing.

Day 180 · August 22

Today, in Latvia, they toppled down the monument intended to commemorate the Soviet victory over Nazi Germany, which in fact, was an offensive reminder of the decades of oppressive occupation by the Soviet Union, which ended in 1991 when Latvia declared independence. It's the latest in the series of demolished Soviet monuments in the Baltic states. It took over 30 years to work up the decisiveness to do it, but even six months ago, it seemed unlikely. I believe it's the result of prayers (not only ours but

Fall of a Soviet monument - Day 183, August 25, 2022

those that started decades ago) for the complete liberation from the poisonous worldview and Soviet heritage.

So let us keep praying, even if our prayers seem unlikely or take too long. Keep praying for the occupied territories (especially Mariupol suffering from a major fire), our POWs, the possible "referendum" in the occupied territories, and for Ukraine's victory in this war against evil.

Today's picture shows the moment when the Soviet-era monument fell into the nearby pond leaving only a splash of water in its way – praying for all the wickedness to do the same.

Day 183 · August 25

So even though I am still grieving the future that was taken away from me, I am trusting God to use me where I am to bring glory to His Name.

Day 184 · August 26

I take comfort in knowing I can call upon the Lord and ask Him to fight our enemies. We are waiting for the day when He will receive victory in this war.

Day 185 · August 27

We are patiently and eagerly awaiting the day of our victory. According to the Estonian intelligence prognosis, the active hostilities will die down in seven to nine weeks due to the weather change, and the war will enter its positional stage where both sides hold their ground without much activity. It's vital to reclaim as much of the occupied territories as possible during this time because life in occupation is unbearable.

Day 191 · September 2

Today's news filled me with cautious hope as we see answers to our prayers. According to Ukraine's intelligence,[xxxiii] most of Russia's modern weaponry was used during the first months of this invasion. Now, they need to unseal their storage to equip new brigades, but as much as 40% of the stored weapons need serious repairs and cannot be used. We praise God and ask for all Russian weapons to malfunction.

The intelligence services of the UK Ministry of Defense report that the Russian troops are suffering from fatigue and low morale.[xxxiv] According to the reports, the Russian soldiers in Kherson are rebelling against their commanders because of insufficient provisions. I've mentioned before that the primary motivation for most Russian soldiers is their pay, but it looks like they do not get the money they were promised which significantly lowers their motivation. The Ukrainian army, on the contrary, is highly motivated to defend their land and their loved ones. We keep praying for all Russian soldiers to sabotage the evil orders, surrender or repent, return home and stop killing Ukrainians.

The Russians use their usual military tactic of scorched earth when they level a city entirely with the ground before advancing in its direction. It's unthinkable cruelty that shows no mercy and no value for anything living. We know that our army wouldn't be capable of anything similar, which explains their relatively slow advances. However, according to the American Institute for the Study of War, the Ukrainian army successfully uses the strategy where they drain the resources of the enemy and cut off their supply chains, so they are forced to surrender or retreat. This strategy takes time but is more gentle on the people in the war zone. We praise God for these reports and ask for His fear to enter the hearts of the enemy soldiers so that they surrender or repent and run in fear.

The commander of an air-defense division shared about the miracles they witnessed.[xxxv] For example, they took down a Russian military plane without even firing at it – the pilot realized that his aircraft was caught on the radar and jumped out of it in fear. That plane crashed into the ground. Another time our air-defense forces had to take down Russian missiles with an old Soviet air-defense rocket. There were two missiles headed in their direction, but they could launch only one rocket and weren't sure it would be effective at all. However, they were in for a surprise – their rocket exploded in the air at such a place that its debris shot down both missiles. They said it was a miracle. We keep praying for more miracles and for the Lord to shield our skies.

Day 193 · September 4

Every day we keep praying for Russia to stop being a threat to Ukraine and the rest of the world. We pray for the ultimate end of this war so that Russia won't be able to return as it happened with the Chechen wars. We pray for all of us to be transformed by this war for the glory of God.

Day 197 · September 8

This semester, I am helping out online at my son's school, teaching English to our middle schoolers who are spread all over the world. I don't think that a year ago, I would have dared to agree to this challenge. I love teaching and have experience teaching English, but I would have been afraid of this new setting. However, God knew about it, and He had a plan. In January, just weeks before the invasion, the English teacher had to take a course and couldn't teach on Fridays, so they were looking for a substitute. It "just happened" to be that they needed the replacement for the few weeks I was free between the Bible schools at YWAM. I could get to know the students, observe the teacher in class, and gain a new experience. I even got to teach online as our school had to go into that mode at some point. That's why today, I felt as if we picked up right where we left off in February. Preparing for my lessons now, I was amazed that God had it all planned out over six months ago! How many more "coincidences" do we fail to notice?

That's why I remind myself to trust God, His ways, and His thoughts as I read news reports. It looks like our army is successfully counterattacking the Russian forces not only in the south (Kherson region) but also in the east (Kharkiv region). There are no official reports yet (they are waiting to clear up and demine the city before making any announcements), only bits of intercepted conversations and information from the locals. Please, keep praying for the complete liberation of Ukraine and the special protection for our defenders and the people in the occupied territories.

Day 195 · September 6

There are numerous reports and intercepted conversations that show that Russian soldiers refuse to go into battles and are trying to desert the battlefield. The news from the east of Ukraine brings fear into the Russian soldiers in the south. There were reports of sightings of buses with unarmed soldiers going from the Kherson region into Crimea. We don't get our hopes up yet, fully understanding what a long and complicated process is ahead of us, but these reports are a clear answer to our prayers, so we keep interceding.

Day 198 · September 9

Our army has liberated the north and northeast of the Kharkiv region and pushed the enemy across the border. In the intercepted conversations, the Russian soldiers call home to say goodbye to their loved ones because they were abandoned by their commanding officers and left without ammunition.

In the south, our army was able to move the front line by as much as twelve kilometers. There are reports of whole detachments of the enemy army in the south of Ukraine getting in touch with our officials to find out how they can surrender and be granted the protection of the POW status because they are completely demoralized – we keep praying this becomes a reality (as our son often prays for the enemy soldiers to have a change of heart and join our army in the fight with the evil). Wouldn't it be surreal if whole Russian battalions willingly surrendered, and this caused turmoil inside of Russia, leading to a complete change there? Wouldn't it make people stop and ask how it was possible if it weren't a miracle of God? Wouldn't it be a testimony for the generations to come? We keep praying for more and more miracles, for all glory to be given to God.

Day 201 · September 12

This night was a night of miracles. Please, keep praying for all the POWs to be set free, for all occupied territories to be liberated, and for justice to be restored. "Therefore the Lord waits to be gracious to you, and therefore he exalts himself to show mercy to you. For the Lord is a God of justice; blessed are all those who wait for him" (Isaiah 30:18).

Day 210 · September 21

How can those who do it still be called people? The beasts seem to be more merciful. For some reason, I thought about the book of Revelations and the description of the defeat of wickedness. The war crimes committed by Russia are so numerous and unthinkable that they reminded me of those descriptions of evil. Thankfully, we know that justice will prevail.

Day 212 · September 23

I saw a video today. In it, a boy is asked what the first thing he would do when the war is over is. In response, he closes his eyes and says, "Yes! We have won!"
We look forward to the day when we'll be able to do the same.

Day 217 · September 28

About 2,500 Russian troops seem to be surrounded in Lyman (Donetsk region). Their supply chains have been cut off. Unless Russian officials request permission for their army to retreat from the city (which is quite unlikely since they keep denying the problem), those soldiers will most likely perish unless they surrender. What were they fighting for? What future can await the country that treats its citizens as cannon fodder?

Meanwhile, the Kremlin celebrates the annexation of the temporarily occupied territories. Does it change anything? No, because no one will ever recognize these actions as legitimate. A few Ukrainian businesses mocked Putin's order by posting online their own annexation claims of the Russian territory "in response to the will of the common people."

The Ukrainian government did react to the annexation by formally submitting an application to join the NATO alliance. Of course, this doesn't have any immediate effects, but it is a historic moment for Ukraine. Even though Putin started this war claiming that he was fighting NATO, he couldn't be further from the truth. Even a year ago, NATO membership seemed rather impossible, even in the distant future. The support for this decision among the people of Ukraine kept rising with the level of Russian aggression. Today, Latvia, Lithuania, Estonia, and Canada have already supported Ukraine's decision. The Armed Forces of Ukraine have shown the world that they know how to fight, they are ready to learn how to use new weapons in days, and they are ready to improve the weapons at the front lines by discovering the capabilities not accounted for by the manufacturers. I am fascinated by the speed and scale of the events we are witnessing and pray for God's glory to be revealed in the outcome.

Please, pray for the people in the temporarily occupied Kherson, Zaporizhzhia, Donetsk, and Luhansk regions. The annexation gives Russia "legal reasons" to recruit local men to be sent straight to the front lines and to speed up other oppressive mechanisms there. Pray for the protection of all our people there. Pray for them not to feel abandoned or uprooted. May they know that God will restore His justice soon.

Day 219 · September 30

Chapter Six
Blackout Season
October 1 - December 31, 2022

A year ago, in one of our favorite parks outside Kyiv, we saw red guelder rose berries. They traditionally symbolize the blood of the soldiers laying down their lives for their land. May the Lord stop this bloodshed and bring victory over this evil.

Day 234 • October 15

I didn't expect to see pictures of small vegetable gardens in trenches – our soldiers would often plant sprouting onions and other greens or basic vegetables to enjoy the food they love.

Day 282 • December 2

Today's picture – the National Philharmonic of Ukraine holds concerts with candles and flashlights despite the blackouts. We are not broken, as long as we have room for art.

Day 291 • December 11

May the truth never be silenced.

Day 295 • December 15

2022 was not an easy year. It was a year we will never forget. In all honesty, I can say that I am grateful to God for every single day of this passing year. He was faithful in every detail, and I hope that one day we'll be able to see the big picture and praise His name in awe of His mercy and grace. 2022 was a year of our resilience. May 2023 be the year of our victory.

Day 311 • December 31

Hope Based in Past Memories

A season to plant: *Planting tulips is an expression of hope, based on past experience. After a bulb is placed in the ground, half a year passes before the gardener knows whether their hope is realized.*

I was stunned and kept thinking back to the morning reports from Kyiv and the evening ones from Yeisk, yet I praised God for being able to come to him with my mixed feelings and to trust in His justice and goodness when I can't make sense of it all.

Day 236 · October 17

Also, our intelligence services report that the risk of a new invasion from the territory of Belarus is increasing. However, this time they may aim at the western regions of Ukraine to cut off aid supply channels. Over the past eight months, we've seen many miracles, so let's pray for all the enemy plans to fail.

Day 239 · October 20

We are adjusting to the rolling blackouts and do our best to keep a positive attitude. We had no electricity in the morning, so we decided it was a perfect opportunity to work outside in the garden. It was an easy solution because the day was relatively warm despite the clouds. I know we may not be as cheerful on rainy days, so I am making mental notes of the activities we could busy ourselves with once the weather gets nasty. I remember rolling blackouts in my childhood, in the 90s. We wouldn't have electricity from 6 pm till 8 pm every night. Even though it was inconvenient, I enjoyed those hours when we got to light up candles, do a shadow show on the walls, sing songs, or sit and talk with my sister and parents. Those blackouts turned into uninterrupted mandatory family bonding, and I missed them once they were canceled. I remember once when I was already a university student, we lost power on New Year's Eve, and my sister and I were very excited that we could have a candle-lit dinner. That night, the power went back on in an hour or so, but we refused to turn on the light and ruin the ambiance. I hope our children will also have warm memories from these blackouts despite the circumstances.

Day 243 · October 24

We lost cell phone reception for over six hours and had no electricity for over eight hours. The power went back on while I was writing this post at 10:30 pm.

It feels like these days of isolation, when we are left without a connection to the outside world, are even more trying than the early days of this invasion. Back then, there was a lot of uncertainty and a lot of fear, but at least we had the luxury of staying connected, which was really empowering. In those first days, I received words of prayer and encouragement from all over the world – from Asia to Australia, to Africa, to South America, to North America, and many European countries. Through this war, I found new friends I've never met in person but whose unexpected love and friendship helped me when it was tough, and I am forever grateful to God for sending them into my life.

Now, more than ever, we are to live by faith. We cannot make even the simplest daily plans because of the emergency blackouts. We don't know how long they will last. We don't know how long until Russia chooses to strike again (because we are certain that more strikes will come). We cannot check on our loved ones and simply trust them in God's hands.

However, we know that we are not abandoned. We know that our God is in control even when we are in the dark. We learn the art of small steps, being thankful for what we have, and trusting God with the big unknown. And we know that we are not abandoned by our prayer warriors.

Day 266 · November 16

Nine years ago, November 21, 2013, became the day of the beginning of the Revolution of Dignity, which laid the foundation for our current events. Back then, Russia tried to consume Ukraine in what they thought was a cunning way.

On November 21, 2013 one and a half thousand people came to the central square in Kyiv as a sign of protest against the refusal of the pro-Russian then-President Viktor Yanukovych to sign the Agreement on the Associated Membership of Ukraine in the European Union. On November

30, at night, when only several hundred activists remained on the street, they were brutally chased by police. In response, on December 1, hundreds of thousands (up to one million, according to some estimations) of people came to the center of Kyiv. They were protesting against corruption, the usurpation of power, police brutality, the violation of human rights in Ukraine, the policy of Russian cultural domination, and the rapprochement with Russia.

In February 2014, these protests escalated. Ukraine lost over 100 people brutally killed by snipers and special police forces – they are called the "Heavenly Hundred" and can be considered the first victims of this Russian-Ukrainian war. On February 20, 2014, when the pro-Russian president and officials fled the country, the parliament took over and managed to stop the violence. On that same day, Russia started its "special operation" in Crimea, which resulted in its annexation and gave way to the invasion of the Donetsk and Luhansk regions.

Today we commemorate November 21 as the Day of Freedom and Dignity, for if not for these values that stood stronger than self-preservation instincts, we could have turned into another Belarus, and today's war could be taking place in a different European country bordering Russia. However, values are something you are willing to pay the price for, and Ukraine is paying a great price to keep its freedom and dignity, to make sure we are not ashamed of our choices before our children and grandchildren.

Day 271 • November 21

You may be familiar with the names of Janusz Korczak or Irena Sendler. I remember hearing about these people and thinking those were shocking yet distant WWII stories since we all say "never again." Today I read about an orphanage near Kherson.

There was a small orphanage in the village of Stepanivka (Kherson region) – it was a center for social and psychological rehabilitation for the orphaned and the children of parents who could not care for their children for physical or financial reasons. In October, the Russians brought 15 children from the Mykolaiv region to stay there (they were forcefully taken from their orphanage when the Russians were leaving the village). However, the Russians didn't know that about a dozen children were already living in that orphanage. The orphanage teachers knew several stories when the vulnerable orphans were forcibly "evacuated" in an unknown direction, so they decided to hide the children in their care and later even snuck them out and hid them in their own homes. Most of the children were reunited with their relatives, but three children had no one to take care of them.

When it became evident that the Russians were preparing to retreat, the staff knew they could not stop them from taking away the children brought from the Mykolaiv region, but they knew they could at least try to save their own. That's when one of the teachers took these three children to her home in Kherson and told everyone they were her niece and nephews. That's where they were when the right bank of the Kherson region was liberated.

According to the orphanage headmaster's information, that group of children from Mykolaiv were accompanied by their headmistress, and they somehow managed to get to Georgia and are safe now.

I am still shaking and weeping after reading this story, but I know this is not the only story. My friends from YWAM Kyiv stayed back in Kyiv during the early days of the invasion to be with the vulnerable orphaned children they had been ministering to. He can share his stories of foster parents and orphanage leaders doing the impossible and rescuing their children.

Day 272 · November 22

"Those who sow in tears shall reap with shouts of joy! He who goes out weeping, bearing the seed for sowing, shall come home with shouts of joy, bringing his sheaves with him" (Psalm 126:5-6).

The fourth Saturday in November is when we remember all Holodomor (the Great Famine) victims. The Soviet Union used famine to force a nation into submission. God blessed Ukraine with fertile land, and our people were self-reliant, working the soil to provide for their families. This went against the communist idea that everyone had to depend on the government. That's why the Soviet regime chose to starve Ukrainians into submission with artificial famines in 1921-1923, 1932-1933, and 1946-1947. The famine of 1932-1933 was recognized as the genocide of the Ukrainian nation. During those years, millions of Ukrainians died from starvation as they were required to give all grain (and other foods) to the government. It is one of the greatest traumas of my people, which is why, ninety years later, we cherish food, refrain from playing with food, and always try to feed those we love (there's an observation made by many foreigners that if you're invited over for a cup of tea in Ukraine, be ready for a full meal).

The stories of the days of the Great Famine are filled with horror, and we remember them today, especially as we see Russia weaponizing hunger once again in the best traditions of the Soviet Union. While the people in Africa and Asia are starving, Russia is trying to stop grain exports or set our harvest on fire.

Today, our President announced the "Grain from Ukraine" initiative to deliver at least 60 vessels with grain to the poorest countries of Africa in the next six months. No one should starve, and no one should compromise their dignity to feed their family.

I'm once again amazed at how the psalm of the day fits the topic. Today's verses talk about sowing in tears and reaping with joy, and it reminded me of the law passed in 1932-1933 – the Law of five spikelets of wheat. Anyone possessing the equivalent of five wheat spikelets had to be arrested and could even receive capital punishment. Think how different it is from the Biblical law of gleaning set to provide for the neediest. In the Soviet Union, special patrols were going door-to-door and searching houses for hidden food. There was a ban on selling bread to the villagers and traveling to other regions in search of food, while the piles of confiscated grain and potatoes were often left to rot in government storages.

My great-grandmother told a story of her mother finding some grain and making some flatbread. When they saw a patrol coming, they hid the bread behind the icons set in the corner of the room. As the patrol entered the house, they slammed the door, and the icons fell, revealing the bread. Thankfully, the patrol officers were also starving, so they quickly grabbed the bread and ate it. This saved my great-grandmother's family from being arrested for the possession of bread (what an unspeakable charge!)

On this Remembrance Day, we light up a candle and put it in the window in memory of those who died from starvation as the Soviet regime tried to subdue or exterminate our nation.

Day 276 · November 27

While we have little news from the frontlines (our army officials try to avoid making hasty announcements), there is some news from the international front.

The German Bundestag recognized the Holodomor of 1932-33 (the Great Famine) as genocide of the Ukrainian people. A bunch of governments passed the same resolution last week. It is an important step. It recognizes our past and raises awareness regarding our present. Many people, even in Ukraine, learned about the famine only after the collapse of the Soviet Union. Many governments ignored this page of our history since they didn't want to offend Russia. However, now justice is slowly being restored. It pains me to know it took 90 years, yet it is a tribute to the millions of those starved to death by the bloodthirsty Soviet regime. It gives me hope that justice will be restored once again, even if it takes longer than we wish.

Day 280 • November 30

Everything looks magical when it snows. The snow graciously covers all the imperfections and silences your anxieties. It brings up happy childhood memories and makes you long for wonder.

Interestingly, today marks the 145th anniversary of the birth of Mykola Leontovych, an outstanding Ukrainian composer and the author of the "Carol of the Bells", which has become a symbol of Christmas for millions of people around the world. Mykola Leontovych was one of the first to interpret Ukrainian folklore in a new way, using the heritage of European choral culture. Throughout his life, Leontovych led a number of choirs, starting from the time of his studying at the Kamianets-Podilskyi Theological Seminary. Unfortunately, the life of Mykola Leontovych was cut short by the hand of a KGB agent since anything Ukrainian was perceived as a threat to the Soviet regime. However, God works in mysterious ways, so the works of Leontovych survived the Soviet genocide and are known all over the world. You can watch the short video made by the Ukrainer media project, which tells the story of Mykola Leontovych and his "Carol of the Bells".[xxxvi]

Day 293 - December 13

Merry Christmas, dear friends.

May God's presence be your reason for joy in this holiday season. We rejoice in Christ's coming to earth and in the great victory we gained through His sacrifice. This year, when rejoicing takes effort, we are more aware of the joy and the price it comes with. This year, when many of us might not have the traditional outward elements of the Christmas season, may we be able to focus more on its real meaning.

Christmas is a great reason for joy, but this joy magnifies once you look at it with Easter in mind. Many times, when we are having a good time as a family now, I tear up because thousands of families can't do that because they are separated by miles of the battle zone. Thousands of families have lost their loved ones because they gave their lives so that we could be together and have this good time. So, while I still have joy, I am aware of its value.

This Christmas, we rejoice in knowing that God sent His Son to save us – "For to us a child is born, to us a son is given; and the government shall be upon his shoulder, and his name shall be called Wonderful Counselor, Mighty God, Everlasting Father, Prince of Peace" (Isaiah 9:6). Yet this joy grows into awe once you think of what He was sent to save us from and what He had to go through to do it – "But he was pierced for our transgressions; he was crushed for our iniquities; upon him was the chastisement that brought us peace, and with his wounds we are healed" (Isaiah 53:5).

May we all have the joy of knowing that God loves us and cares for us. "In this the love of God was made manifest among us, that God sent his only Son into the world, so that we might live through him. In this is love, not that we have loved God but that he loved us and sent his Son to be the propitiation for our sins" (1 John 4:9-10).

May we have the joy of knowing that we are worthy in God's eyes and that He is faithful even when the world around us is a whirlwind of chaos. "He who did not spare his own Son but gave him up for us all, how will he not also with him graciously give us all things?" (Romans 8:32).

May we have the joy of knowing that the victory belongs to the Lord and He has already defeated death and evil on the cross, so we can rejoice in knowing that justice will be restored and every tear will be wiped away. "He will wipe away every tear from their eyes, and death shall be no more, neither shall there be mourning, nor crying, nor pain anymore, for the former things have passed away" (Revelation 21:4). May we have the quiet joy that we can have in our hearts despite the circumstances or even against the circumstances.

Merry Christmas, dear friends. We thank God for each one of you and pray blessings upon your families.

Day 304 · December 24

Late last night, after I wrote my daily update, I was getting ready for bed when I heard the sound of airplanes. I knew right away that it meant that there must be another aerial threat. This morning we read about sixteen kamikaze drones launched at Ukraine. Thankfully, all sixteen of them were shot down.

In Ukraine, as in many post-Soviet countries, the New Year celebration has always been far more important than Christmas. Christmas was celebrated with family, but the New Year was the time for big parties. This year is different. I notice more and more people focusing on Christmas and its meaning rather than on the new year festivities. This war is transforming and shaping us on so many levels. May it all be for God's glory.

Day 310 · December 30

The Experience of Survival

A season to make roots: *Having planted our tulip bulbs, we move forward into the busyness of preparing for winter. This is a practical time, built around survival.*

We live ordinary lives every day, and sometimes I forget about the war for a moment. Working in the garden, doing household chores, homeschooling, or just having fun with our son, I catch myself wondering if this whole war was just a product of my imagination. Perhaps, that was a nightmare that kept haunting me and not the reality we are living in. But then I hear an airplane or someone revving up the engine, and I freeze for a moment and feel panic wash over me. I usually need just a second or two to compose myself and return to what I was doing.

Sometimes I am impacted by someone's post on Facebook. Someone's story can easily leave me in tears (either sorrow or joy), and I would keep thinking back to it throughout the day, trying to see beyond the words shared and into the long-term consequences.

I dream of the day when we can return to our boring, peaceful lives, but I'm afraid this day will never come, even when the war is over. This war is something that's changed us forever, and it will remain with us for the rest of our lives in one way or another.

We will keep seeing reminders in ordinary things. When we were leaving Kyiv on February 24, we stopped at a store to get some supplies, but the shelves were mostly empty. My aunt managed to buy a couple of items, including nutmeg. Why nutmeg? She couldn't explain it herself. She saw it on a shelf and thought it was better to buy it because spices may become scarce. We keep teasing her about that event, but I know that every time I use nutmeg, I will be reminded of the day we were leaving Kyiv.

I notice that about myself, who has had a very limited war experience, and my heart breaks for the people who live in the temporarily occupied territories, who go through filtration and deportation, who are not able to evacuate, who see and experience something that should never be seen or experienced by anyone in this world. We witness the genocide of our nation. We see cities turn into ruin. We live in the days when nuclear strike threats are casually tossed around. We carry burdens that are too heavy of a load for any human, yet it's something that we must deal with.

When I was a kid, I often wondered why my grandma talked about her war memories so much if almost 50 years had passed since WWII ended. She was twelve years old when the war started. She had just finished 4th grade. She never went back to school because she needed to work.

Now, my son is eight years old. He just started second grade, and tonight at bedtime, he said he missed his classmates. He said, "I feel a void inside without my friends. I wish we could all be together again." And we proceeded to pray for his friends and classmates, now scattered around the world. As he fell asleep, I kept praying for our children not to be traumatized and crippled by this war, I kept praying for the Lord's consolation and healing for their little hearts. I kept wondering if my son's children and grandchildren would also complain about his sharing too many war memories years after the war is over.

Day 222 • October 3

Over the past few days, we've had fewer missile strikes (they are trying to save them for important targets) but more attacks using unmanned aerial vehicles (kamikaze drones supplied by Iran). They are harder to detect and will most likely be used against critical infrastructure objects. Last night, they sent twelve drones into the Kyiv region, six of which were shot down, but the other six hit infrastructure objects in a city about 70 km (30 miles) from where we are staying.

Please, keep praying for the Ukrainians from the occupied territories trying to get to Europe through Russia. The Minister of the Internal Affairs of Estonia confirmed that about 1,000 Ukrainians were waiting at the border on the Russian side, but they all were loaded up into large trucks and taken in an unknown direction.[xxxvii] They suspect that it may be used for provocations along the border, or it could be an attempt to get some Russian secret service officers or illegal immigrants into Estonia. Please, pray for God's protection and for all evil plans to fail.

Day 224 • October 5

Many cities suffered from power outages because of the strikes on the energy branch infrastructure. Lviv region and the city were in a blackout most of the day. Our neighbors in Kyiv spent over twelve hours without electricity, which meant a complete collapse for our apartment building (we have electric stoves and need electric pumps for water supply). However, most of our neighbors didn't panic but started devising backup plans in case such attacks happened again. There were no lines at the stores or gas stations. People were mentally prepared for it because what happened today was not new. It was the same evil, only in a concentrated form and on a larger scale.

Most cities and regions will continue going through power outages for the next few days. The government asked the people to cut down energy consumption in the evenings to help our energy system cope with the load, and the first reports from the Kyiv region show that the energy consumption was down by 26%, which once again shows the readiness of our people to give up some personal comforts for the sake of our victory.

Tonight, hundreds, if not thousands, of people went into the streets of large European cities in solidarity with Ukraine, demanding to recognize Russia as a terrorist state and asking to arm Ukraine now. Overall, this massive attack brought much discomfort to the civilians in Ukraine, yet it was just a tiny glimpse of what our defenders and people in the war zone go through every day.

Today, I pray imprecatory psalms and look forward to the fulfillment of the last chapters of Revelations. Today's attack made us more aware of what should be expected this winter, yet it didn't break us or throw us into despair. However, it made us more confident in our victory because this is the agony of the beast. These are the darkest hours before dawn. This is the passion Friday before the resurrection Sunday. The enemy may rejoice now, but the Lord will not delay his justice.

Day 229 · October 10

Sometimes I wonder what it would be like to see the truly "big picture", to get a glimpse of how God views things. I'm sure it would make us reconsider some of our conclusions and find purpose behind things that don't make sense.

I was thinking about it in light of the Monday missile attacks. According to our intelligence, Russia was planning it in advance, so it was not a retaliation for the Crimea bridge. We knew that attacks on critical infrastructure were in store for us this winter, and we were getting ready. Of course, we wish this hadn't happened, yet there are reasons to praise God. Had Russia waited and conducted this attack in the middle of winter when the temperature was extremely low, it would have been a great shock and would have had much more severe consequences for the people. However, they wanted a "big gesture" now, which helps us better prepare for the winter, and now even skeptics are stocking up on candles and warm clothes.

The blatant Monday attack on critical infrastructure also left no choice to the civilized world but to side with Ukraine and commit to the support. Today, we've seen a few countries promise to provide air-defense systems as soon as possible (to be honest, that's what we'd been asking for since the beginning of the invasion), and other much-needed weapons are also on their way.

These are two of the most obvious reasons to praise God amid this current storm, and I wonder how many more are left unnoticed. May we always be able to see His hand, even at the darkest of times.

Day 231 · October 12

Our Ministry of Infrastructure announced that thanks to the fact that Ukrainians have demonstrated unity in cutting down energy consumption at peak hours, there's no need for the rolling blackouts at the moment. There may be emergency power outages, but they shouldn't become regular.

Day 232 · October 13

There are days when all the news reports blend in together, and by the end of the day, I have a hard time remembering if something happened today or if it was from days ago.

The terror of civilians continues. Missile attacks and kamikaze drones aimed at critical infrastructure, air-raid alerts lasting for hours every day, preventing us from getting anything done, kids switching to distance learning or studying in bomb shelters. Yes, we are weary of it. Yes, we want it to be over. No, we are not ready to give up.

Over the past couple of days, I saw the following reports. There are parents who ask if they can bring the kids to school as soon as the air-raid warning is lifted, and the teachers ready to teach online, in bomb shelters, or during after-hours. Our neighbors from our apartment building in Kyiv are discussing alternative solutions in case of prolonged power outages. It seems surreal – people during the war not panicking but debating the efficiency of solar panels in a large apartment building. People are debating the most efficient energy-saving actions (do you lower the temperature on your water heater, turn it off during peak hours, or use it at night? should you boil water on a stove, in an electric kettle, or use a microwave?). People are offering their services at a discounted price (out of understanding the economic hardships of their customers) get paid the full price (despite the financial hardships and out of understanding the needs of the service provider) and donate the "extra" to charity funds (out of understanding the greater needs).

Day 237 · October 18

Please, pray for the temporarily occupied territories. Children and adults are kidnapped in the Kherson region under the pretense of retreat or evacuation, yet we know this is the same scheme used in Mariupol and the Kharkiv region.

Also, there is a high risk of the Russians blowing up a Kakhovka hydropower station in the Kherson region (by Nova Kakhovka), which would flood the right bank of the Dnipro River. The propagandists started spreading rumors of Ukrainians planning to attack the dam there, which usually means that's what they plan to do and are simply preparing the ground for the false-flag operation. The occupational authorities have been moving their families to the left bank, which makes this theory even more plausible. Please, pray for this disaster to be averted – thousands of civilians and our defenders will likely perish if the dam is blown up.

Day 237 · October 18

An air-raid warning lasted over three hours today. Our air-defense forces took down four out of six missiles and ten kamikaze drones, yet there were hits on the critical infrastructure. All of Ukraine will go into mandatory energy-saving mode tomorrow. We are asked to minimize energy consumption from 7 am until 11 pm. Rolling blackouts will be implemented if sufficient energy saving is not achieved.

The temperature keeps dropping and will be just a few degrees above freezing for a few days. It's a nasty part of the year to be left without electricity, hot water, and heat. And that's why the enemy keeps attacking our critical infrastructure.

Today, Kyiv heard explosions when our air-defense forces were neutralizing the missiles. It was in the middle of the day, while the kids were in school and the parents were at work. Two messages from a teacher to parents in Kyiv had me in tears. The first one, "The kids are in the shelter. It's noisy here, so they don't hear the explosions." The second one, "You can pick up your kids once it's safe. Someone will stay with them at the school shelter as long as needed." Two simple messages of love and care describe the reality we are living in now. This war has shown us so many ordinary heroes around us – the soldiers, firefighters, rescue workers, doctors, teachers, electricians, plumbers, road service workers, drivers, and so many more we used to take for granted.

Day 238 · October 19

Praise God, we had our electricity throughout the day today, but many cities remain in the darkness after the most recent attacks on our energy infrastructure. I had a two-hour Zoom call today with our neighbors in Kyiv as we were thinking of ways we can prepare our apartment building for the possibly harsh and dark winter. It is draining to think of all the "what ifs". I don't want to imagine our beautiful neighborhood turning into a dreary place with fire pits as make-do warming and cooking stations. However, it is already a reality in so many towns of Ukraine, even those rather far from the frontline. We prepare for the worst but keep believing and hoping for the best.

Day 242 · October 23

Last night, the enemy severely damaged energy infrastructure in the Kyiv region. We need to cut energy consumption by 30%! While the power grid experts try to balance our system to avoid a total collapse, we spent almost half of our day without electricity, had it for four hours in the morning and almost three hours in the evening. The local cell phone tower can function only up to three hours without electricity. Thankfully, since the beginning of the full-scale war, our phone operators offer domestic roaming where you can connect to the competitor's network if the service of your cell phone operator is down. This allows us to call someone in case of emergency and even sporadically catch some mobile internet (which I'm relying on to post this).

Trying to look for the silver lining, we once again realized that we are blessed to be in the village and not in Kyiv. Here you can always find chores and do something useful outside instead of constantly checking and waiting for the power to return.

Please, pray for Ukraine's winter. Pray for our perseverance as we adjust to our challenging circumstances. Pray for the children who go down to the bomb shelters during sirens. Pray for the teachers who manage to teach classes in bomb shelters even when there's no electricity. Pray for the children who are afraid of the darkness. Pray for God's light to shine through the thickest of darkness.

Day 246 · October 27

On a personal level, we don't suffer much from rolling blackouts. Ivan managed to work the expected number of hours and finish his tasks. I am somewhat flustered by this "routine" where you have to drop everything once the power is out and find jobs that don't require electricity and be ready to drop them as soon as the power is back. We are getting into the habit of recharging all of our devices and refilling emergency water jugs every time the power is back. We are getting more disciplined at doing dishes and more creative at cooking. I'm still trying to figure out the best way or time to do laundry since the rolling blackouts have been somewhat unpredictable. However, we've already had two board game nights and candlelight dinners that help us bond as a family. The blackouts are aggravating, but if the Russians want us to improve our survival skills and make us even more resilient, so be it.

We don't know how much longer we'll have to keep up this routine, but most of us agree that this is just the beginning of a long, challenging winter. One interesting thing that has happened – because getting stuck in an elevator during a power outage is a serious problem, people are trying to help their neighbors by leaving a "survival kit" in an elevator. The contents differ and may include a water bottle, snacks, a warm blanket or scarf, and a foldable chair or cushions. Yes, the circumstances are horrible, but Ukrainians keep amazing me. May the Lord bless this nation.

Day 247 · October 28

Over the past few days, there was a phrase that caught my eye a couple of times, "Life doesn't stand still during the war, so we must keep on living." I felt the truth of it today when the beautiful and ugly were woven together once again.

This morning I woke up to a bright sun and the birds chirping. It was the perfect fall day. I also woke up to the news of another massive missile strike on Ukraine. This morning, for the first time since the invasion, a missile hit an object of critical infrastructure a few kilometers away from my hometown, where my parents live. Thankfully, there were no casualties, but the hit will have severe consequences for the energy system of Ukraine. Some debris from a missile that was shot down by our air defense forces even fell in Moldova in a town at the Ukrainian border.

Overall, there were over 50 cruise missiles launched at Ukraine this morning, and 44 (!) of them were destroyed by the air defense forces of Ukraine. However, the missiles and kamikaze drones still damaged eighteen objects in ten regions of Ukraine (the Chernivtsi, Kyiv, Kharkiv, Zaporizhzhya, Dnipropetrovsk, Cherkasy, Kirovohrad, and other regions). This seems to be the most destructive attack so far, especially since our energy company reported that they are running out of spare parts because of the constant need to repair the grid.

Because of the morning attack, almost 80% of Kyiv residents were left without water and electricity. In Kharkiv, they damaged the power supply of the metro stations and public transportation. We also lost electricity for most of the day, which also meant poor cell phone reception and a sporadic mobile internet connection. However, the moon and stars were shining so bright in the crisp night air that you didn't need any additional light sources outside. Please, keep praying for our cities and our people, because we are getting weary, restless, angry, and even more ready to resist.

Day 250 • October 31

We had electricity for a couple of hours in the morning and then for half an hour in the afternoon. We somehow got an internet connection at the moment, which is a miracle. We had no connection most of the day, and Ivan had to walk through the fields trying to catch cell phone reception for his work call. On the one hand, it's easier to be in the village since we have heat (a gas heater and a wood heater) and a gas stove to make food. We can walk outside and don't have to worry about the sewerage (which may become a severe problem for our neighbors in Kyiv). On the other hand, the connection is more stable in a big city, and it's easier to find a coworking station with Wi-Fi available there, but you have to survive without heat and water supply.

Day 278 · November 28

Meanwhile, Ukraine keeps preparing for another massive missile attack. Kyiv city officials share available provisions in case of a total blackout. They've made a list of stores that will continue working without electricity. People will be able to use metro stations as shelters and sources of electricity and water. After the past nine months, the thought of a possible extended blackout scares me, yet it also makes me wonder what other creative solutions we will be able to discover through it.

Someone said they noticed that Ukrainians are excellent at normalizing the abnormal. And it's true. We long to bring our peaceful lives into the turmoil we live in. In March, when the Russians were several kilometers away from Kyiv, many of our neighbors spent nights in a bomb shelter. When I asked one of them how they were surviving, she sent me a video of a cozy corner with throw pillows, a microwave, and a play zone for the kids. It was not what I expected to see.

Day 282 · December 2

It's been over a month since the regular rolling blackouts, and we seem to have caught onto its rhythm. A few hours without an internet connection or cell phone reception no longer cause me to panic. It is still inconvenient, and I get frustrated when I fall behind on my tasks, but I am learning to manage this new routine. I've figured out the night hours when you can do laundry and adjusted to cooking dinners without electricity.

There's a repeated joke that's not really a joke. They say that when we get old, we'll keep our power banks fully charged at all times, we'll keep a stash of water, dry foods, and cans with generator fuel somewhere in the garage, and we'll always be in a hurry to get everything done in three- to four-hour slots. And our grandchildren will think that we're weird, and our children will explain to them that we got those habits from living through the war.

Please, keep praying for the occupied territories. Life there is often reduced to survival. May God be with those people in their circumstances, and may we hear of many miracles of His grace.

Day 283 · December 3

❦ By the waters of Babylon,
there we sat down and wept,
when we remembered Zion.
(Psalm 137:1)

This psalm (137) was written when God's people were taken into Babylonian exile. They were remembering the lives they used to have and wept in the foreign land. According to the UNHCR, 7.8 million refugees from Ukraine have been recorded across Europe. Also, about 2.8 million Ukrainians have been forcefully deported or pressured to move to Russia. In total, it makes up 25% of Ukraine's population. Add to this number almost 5 million internally displaced people and those who left their homes for safer regions but never registered for government support (like our family). Each of us left something dear behind, but as we weep, we also hold on to the hope of the bright, peaceful future that will definitely come.

Russia hoped to win this war in three days; ten days at the most. We're well into the tenth month. This war turns into a test of endurance both for the civilians and the armies. Russia has many resources. We have a lot of support. They are motivated to kill. We want to live. This is such an obvious fight between evil and good that one couldn't make up a more contrasting story. We know that good will win in the end, but we can't help but ask God how much longer we must endure. So, when it gets tough, I remind myself that the people living in the active combat zone and our defenders face much greater challenges, so now is not the time to complain.

Day 287 · December 7

All the verses about light and darkness shine even brighter during our blackouts. They introduced a new schedule for power supply in Kyiv – electricity is guaranteed for two hours in the morning, during the day, and in the evening. It is also certain that they will not have electricity for at least twelve hours in the day. The rest will depend on the power-generating capacity.

I may have worn you out with the talks about the blackout, but as time goes by, we see more issues arising. The drivers were the first to speak about the difficulty of driving in complete darkness when the traffic lights are off and you can only guess if a pedestrian is trying to cross the road.

Picking up a package from a post office can become a multi-level challenge when you need to factor in their hours of operation and power supply and make sure you don't come during an air-raid warning. We memorize the list of stores that have generators since it not only means they would be working when there's no electricity but also that their fridges will keep the groceries at a safe temperature when the power is out.

We return to the habit of keeping larger amounts of cash at hand since bank terminals would not work without an internet connection. And don't even mention the minor inconveniences such as using the stairs instead of an elevator, showering and doing laundry in the middle of the night (or whenever your lucky hours are), and adjusting your work hours to the power supply schedule.

However, while most of those are inconveniences, some serious threats come with the absence of electricity. Tonight, our elderly neighbor came in asking for help as she got a bad burn on her hand in a kitchen accident when the power went out. Burns, cuts, and other injuries become an inevitable hazard in the dark.

Day 298 · December 9

There have been no massive missile attacks in over a week, which means that the enemy is preparing and waiting for the perfect timing for the next strike. I've noticed that I get tenser when we have more extended periods between attacks because the strike may come at any moment, and we don't know what it might bring. So, once we get past the fifth day after the attack, I do my best to keep my phone battery fully charged and make sure we have enough clean clothes in case we can't do laundry for over a week.

Our air-defense forces are getting better with every attack, but the Russians are also changing their tactics. Last week, the Security Service of Ukraine uncovered a network of agents who were spying in the Donetsk region and making lists of targets (schools, maternity hospitals, power stations, and student dorms) for the Russian army. Some of the detained agents turned out to be locals. I can't understand what was going on in their heads, especially as they knew what the list of targets would be used for.

While most Ukrainians are adjusting to power outages (which are an inconvenience we are ready to bear if that's what it takes to keep our freedom), the situation is getting critical for some. Many people along the front lines have to live in inhumane conditions. In Mariupol, people survive without water, electricity, or heat. Most apartments also don't have windows, which means it's as cold inside as it is outside. More and more people get sick with the flu or a seasonal cold, and the mortality rate is rising.

Day 292 · December 12

This morning the air-raid warning lasted for over three hours as the Russians were attacking Ukraine with kamikaze drones. Thankfully, our air-defense forces shot down all thirteen drones aimed at Kyiv, and they didn't cause any damage to our power lines (even though the debris did cause some damage to a couple of buildings).

Our power engineers do wonders, so the power outages mostly stick to the schedule and sometimes even are reduced. We enjoy it while it lasts, as we know that another massive attack may come any day, and we keep praying for God's protection. We also thank God for all the support provided to Ukraine to overcome the consequences of the attacks on our energy system.

Day 294 · December 14

After yesterday's missile attack, the whole energy system went into an emergency blackout for over six hours. Thankfully, our engineers managed the system back into control, which meant the enemy did not achieve their goal. We had electricity most of the night, but the power was cut early tonight. Our neighbors in Kyiv had no water or electricity for over fifteen hours and are still waiting for the centralized heating to power up, but hopefully, it's back, even if just for a few hours a day.

Day 297 · December 17

Last night, I checked the news before going to bed. The air-raid warning was issued to the southern regions of Ukraine as the Russians sent out the Iran-made Shahed kamikaze drones. We lost internet connection shortly after that, so when I was already in bed and heard a loud noise in the sky, I had to guess the drones were sent not only to the south of Ukraine. This morning we saw the reports that 30 drones attacked at night (23 of them coming at Kyiv), and our air-defense forces shot down 25 of them. Apparently, these drones came from the new shipment received from Iran – according to our intelligence; they received 250 of those.

Severe damage was caused to several infrastructure objects in Kyiv and the Kyiv region. Our neighbors in Kyiv spent over 12 hours without electricity, heat, or running water. A power company representative said that 10-hour-long blackouts may become their new reality.

Our part of the region did get electricity on schedule, but one of our outlets showed a voltage of 340 V (instead of the required 220). That was concerning, so we unplugged our appliances to be safe. I was a bit frustrated that the hours with electricity had to be wasted, but we hope it was a wise decision.

Day 299 · December 19

We know Russians would love to see us miserable during this holiday season, so we are bracing ourselves for the upcoming attacks.

This is why this year, we honor the power engineers with special gratitude. All the technicians, electricians, and power station workers used to be invisible to us, but today we realize they are as heroic as those who defend our land with arms. They work 24/7, and they risk their lives, knowing that energy infrastructure is the primary target for the enemy, yet they do what they can to bring light into Ukrainian homes.

Day 302 · December 22

When Hope Felt Distant

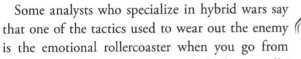

A season to cool: *Winter buries the memory of the hopes that we had planted with our tulip bulbs.*

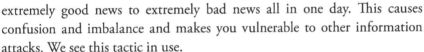

Some analysts who specialize in hybrid wars say that one of the tactics used to wear out the enemy is the emotional rollercoaster when you go from extremely good news to extremely bad news all in one day. This causes confusion and imbalance and makes you vulnerable to other information attacks. We see this tactic in use.

Today, the Security Service of Ukraine discovered another convoy of civilians shot by the Russians in the "gray zone" around September 26. Twenty-four victims, including 13 children and a pregnant woman. The people were driving from the temporarily occupied Svatove (Luhansk region) to the newly liberated Kupiansk (Kharkiv region) when they were shot to death at close range by a Russian sabotage and reconnaissance group.

May the Lord comfort all who mourn...

Day 220 · October 1

The Ukrainian army keeps advancing in the east. They find new bodies of people who went missing months ago during an attempted evacuation. They are also surprised by the number of victims among the enemy soldiers. They say that despite the heavy fighting in the area, such a great number of victims can only be explained by anti-retreat forces killing saboteurs and deserters and those who tried to flee from the battlefield. We've already heard about those barrier troops back in spring, which was also a common practice in the Soviet Red Army.

One day in the future, when someone thinks about writing a dystopian novel, they wouldn't need to spend much time coming up with wild ideas; it would be enough to read about Russia nowadays. Sending your citizens to invade another country and presenting it as a "sacred duty" and "self-defense." People protesting not against the unjust war or atrocities (they don't mind being a passive bystander) but against mobilization (so it's not about justice, just self-preservation). Thousands of people calling themselves "war refugees," yet there's no war in their country, and surprisingly very few women and children among the "refugees." Men running for their lives, leaving behind their women and children in the country run by a mad maniac. Pastors justifying illegal annexation and total mobilization with words, "Our president is our God-given king, and we must serve him." What an upside-down world they live in!

I keep reminding myself that nothing is impossible for God, and even Nineveh repented after all the committed atrocities when Jonah brought the message from the Lord. May the light of God's truth shine brightly in Russia and open up the eyes that refuse to see it. May the Lord restore His justice and avenge the innocent.

Day 221 · October 2

Also, new reports come from Mariupol and the occupied territories close to the Russian border. For a while, the only way for the people to get to the territory under Ukraine's control was to go through Russia, cross the border into Estonia, and continue their journey from there. It was a long and expensive trip, but it was the only way out for many. However, now there are reports of "filtration camps" set up by the Russians at the Estonian border, and people from Mariupol and the occupied territories must go through humiliating "filtration" and wait for days until they are let out of Russia. Also, with the great number of Russians leaving their country, the people from Ukrainian territories are told to wait and let them go first. I can't imagine how hopeless they must feel.

Day 223 · October 4

Today's morning was tough. Massive missile attack came in two waves all over Ukraine. They launched missiles from the air, the Black Sea, the temporarily occupied territories and sent kamikaze drones from the territory of Belarus. Overall, there were 84 missiles and 13 kamikaze drones targeting the critical infrastructure (mostly power stations) in 20 cities of Ukraine. Our air-defense forces did the impossible and downed 43 missiles and 10 kamikaze drones without modern air-defense complexes. God was gracious to us because an attack of such scale was unheard of. Unfortunately, 11 people were killed during the attack, and up to 100 were wounded.

Today, just like on February 24, the Kyiv metro stopped working, many businesses closed, schools told the kids to stay home, and people went into bomb shelters. People were checking on their friends and loved ones. Neighbors once again came together to help those in need. It was a powerful flashback, but there was a distinctive difference. In the bomb shelters, neighborhood chat groups, Facebook feed, you could see jokes, rage, annoyance, despisal, bitterness, but there was no room for fear. Don't get me wrong, we still worry for our loved ones, mourn the losses, and do our best to protect our children, but there's no paralyzing fear the enemy tried to cause. We were afraid in February, before the invasion, and in the morning of the 24th. We were afraid of the unknown, yet we knew Ukraine would resist.

Day 229 · October 10

Today wasn't an easy day.

We woke up to the news of Kyiv being bombed with Iranian-made kamikaze drones. Five explosions in the downtown area. One of them hit an apartment building, killing four people. Among the victims were a 6-months pregnant woman and her husband. This report made me feel sick with pain. However, one of the rescue workers said that had the drone hit the building a few meters to the left, all residents would have died. When I read that 37 of the 43 launched kamikaze drones were taken down by our air-defense forces, I felt like praising God despite the pain, for we can only imagine how much greater tragedy He has averted.

Day 236 · October 17

I trust that God is doing something great in people's hearts (not only in Ukraine but in the world). Yet today, we are broken, shattered, and puzzled. I dream that one day, He would reveal how all these puzzle pieces fit into His perfect picture. Until then, let us hold fast to His faithfulness.

Day 237 · October 18

We spent four hours without electricity today due to the rolling blackouts. It was (almost) fine until the beginning of the fourth hour when we lost cell phone reception (and internet) because the emergency battery on the telephone tower died. That's when I started feeling uneasy. Thankfully, the power and cell phone coverage were back almost according to the schedule.

As I was trying to cheer up our son tonight (he wasn't happy about the power outage), I explained that this was our share in fighting the enemy. I told him about many boys and girls who lived in bomb shelters without electricity for months and encouraged him to be thankful that we can stay in our warm house far from the active war zone. He was understanding, but he was upset, with tears in his eyes, and I had tears in my eyes for having to talk to our eight-year-old boy about war, something children shouldn't be familiar with.

Day 245 · October 26

Yesterday was the first time since the beginning of the full-scale war when I didn't post my daily update. We lost electricity around 4 pm, we lost cell phone and internet connection around 8 pm, and the power did not return until after midnight. At 8 am the power went out again.

Over the past 24 hours, we had electricity for a total of twelve hours but eight of them were at night.

Thankfully, our basic needs are not affected by the blackouts – we have a gas stove and a gas heater here. But the loss of means of communication is the greatest challenge for me. When you sit in the dark in complete isolation from the outside world, different thoughts start crawling into your mind, and only the "direct line" with God helps you not to believe your doubts and not to fall into despair. Last night's blackout made me realize what a tremendous privilege and support your prayers and encouragement have been throughout the past eight months.

We see the oppressive governments getting together and plotting even more evil. Yesterday, Saudi Arabia shared intelligence with the U.S. warning of an imminent attack from Iran on targets in the kingdom. In the beginning of this full-scale war, many governments were slow to support Ukraine because they were afraid it could start WWIII. Our diplomats kept crying out that it was the other way around, that if the evil is not stopped, if they see the helplessness and uselessness of international organizations, then other despotic governments will try to take advantage of the situation knowing that they can do what they will without any real consequences. We see that happening now, and once again we call on the world to act fast before it's too late.

I don't know if I will have electricity tonight for another daily update. Like my husband noticed this morning, the blackouts teach us to live in constant anticipation and are a good reminder of the Biblical encouragement from Matthew 24:44, "Therefore you also must be ready, for the Son of Man is coming at an hour you do not expect."

May we all be ready and found worthy at the time of His coming.

Day 251 • November 1

Please, keep praying for the occupied territories, especially the Kherson region. The occupiers kidnapped 34 children from the village of Preobrazhenka (Kherson region). The parents were promised that their children would go to the city of Anapa (Russia) for the alleged recreation and would return by the end of the week, but then the time of stay was extended again for another week. The Russian invaders deported 12 children from the Oleshky boarding school to Russian-occupied Crimea.

In total, as of October, since the beginning of the full-scale war, 8,732 Ukrainian children are considered deported to the Russian Federation, and 238 more are considered missing.

Lord, have mercy and pour out your judgment.

Day 255 • November 5

We've had an incredibly mild fall so far (the extended weather forecast promises no freezing temperatures until December). This weather favors our troops, men, and women who have to live in trenches. It also helps us save coal and gas needed for centralized heating. God is good.

We haven't had much news from the frontline, but there was some disturbing international news, and once again, I will say that the whole world is a battlefield. Russia is waging war on freedom, dignity, and truth. And Russia is not the only one. The world must stand up for the truth. Please, pray for God's victory in Ukraine and across the globe.

The disturbing news came from Iran – its parliament adopted a resolution calling for the death penalty for more than 14,000 detained during the protests. Pray for God's mercy. If we keep silent and find justifications for this, we side with evil. May the Lord show His power in Iran, and may many find Christ during these trials.

North Korea keeps siding with Russia. Its factories began mass sewing military uniforms for the Russian army from materials supplied by Russia. It may not seem a great help, and it does show Russia's inability to provide for the military, but it is disturbing to see tyrannical governments supporting each other.

Russia is trying hard to spread its propaganda far and wide. Rumors will be spread; respectable people will insist that "it's very unclear" and will try to offer simple solutions to complex problems. I pray that in this war for the minds, we will be responsible and guided by God's wisdom and His word, "Rejoice always, pray without ceasing, give thanks in all circumstances; for this is the will of God in Christ Jesus for you. [...] Test everything; hold fast what is good. Abstain from every form of evil" (1 Thessalonians 5:16-18, 21-22).

Day 258 · November 8

Today, we were blessed to have electricity according to the schedule (and even had a few extra hours throughout the day!). Interestingly, our joy was mixed with suspicion – why? what does it mean? will they overcompensate for it later? I was concerned by this attitude. It reminded me of the impression many missionaries shared from visiting Ukraine during or recently after the collapse of the Soviet Union: Grim faces of people who never smile and are always suspicious of your kindness. If you are kind, then you expect something in return. Those years under the communist regime took a toll on our nation's ability to experience joy to the fullest. You had to expect the worst and never rejoice too much. Many older people still keep this attitude despite the decades that have passed.

As I noticed this change in my attitude, I was made even more aware of the long-term consequences this war is going to have on our hearts. May we always be able to find the joy God wants us to have.

Day 268 · November 18

Another massive missile attack right now (day 283). Lots of explosions in Kyiv. Many areas of Ukraine (and even Moldova) without electricity. Our power also just went out and we're not sure when it will be back.

Please, pray for Ukraine.
Ironically, today the European Parliament passed the resolution recognizing Russia as a terrorist state.

Day 273 • November 23

Thirty-one years ago, on December 1, 1991, the people of Ukraine voted in a nationwide referendum to confirm the declaration of Ukraine's independence. Over 90% of citizens voted "yes" (including 54% in Crimea and 83% in the Donetsk and Luhansk regions), which became overwhelming proof of the right to Ukraine's existence in the eyes of the western governments. It was yet another restoration of justice. After World War I, when several European countries gained independence, Ukraine didn't have enough military power and international support to stand against the Russian empire and the Soviet Union. To be honest, the western governments weren't quite ready to accept the collapse of the Soviet Union, so this referendum became something they couldn't ignore, something that convinced them to recognize Ukraine as an independent state.

Back then, in 1991, Russia wasn't ready to fight for Ukraine (especially since Ukraine remained under its strong influence), so we gained independence in a bloodless way, but we are paying for it now.

Looking back at our history, we recognize that we have been suffering from Russia because of its thirst for power and its system of values. And we are well aware that until those change, Russia will remain a threat to us and the rest of the world.

We saw proof of that today when several Ukrainian diplomatic institutions, a US embassy in Spain, and a few Spanish institutions received envelopes with bombs or threats. It looks pathetic yet goes in line with other terrorist tactics used by Russia. We pray that no one will be shaken or dismayed by these threats but that they will only increase the support for Ukraine.

There was an hour-long air-raid warning today for all regions of Ukraine, which caused all of us to tense up, but we are grateful it passed without the missile attack. However, there were a few powerful explosions in Kherson. The Russians shoot aimlessly to get satisfaction from destroying the people who refuse to welcome them.

Day 281 • December 1

We had a strange day today with a very sporadic power supply (and internet connection). It was frustrating and exhausting as we've adjusted to the scheduled blackouts and were planning accordingly. I'm not complaining, we still managed to get things done, but it added to the general weariness.

I think I've shared before that one of the main challenges for me is the lack of the predictable. When you know what to expect, you plan and adjust. But our lives are far from predictable now, which leaves you second guessing every decision and feeling like you must be ready to act anytime.

'How long, o Lord?' seems to be the question I ask God the most. It feels like it would be easier to endure if we knew when it would be over. However, it doesn't work like this. And that's why I often think about faith.

Now faith is the assurance of things hoped for, the conviction of things not seen (Hebrews 11:1). Many of us know this verse, yet living by it is so much harder than just knowing it. And as you hope for the unseen, you also need to fight the overwhelming doubts and lies that crawl in quietly. It takes focus to remember the truth and to boldly proclaim it against the doubts.

In a childish way, I want to believe that God doesn't give away His timing just so that He could surprise us with unexpected victory sooner than expected. We also know that among the few tasks that are given to us as Christians is the command to keep watch and to be sober, "But since we belong to the day, let us be sober, having put on the breastplate of faith and love, and for a helmet the hope of salvation" (1 Thessalonians 5:8). Continuing in this image, faith and love can protect our heart as a breastplate, and the hope of salvation is the helmet that can protect our mind from doubts and despair.

May the Lord fill us with His faith, love, and hope so that we can stand strong in this battle.

Day 288 · December 8

Today's post mainly focused on international relations and made me think of the fragility of our world and the apparent peace. It reminded me of the domino tower my son built the other day – it may look glorious and impressive but can easily collapse if we are not careful with it.

Day 290 · December 10

When Ukraine didn't fall in three days, our hope started to grow. When the north of Ukraine was liberated in April (Kyiv, Chernihiv, and Sumy regions), we were reassured of our ability to drive the enemy away. When we see the massive support, we are confident that we will prevail over this evil. However, no one said it was going to happen soon. And this is the hardest thing to accept.

In a recent interview, the Commander-in-Chief of the Armed Forces of Ukraine, Valeriy Zaluzhnyi, said that Russia might be planning another massive invasion at the end of January or in February.[xxxviii] They could attempt to attack Kyiv once again, or they could attack from the territory of Belarus. This thought was also repeated by our Minister of Defense and the Minister of Foreign Affairs. I don't want to believe this is possible, but I know that Russia is still capable of causing a lot of damage. That's why Ukraine needs more ammunition, long-range rockets, and more air-defense systems. The enemy must be stopped.

We see preparations for another massive missile attack. The Russian Kalibr missile carrier is back in the Black Sea, and airplanes with Kalibr missiles were also spotted in Belarus. While we have almost recovered from the last missile attack, our power grid is still highly vulnerable, especially because of the weather conditions (snow, ice, and strong winds). We pray for God's protection.

Day 295 · December 15

In this war, the Russian army has killed 450 Ukrainian children, at least 863 were wounded, and 331 children are missing. They have forcefully deported 13,613 kids, of which 8,281 have been found, but only 121 have returned to Ukraine.

This is something we will never be able to forget. They are setting up the municipal Christmas tree in Kyiv with minimum decorations and a generator-powered illumination with a phone charging station next to it. Some schools decorate not only their hallways but also their bomb shelters for Christmas, as on days like yesterday, that's where children spend most of their time. Today, we long for the arrival of the Messiah, as He will surely put an end to this cruelty. What a blessing it is to know that Christmas is only a week away.

Day 297 · December 17

There are days when I don't know what to write here. It feels like all the words that fit have been used thousands of times over the past 300 days.

Someone wrote today that this year had only two months – January and the never-ending February. I guess that explains why we are so anxiously waiting for spring.

My son and I went for a stroll today. It was sunny and warm (too warm for December!). My son said this weather reminded him of Kyiv and a park we used to go to on weekends. He went on and on sharing his memories from home and dreaming (planning in every detail) about our return to Kyiv once the war is over. I was listening to him with tears in my eyes, dreaming of that day with him.

Day 308 · December 28

Defiance in the Face of Aggression

A season to grow: *In spite of the sometimes-returning onslaughts of fading winter, tulips start growing below the surface. This is a time of defiance and hope.*

Today I saw a picture that reminded me of hope and God's strength. The Russian missile landed in the field of sunflowers, yet did not explode and did not break the flowers. Russian threats and cruelty may land around us, yet they will not break our spirit.

Day 223 · October 4

After the horror stories from the liberated Bucha, we lost the fear because we realized that we are against the utmost evil, so there was no need to be afraid, but it was time to act, for God and truth were on our side. There isn't a single soul in Ukraine now who hasn't actively joined this war – we all, old and young, stand at our own frontlines, and we will keep on fighting to the end. They thought this massive attack would cause us to compromise and "seek a truce" with our murderers, but instead, it only made us more enraged, united, and determined.

Day 229 · October 10

There have been a few unlikely yet very symbolic events in this war. For example, you may remember a kitchen cabinet in a destroyed apartment building in Borodianka – the walls collapsed, but the kitchen cabinet was "hanging in there," with all of its contents intact and even an undamaged ceramic rooster on top of it.[xxxix] It became a symbol of Ukraine's fortitude.

Yesterday's attack gave us one more symbol. A few years ago, in 2019, they opened a new pedestrian and bicycle bridge over Saint Volodymyr Descent in Kyiv's downtown. It offers a beautiful panorama of the Dnipro River, and the fun part is that it has some glass floor panes, which you can walk over. Yesterday's missile hit right next to it, shattered protective panels, and left a massive crater at its base, but it did not break the bridge or harm its construction.[xl] It raised the spirits of many Ukrainians to see the bridge standing (especially since it happened days after the Russian Kerch bridge partially collapsed). Still, an even more beautiful and symbolic story behind it is that this pedestrian bridge was constructed with steel produced at the Azovstal Steel Plant in Mariupol. This fact brought forth a new Ukrainian axiom, "Azovstal (Mariupol) did not give in. The bridge did not give in. Ukraine will not give in. We all are made of Azovstal steel."

Day 230 · October 11

Some days are about thanking God for the small things.

This morning, Russia launched an air attack and hit a critical infrastructure object in the Kyiv region, which could mean emergency blackouts throughout the day. However, thanks to the willful decrease in energy consumption and the amazing work of those fixing the power lines, there was no need for the blackouts in the region.

Day 234 · October 15

There was a joke shared yesterday that government warnings have gone from "Please, do not panic" on February 24 to "Please, do not attempt to take down Russian drones on your own. Let the military do their job" today. And it is true. We are getting weary, yet we are getting more resolved.

Day 237 · October 18

I need to keep today's post short as we're out of electricity, and I have to type on my phone.

This morning, Russia hit Ukraine with 40 missiles and sixteen kamikaze drones. The Armed Forces of Ukraine shot down 20 enemy missiles and eleven drones. The missiles severely damaged energy and critical infrastructure facilities in the Volyn, Rivne, Kharkiv, Khmelnytskyi, Kirovohrad, Cherkasy, Zaporizhzhia, Odesa, and Mykolaiv regions. Most of Ukraine is experiencing rolling blackouts to lower the load on the working power stations. Some experts say today's damage may be even more significant than that caused by a massive attack on October 10.

"You will not fear the terror of the night, nor the arrow that flies by day, nor the pestilence that stalks in darkness, nor the destruction that wastes at noonday. A thousand may fall at your side, ten thousand at your right hand, but it will not come near you. You will only look with your eyes and see the recompense of the wicked" (Psalm 91:5-8).

Day 241 · October 22

Today's picture comes from the recently de-occupied Kharkiv region. A man who left his village during the occupation asked his neighbors to contact the Ukrainian soldiers and ask them to dig out the Ukrainian flags he hid in his garden before leaving his home. He knew he could be killed if seen with a Ukrainian flag, but he couldn't bear the thought of the invaders getting hold of the flags. To some, a flag may seem like just a piece of cloth, but it has become a prized possession for us as it represents what we are fighting for.

Day 257 · November 7

Thankfully, the power was back on this morning. So far, we mostly follow a 4-hour schedule (4 hours with electricity, 4 without) unless there is an emergency, such as yesterday. The Russians chose the tactic of damaging the key elements in our energy system that distribute and transport the power to the consumers. That increases the load on the working channels, which may lead to even greater damage. That's why we have to deal with the rolling and emergency blackouts. It's frustrating, but it's better than living under Russia.

The people of Kherson are a great testimony to that. For the third day in a row, they keep going into the city square to celebrate their liberation. They haven't had electricity, heat, running water, cell phone reception, or internet for a couple of weeks, yet it's nothing compared to the joy of liberation.

We are well aware of the great work still ahead of us. However, we can do it if we persevere in hope and set our eyes on the goal. I was reminded of it today when I read about a fundraising event organized in cooperation with the Ukrainian railroad company. They started selling tickets from Kyiv to the first three trains going to Kherson, Luhansk, Donetsk, Mariupol, and Simferopol (Crimea) once they are liberated and safe. The symbolic name of this fundraiser is "Train ride to victory." Over 1,000 tickets were sold in the first few hours. All proceeds will go to purchasing "last-mile vehicles" to help people from the areas in need of evacuation get to the nearest train

Buried flags - Day 257, November 7, 2022

station. I was struck by the faith of people purchasing the tickets, doing it as a prophetic act. Then I remembered how this spring we were purchasing zoo tickets to support the zoos (in Kyiv, Kharkiv, and Mykolaiv) while they couldn't invite the visitors.

Day 263 · November 13

It was the largest missile attack since the beginning of the full-scale war. Russia launched over 90 missiles and ten kamikaze drones. Our air-defense forces shot down 80% of the missiles and all of the drones. However, the remaining missiles did cause significant damage. Almost all regions were hit.

According to some reports, a missile or its fragment crossed the Polish border and killed two people. The official reports are yet to come.

We haven't had electricity for the past ten hours (first due to the scheduled blackout, then due to the missile attack). We got power back for about 20 minutes, and it was a literal glimpse of hope but there's no electricity at the moment (10 pm, Tuesday night).

While we were sitting in the dark, not knowing the news (the battery on the local cell phone tower died after an extended blackout), we were nervous, but we chose to stay positive. So, we celebrated Russia's demise (that is yet to happen) with hot dogs and traditional Ukrainian songs.

We may sit in the dark for a few hours, but it's better than having the darkness consume our inner being.

Day 265 · November 15

On days like this it's hard to come up with words. All of them seem inadequate. My mind refuses to process the brutality we've been living in for the past nine months.

This morning started with a report on a shelling of a maternity hospital in Vilniansk of the Zaporizhzhia region. A newborn baby was killed, and the mom and a doctor suffered injuries.

In the afternoon, we went through yet another massive missile attack. About 70 missiles were launched (30 of them targeting Kyiv), yet by the grace of God our air-defense forces intercepted 51 missiles and five enemy drones.

I wonder what the people doing it are thinking. I wonder what the ones cheering them on are thinking. They may be rejoicing now, but they don't understand that we will come out of these trials even more resilient, and they will have to be held accountable for every wicked deed they committed or supported.

Russia threw at us millions of dollars seeking blood and terror, but this money could have been spent on the needs of the vulnerable people in Russia. They could choose to create, instead, they chose to destroy. So, it is even more amazing to see how fast our miracle workers are restoring power and energy supply (they expect to have all temporary solutions in place by morning).

As I'm writing this post, we have no connection to the outside world except for the radio. I am listening to the 10 pm news, and as the anchor talks to the reporters from various regions of Ukraine, he asks them if there was any panic. Honestly, I am not surprised to hear that there was no panic in the stores, pharmacies, or gas stations. Our people have been trained well by our "loving brotherly neighbor." The only extraordinary thing was slightly longer lines of people getting on buses since the underground metro stations were used as shelters, and the trams and trolley-buses had to stop because of the blackout.

Over 2,750 "Stations of the Unbreakable" have been set up throughout the country. They will have generators, heaters, internet connection, water and hot meals available. We will come together and we will not be broken. The sun will come out in the morning. We will restore the power stations and we will emerge from this challenge weary, sorrowful, but victorious and standing strong. And the terrorists who are trying to destroy us will have to live with their shame until they repent, and we can only pray that their children and grandchildren will want to live differently.

May the Lord help us to be unashamed of our choices.

It looks like our energy system has passed the critical condition and has almost recovered its pre-attack capacity. Our hours without electricity today mostly followed the schedule of the rolling blackouts. Praise God!

The situation in Kyiv and other big cities is more serious – many city districts are still without electricity, internet, or cell phone reception today. However, it's incredible to see people coming together against this evil. Our neighbors in our apartment building in Kyiv shared tips on how to cook a meal in 40 minutes (that's the amount of time they had electricity for this morning). One neighbor said he woke up at night for a drink of water and saw his wife cooking borscht at 2 am because the power was back on, and she didn't want to waste time.

Another neighbor set up a power outlet in the common hallway and invited neighbors to come over and charge their devices when he runs his generator. The neighbors from the bottom floors invited the residents of the top floors to come over and get water from their faucets since the pressure is not enough to pump the water to the top floor during the blackouts.

Businesses with generators let people use any socket they can find for charging their devices. Restaurants invited people for a free cup of hot tea and a quick charge of their devices. A large internet store turned its order pickup stations into resilience hubs with free Wi-Fi, hot beverages, and charging stations.

I hope that as time passes, we will remember this solidarity and kindness in the face of evil. They will not break us as long as we remember to love each other. "A new commandment I give to you, that you love one another: just as I have loved you, you also are to love one another. By this all people will know that you are my disciples, if you have love for one another" (John 13:34-35).

Day 275 · November 25

We learn to plan our lives around the hours with electricity – that's when we do the dishes, take a shower or work, and it doesn't matter if it's the middle of the night or the early morning hours. At least we have heat and a gas stove here – a luxury unavailable to many Ukrainians.

I caught myself thinking that these days in anticipation of another massive attack and a possible total blackout reminded me of us expecting the invasion. Back then, we knew it was inevitable, we knew we had to prepare, but there was no way to know when it would happen and whether we'd manage to finish our preparations. I know that the enemy wants us to live in fear of a total blackout, and I can't help but feel anxious, wondering if we're prepared enough and hoping for the attack to come later in the week so that we are more prepared. Perhaps it's the accumulated stress speaking, or maybe that's the weakness of my flesh, because my spirit is willing to trust in God's mercy and grace. He's been faithful throughout the past nine months, and I have no reason to doubt Him now. May He shield our skies, our homes, our power lines, and our soldiers.

"The light shines in the darkness, and the darkness has not overcome it" (John 1:5).

Day 279 · November 29

Just think of the scale of destruction, which only includes the tangible things we can restore. We've already lost many irretrievable art and historical objects, and we keep losing our most precious asset – our people. Yet we are ready to persevere, knowing this winter will be harsh for us but hoping it will be the last winter for Russia in its current state.

Day 284 · December 4

This morning Russia sent 76 missiles at Ukraine (40 of them were aimed at Kyiv). Thankfully, 60 of them were shot down by our air-defense forces (37 out of those coming at Kyiv). However, the remaining rockets hit critical energy system infrastructure, which caused the loss of 50% of power generation. All of Ukraine goes into emergency mode. Many regions are in a complete blackout, and there's no running water in Kyiv because of the attack.

We haven't had electricity since 8 am (it's almost 4 pm now), and we don't know when it will return. We also didn't have any connection, but our internet went back just now (we hope it will last), but we may be out of range for a day or even longer.

The terrorists think they can break us into submission, but these attacks only make us yearn for justice, victory, and the complete defeat of Russia. May the Lord be with us.

Day 296 · December 16

Today is the winter solstice, the longest night of the year, after which days start getting longer. Even though it will take weeks to notice any difference, I am rejoicing today because the bleak and dreary days will soon be over. This astronomical phenomenon made me think of our present situation. Ukraine has been going through this longest night of the year for the past 10 months, and even though it will take weeks (or months, to be more realistic) to see our future getting brighter, I believe the inevitable change has already taken place, and with every passing moment we are approaching our victory.

However, we know there is still plenty of darkness ahead of us. Almost 60% of power transformers in and around Kyiv are destroyed, so people get only 2-4 hours of electricity a day, and some districts have had no electricity since the attack on December 19. We can only pray for protection from further attacks.

To show support for Ukraine, over 90 locations around the world participated in the #LightUpUkraine appeal today. This campaign is part of a $10m fundraising drive for generators for hospitals across war-torn Ukraine. In a symbolic act of support for Ukraine, the Christmas lights and regular illuminations were turned off for an hour in London, Paris, New York, Sydney, Warsaw, Prague, Edinburgh, Liverpool, Reykjavik, Sofia, Ottawa, Helsinki, and other cities. You may think it is just a symbolic turning off of lights, but my heart swells with gratitude for this show of solidarity. Thank you, dear friends, for thinking about us and praying for us.

Day 301 · December 21

This morning started with yet another massive missile attack. They began in the middle of the night with kamikaze drones that had to determine the locations of our air defense and allow for the missile attack adjustment. Our air-defense forces shot down 54 missiles (out of 69) and 11 drones. Ten regions of Ukraine suffered from the attack.

One of the missiles was shot down over our city district in Kyiv. The debris destroyed a private house, and they say smaller shards were found in our neighborhood. Ivan also heard one of the missiles going over the (relatively safe) place we are staying in (interestingly, you learn to discern the sounds of missiles and airplanes).

We praise God once again that Russia failed to achieve its goals with this attack. Our part of the Kyiv region got electricity according to the schedule, and even though the attack did cause damage, our power engineers were able to manage it. It's yet another miracle. We praise Him for every rocket shot down and for every life spared.

Day 309 · December 29

Celebration,
While Aware of the Costs

A season to bloom: *The crowning season for the tulips arrives as their flowers reach to the sky. But celebration is vulnerable – the tulip has used huge amounts of the bulb's resources in the hope of future goodness.*

Last night, I wrote about the Russian troops being almost surrounded in Lyman (Donetsk region). Today, the Armed Forces of Ukraine entered the city. Many Russian soldiers were taken captive, and many fled the city, leaving their weapons behind. Our army acquired their tanks and ammunition. May all who seek you rejoice and be glad in you! May those who love your salvation say evermore, "God is great!" (Psalm 70:4).

Today I saw a video that gives me goosebumps. Psalm 91 (90 in some Ukrainian translations) has become a daily prayer of many Ukrainian soldiers and civilians. In this video, the Ukrainian servicemen pray before going on a mission:

⚘ I will protect him, because he knows my name.
When he calls to me, I will answer him;
I will be with him in trouble;
I will rescue him and honor him.

⚘ With long life I will satisfy him
and show him my salvation.
(Psalm 91:14-16)

Meanwhile, Ukrainian troops are also advancing in the south. Today, they reported the liberation of two towns in the Kherson region. The Russian army is fleeing in fear, especially after the reports of recent successful operations in Izium and Lyman. But the enemy is still strong and vicious. Please, keep praying for the miracles and the powerful hand of the Lord over our land.

Day 221 · October 2

There was news today that warmed my heart and stirred up hope. The leaders of Azovstal (Mariupol) defenders, who were miraculously released from Russian captivity and will remain in Turkey until the end of the war, finally got to see their families. This is one of God's miracles, inspiring us to keep praying and believing.

Day 222 · October 3

Our army has liberated eight towns and villages in the south (Kherson region). Some experts say that our troops move with incredible speed. May the Lord's army go before them.

Day 223 · October 4

We praise God for the advances of our army. The Russian troops run in fear for their lives, leaving behind their wounded friends and ammunition. The Armed Forces of Ukraine have already captured 460 Russian battle tanks, 92 self-propelled howitzers, 448 infantry fighting vehicles, 195 armored fighting vehicles, and 44 rocket launchers. We pray for all Russian weapons to malfunction and turn against those who plan evil.

Day 224 · October 5

Today, the enemy attacked Zaporizhzhia again, and a couple of hours ago, they hit Kharkiv downtown with missiles, which led to a fire in one of the healthcare institutions.

While processing this news, I realized what angers me the most. I mean, all of it is wrong, no city should be attacked, and no people deserve to be hiding from bombs and wake up to terror in the middle of the night. Still, the cruelest aspect of these attacks on Kharkiv, Zaporizhzhia, and Dnipro is that those cities are relatively close to the front lines, which means they've become home to the people trying to escape the war and occupation but not having enough courage to go far from home. Zaporizhzhia has been the hub for refugees from Mariupol, Melitopol, Berdiansk, and the southeast of Ukraine. Dnipro welcomes people from the Donetsk region and those going through

Zaporizhzhia who are willing to move just a little further away from the war zone. It's also a city with many military hospitals where wounded soldiers are treated. Kharkiv, having withstood many attacks throughout the past seven months, keeps living and accepting people from the occupied parts of the Kharkiv and Luhansk regions. I believe the enemy chose these cities not just because of their proximity to the front line and strategic significance but also to terrorize further the people who've already been through hell. May the Lord stop the enemy and protect the innocent.

I know that many of you remember the story of the four-year-old from Mariupol, her mom was detained at the filtration camp during evacuation. Some of you were asking if there was any news from them. According to the Deputy Head of the Zaporizhzhia region, Alisa's mom was allowed to call the girl on her birthday. She remains in captivity; her most probable location is Olenivka (the same detention center that was used for a terrorist attack on Ukrainian POWs a few weeks ago). Please pray for her mom and thousands of other POWs and their families.

Day 226 · October 7

This morning we woke up to amazing news – the Kerch Bridge (the illegal bridge constructed to connect Crimea to Russia) partially collapsed because of an explosion. There are no details on who is responsible for it, but we rejoice in the fact for two reasons.

First of all, Russia spent a lot of money and took pride in that bridge, and bragged about its safety, so this is a massive punch in the gut of Russian morale.

However, the Kerch bridge is crucial for Russia's military operations in southern Ukraine. It was used to transport weapons and ammunition to Crimea, so its destruction also means breaking logistical chains and aiding our troops in the Kherson region.

Day 227 · October 8

Today, the attacks continued. The morning air-raid warning lasted for over five hours. Thousands of people have to deal with rolling blackouts to help our energy system cope with the load after the damage caused by the Russian missiles. The situation in the Lviv region is critical. The city and most of the region were left without electricity all day yesterday, and there were repeated hits on the power stations there today.

However, we see God's goodness. This morning, Ukraine was attacked with 28 missiles, and 20 were shot down by our air-defense forces. They also took down most of the kamikaze drones. It is incredible, and we praise God and thank you for covering us with your prayers.

Today, 32 Ukrainian POWs returned home after a prisoner swap. Ukraine has also managed to track down and get back 37 children who had been deported to Russia. The children are now reunited with their families.

Day 230 · October 11

One of the Ukrainian TV channels reported a large group of recently mobilized Russian soldiers getting in touch with the Ukrainian side and surrendering to the authorities.[xli] They were sent to fight without a boot camp, warm clothes, or ammunition but with lots of empty promises and a threat to be shot if they chose to retreat. To save their lives, they killed their commander and surrendered to the Ukrainian armed forces.

We hear some amazing stories from people who survived the missile attacks on Monday. A man who walks on the Glass Bridge every morning was there at the time of the attack and was even captured by the surveillance cameras. He is unharmed and even joking about the incident. A father and son took a detour that morning on the way to preschool and avoided getting hit by the missile debris. A military chaplain whose morning jogging route passes not one but four (!) of the locations hit by the missiles was running late that morning, which saved his life.

The bees have neutralized a boobytrap in Babyntsi (Kyiv region). It has been reported that the Russians booby trap most mass grave sites and anything you can see in the de-occupied territories. Back in March, they set a booby trap in a beehive in Babyntsi village. The beehive owner returned only now, and when he opened the hive, he saw two hand grenades covered with honey and bee wax which prevented them from detonating. I get goosebumps from such stories when you clearly see the hand of God.

Day 232 · October 13

The Ukrainian army keeps advancing in the Kherson region. In a recently de-occupied Velyka Oleksandrivka, they found a large ammunition depot (over 500 artillery shells and over 100 anti-tank guided missiles and anti-tank mines).

We praise God for His protection today, on the day of the defenders of Ukraine. We pray for our defenders – the men and women in the Armed Forces of Ukraine, the National Guard of Ukraine, the Security Service of Ukraine, the volunteer battalions, the volunteers, the emergency services, rescue teams, doctors, teachers, diplomats, every Ukrainian who does everything in their power to defend Ukraine, and for our brothers and sisters from abroad who stand with us.

Day 233 · October 14

The brightest highlight of the day was the news of another POW swap. 108 women were released from Russian captivity, including the mother of 4-year-old, for whom many of you were praying. It's so incredible that I praised God through tears of joy.

Day 236 · October 17

After the past few days with numerous air-raid sirens and rolling blackouts, today felt like a true day of rest. Praise God, we had no power outages today! Honestly, it felt suspicious, and we spent the whole day wondering when the power would go off. But it never did, so we enjoyed the luxury of electricity that we promise not to take for granted.

Today, there was another POW swap, and 52 Ukrainians were finally able to return home. Every person in Russian captivity goes through hell, so we rejoice and celebrate every person released and keep praying for all POWs to return home.

Day 248 · October 29

It's the end of the day, and we've lost electricity for only four hours today. Wow! God is good! We learn to appreciate these simple things. We are becoming even more aware that the reality of war is still different for everyone, and what only recently became a challenge to me had already become mundane for those in Kharkiv or Mykolaiv. My Facebook feed and neighborhood messenger groups consist of stories related to the blackouts, yet there is no whining. Instead, people seem genuinely amused by their own flexibility and share newly found survival lifehacks. Last night, when our son complained about the blackout because he couldn't watch a cartoon or listen to his audiobook, we reminded him that it was not a need but a privilege, so he had to be grateful for having his needs covered and needed to look for other ways to entertain himself. A couple of hours later, I had to remind myself of my own words - be grateful for having your basic needs covered, especially since what you have now is already a privilege to many in Ukraine.

As our days get even more unpredictable, we are reminded to turn to God. May He use these tribulations for His glory.

Day 252 · November 2

Praise the Lord! He is the God of wonders. His works are incredible, and His ways are amazing. I am weeping with tears of joy, trying to make sense of everything that happened today.

Last night, I wrote my post about the liberation of the Mykolaiv region and asked you to pray for our army's advances toward Kherson. In a bit more than 12 hours, the first Ukrainian forces entered Kherson. The liberated area went from 260 square kilometers to over 3,000 square kilometers in a matter of hours! With the approach of our army, the people flooded the streets of the city, pulling off anything with a Russian symbol and setting up Ukrainian flags. They were singing Ukrainian songs in the city squares, cheering for our army, crying tears of relief, and finally seeing their hopes fulfilled. Kherson was among the cities occupied in the first week of the invasion, but they continued holding anti-Russian rallies for over a month until it became extremely dangerous. Seeing those people hugging our soldiers, crying, and repeating, "We knew you would come! Please, don't leave us again!" gave me goosebumps.

I guess it will be a while until we learn the details of this liberation operation. However, one report reminded me of Old Testament events when the enemy was confused and blinded by the Lord.^{xlii} According to the report, the Russians were deceived, thinking the Ukrainian army had surrounded Kherson and gained control over the Kakhovka dam. Terrified of this possibility, the Russians on the left bank started shooting at the group on the right bank of the Dnipro River. Meanwhile, the group on the right bank thought Ukrainians were attacking them from the left bank, so they started shooting back. This friendly fire lasted almost an hour, and hundreds of Russians were killed until they realized what was happening.

"Do not be afraid and do not be dismayed at this great horde, for the battle is not yours but God's" (2 Chronicles 20:15).

While we rejoice, we can't help but feel "the other side" of this liberation. We are painfully aware of the hundreds, if not thousands, of people who gave their lives to make it happen. We are mentally preparing ourselves for the unveiling of the atrocities that took place there during the occupation. We keep praying for the rest of the Kherson region still under occupation. Imagine what it's like knowing that Ukrainian forces are on the other riverbank yet unable to change anything. We pray for God's protection upon our military as they prepare to de-mine and inspect every inch of the liberated territory. Thousands of Russians remain on the right bank of the Dnipro River (mostly dispersed, hiding, and dressed as civilians) and may sabotage or attack our troops and civilians.

We brace ourselves, realizing that the terrorist revenge will come soon and that retaliation will most likely include attacks on the civilian infrastructure all over Ukraine. We pray for our troops in all other locations, especially around Bakhmut and Soledar. The intensity of the fighting is extreme there, and our troops desperately need ammunition and God's protection. Today was a historic day for Ukraine, but we know that our army couldn't do it on its own. That's why today, on the traditional Armistice Day, we thank all veterans who stand with Ukraine and share their experience for our victory. We also join Poland in celebrating its Independence Day. Thank you for opening your doors and hearts to our people, and thank you for standing with us. Za naszą i waszą wolność (For our freedom and yours)

Day 261 · November 11

We were blessed today to have the blackouts according to the announced schedule. However, we don't know what tomorrow may hold.

Back in the summer of 2014, when the war was limited to the east of Ukraine, an airliner MH17 was shot down over Russian-controlled territory, killing 298 people who were on board. Today, the District Court of Hague recognized that Russia controlled the so-called "DNR" at the time of the downing of the plane and sentenced three executors to life imprisonment in absentia.

Day 267 · November 17

Our days for the past (almost) nine months have been one long rollercoaster ride. We all feel dizzy and cannot wait for this ride to be over. Tonight, the enemy forces shelled the city of Zaporizhzhia, hitting a critical industrial object. People may still be buried under the debris. Over half the city lost electricity and heat.

This evening, the first train with about 200 passengers left for the recently liberated Kherson. We want to believe that one day soon, we will have trains going to the liberated and restored Luhansk, Donetsk, Mariupol, and Crimea. While we rejoice for Kherson, we remember that a large portion of the Kherson region remains under occupation. We pray for their protection and liberation.

Our news (and my reports) often focus on the parts of the frontline with new developments, and it is easy to overlook the incredible endurance of our soldiers fighting in the east of Ukraine. Bakhmut has been the location of the fiercest battles for the past three months. Even experienced veterans say they have never seen anything like that - the intensity of the fighting, the extent of the losses, the unyielding resolve of our soldiers not to give the enemy even the tiniest bit of our land. May Bakhmut be the new victory of our army, and may the enemy army flee in fear.

We had the first real snow of the season. Our son was squealing with excitement, but we kept thinking about our soldiers freezing in the trenches, about those who lost their homes in the enemy attacks, and those who kept their homes but were left without electricity and heat. Who knew that snow could bring up so many thoughts?

Day 268 · November 18

Last night and this morning, there were a few important online calls we needed to make, but we had no electricity or cell phone reception. Just as we were getting ready to get in the car and drive around searching for an internet connection, the power went back on as we were putting our shoes on. Those times felt like gentle, loving presents from God, His reminder that He is in control, and He cares for us. I am in awe whenever I realize that the great Maker of the Universe is small enough to know my heart.[xliii]

Every evening, praying at bedtime, I thank God for keeping our loved ones and us safe.

Day 280 · November 30

In the spirit of God's mysterious ways, let me share an amazing story of His faithfulness. A couple of weeks ago, I received a message request from someone I didn't know, a fellow sister in Christ from Puerto Rico. She wrote that we had mutual friends and asked if we had any needs and how they could pray for us. It was around the time of one of the massive missile attacks, so I shared my anxieties and asked her to pray for God to provide for us a way to stay here in the village despite the possible blackout.

To cut a long story short, fast forward a couple of weeks. I received another message from her, in which she shared the desire to share our story with her church and collect an offering for us. Around the same time, we learned about a family here in the village. The elderly husband has a chronic lung disease and depends on oxygen pumped by a ventilator. During prolonged blackouts (on some nights, we have over 8 hours without electricity), he suffers greatly, and his wife anxiously prays at his bedside. Ivan immediately felt God told him he had to help this family. He got in touch with their son, and they found a power station that could power the ventilator for at least a couple of hours during the extended blackouts. At the time, they didn't have the money for the power station, and neither did we, but we knew that God must have a plan. Imagine our amazement when the next day we received a money transfer from the Puerto Rico church, which was the exact amount needed for the power station! It was such a powerful reminder that God is in control and that we are united into His body here on earth, so it is not unusual for Him to urge a family in Puerto Rico to collect a church offering to bless an unsuspecting family in a small village in Ukraine. It was a great testimony to that family, and the wife of the sick man keeps saying that she wants to kneel and thank the kind people and God who gave her husband a chance to live.

I believe that this was just the first of the amazing Christmas miracles we are going to see this year.

Day 293 · December 13

Over 30 countries have publicly announced the provision of support for the energy system of Ukraine, and now add here the unannounced aid coming from kind people from all over the world. Russia's attempt at degenerating life in Ukraine generated solidarity and support for Ukraine instead. Indeed, "you meant evil against me, but God meant it for good, to bring it about that many people should be kept alive, as they are today" (Genesis 50:20).

Inspired by this news, I keep praying Psalm 144 over every nation and every family who chooses to respond with kindness and mercy to the trials we experience today:

❧ May [your] sons in their youth
be like plants full grown,
[your] daughters like corner pillars
cut for the structure of a palace;

❧ may [your] granaries be full,
providing all kinds of produce;
may [your] sheep bring forth thousands
and ten thousands in our fields;

❧ may [your] cattle be heavy with young,
suffering no mishap or failure in bearing;
may there be no cry of distress in [your] streets!

❧ Blessed are the people to whom such blessings fall!
Blessed are the people whose God is the Lord!

Day 294 · December 14

Today, the Russian army shelled a maternity hospital in Kherson. We were deeply shocked when they did the same thing in Mariupol back in March. We shouldn't be surprised now, but we are infuriated. Thankfully, no one got hurt in today's shelling. Two babies were born in that maternity hospital today. In fact, the doctors had just finished a c-section shortly before the attack. Even in the cruel crime, we can see God in the details.

One of Russia's plans (and a pillar of domestic propaganda) was to make Europe freeze this winter. That was the plan behind the attacks on the critical infrastructure of Ukraine. However, this plan was crushed by natural phenomena. While some of my dear friends suffer from unusually low temperatures, we've had an unusually warm winter. The forecast for New Year's Day is +10°C (50 F). The higher temperatures also decrease electricity consumption, which allows for shorter scheduled blackouts. The power company even said that we might have a couple of days with electricity for the New Year celebration if no new attacks take place. We keep hoping and praying.

Day 307 • December 27

Loss and Lament

A season to regenerate: *Far too quickly are the days of the beautiful flowers gone. The tulip begins to replenish its stores under the ground. This stage is not lovely to look at, but if the stage is cut short, tulips are at risk of dying.*

Early this morning, there was a missile attack on the downtown of Zaporizhzhia; seven people were killed, and five are still missing (they could be buried under the rubble). It makes me sick how they go from one city to another, bringing death and destruction, but I know that they will not prevail.

Day 225 · October 6

Please, pray for Zaporizhzhia. I am losing count of the number of times the enemy has attacked the city with missiles. Last night, at around 2 am, missiles hit residential buildings killing at least 13 people and leaving over 60 injured. The rescue operation continues, and more people may be found in the debris.

This night again, at around 2 am, another missile attack on Zaporizhzhia (as many as ten missiles reported). The consequences are to be announced later.

Please, uphold the people of Zaporizhzhia in your prayers. Terrorism is Russia's last resort, but at least we hope the world would recognize them for who they are and stop offering compromises with murderers and terrorists.

Day 228 · October 9

Russia keeps attacking Kharkiv, Zaporizhzhia, and Mykolaiv as the cities closest to the front lines. In one of the recent attacks, the missiles hit an apartment building in Mykolaiv, burying the residents under the debris. The rescue team found an eleven-year-old boy who spent six hours under the rubble, but the boy died at the hospital.

Day 232 · October 13

Lately, all of my thoughts are consumed with the Kherson region. I have mentioned before that that region has a special place in my heart. That's where my dad was born, where his mother lived and where some of his distant relatives live today. Growing up, I heard many towns mentioned over and over again, so I learned to love them even though I had never been there.

Beryslav is one of those towns. It is the oldest settlement in the Kherson region and was the southernmost customs point in the Grand Duchy of Lithuania (late 4th century). It is located on the right bank of the Dnipro River, across from Kakhovka. A bit lower down the river is the Kozatske settlement, where my grandma grew up. It's the site of Prince Trubetskoy's winery and mansion. It is located on the Nova Kakhovka hydropower plant (HPP) dam. And if you go further down the river, there is a tiny village Lvove, where I spent the first year of my life as my parents were sent there on a job assignment. Honestly, I've visited those places only once (when I was a teenager), but they feel like a large part of me, especially now.

Today, those places are under occupation. However, there are reports that all occupational authorities have ceased operations in Beryslav, and collaborators are leaving the city en masse. In the Kherson region, the occupiers loot homes, hospitals, supermarkets, etc., stealing whatever happens to be on their way.

There are high risks of the Nova Kakhovka HPP being blown up by the retreating Russian army as they have mined everything around it. Some experts say that blowing up the HPP is illogical because it would mainly harm the Russians (and the temporarily occupied Crimea).

Day 240 · October 21

Meanwhile, the Russian troops keep leveling Bakhmut with the ground, and a Russian media outlet incites genocide.[xliv] One presenter said children who criticized Russia should have been drowned. Alternatively, he said, they could be shoved into huts and burned. In a short segment shared on social media, he also laughed at reports that Russian soldiers had raped elderly Ukrainian women during the invasion.

Day 242 · October 23

Today's pictures show our beautiful Kyiv before the Russian invasion and now in energy-saving mode. I almost cried when I saw these pictures, yet someone pointed out on the internet, "The Russians naively thought they could take away our light. They can't do it, for we are the light, and the light is within us!"

Jesus spoke to them, saying, "I am the light of the world. Whoever follows me will not walk in darkness, but will have the light of life" (John 8:12).

Day 243 · October 24

The story that broke my heart today is about an eight-year-old from Bakhmut. His parents died when the city was heavily shelled. His mom was seven-months pregnant. He was left alone with his dog in a completely destroyed city district. He somehow got to the city, and the police officers somehow learned about him and organized a rescue operation. They had to walk on foot for a certain part of their route. Now, he is safe, and his aunt will take care of him. His name means "given by God," and this story of a dozen "coincidences" proves it correct.

Day 244 · October 25

Today, Ukraine was able to retrieve 107 POWs. Most of them were defending Azovstal in Mariupol. Many were wounded back in spring, received close to no medical care in captivity and are in a critical condition now. Please, pray for their complete restoration – physical, emotional, and spiritual.

Amid the heavy and terrifying reports about being a POW in a Russian prison, there is a bright star of hope. Some of the Ukrainian soldiers from the Azov steelworks in Mariupol have become Christians in Russian captivity. This was reported by a pastor after his trip to Ukraine where he met two fighters from Mariupol. They shared about their experience and said they managed to get a copy of the Holy Scriptures, even though this request was not granted immediately. Eventually, some of the men had a conversion experience, the pastor said. He was unable to find out how many made a decision of faith, he said: "I was told there were many."[xlv] We know that our God is the God who goes after His sheep, and we praise Him that the prison walls cannot stop Him.

Day 253 · November 3

We've noticed a pattern – the Russians carry out a massive attack on Monday, things get crazy, and by Friday you have figured out a few solutions

Kyiv in the dark - Day 243, October 24, 2022

and are mostly used to the new reality. The worst part is that now you start anticipating the attacks. Oh, how I long for the day when we won't need to think about those... How I hate that we learned to think about air-raid sirens, blackouts, and the possibility of a nuclear strike...

Over the past few days, I had a few conversations with people who had to leave Ukraine and seek refuge abroad. We may be tempted to think they got an easy way out while they go through as many challenges as we do in Ukraine – the feeling of being plucked out from your home, the uncertainty in a foreign land, the dependence on the government of the host country, the longing to be with your loved ones who stayed behind, feeling alienated and powerless to help. Many Ukrainians abroad experience these feelings at various times. Add to that the fact that oftentimes it is just the mother and her kids (because their father cannot leave Ukraine). Imagine living through this experience as a teenager when life is hard as it is only now you don't have your close friends or favorite spots to share it with. Please, pray for God's comfort and healing for those who had to leave Ukraine but whose hearts stayed here.

Day 254 • November 4

One of the hardest things for me is the total loss of control and complete unpredictability of life. It can be good because it teaches us to trust God, yet it is draining.

Kyiv city authorities discussed the possibility of a total blackout if the attacks continue. They advise the population on preparation, develop evacuation plans (for a city of 3 million people!), and try to think of possible solutions. And we are left with all the questions – will it come to that? If it does, how long will it last? If we lose electricity, will we at least have cell phone reception to keep in touch with our loved ones? There are more questions than answers.

At the same time, Ukraine's energy company announced that the expected energy deficit in Kyiv tomorrow will be 30% more than the scheduled rolling blackouts can cover. This means the blackouts may last longer and cover more districts. After this announcement, I wonder if the expected energy deficit will result from the expected massive missile attack on Ukraine (the Monday morning "tradition" the Russians love so much). We don't know if those prolonged blackouts will also include our area. We've had the blessing of scheduled blackouts for the past four days and learned to plan our days around them.

Day 256 • November 6

Today, a train left from Kyiv to Mykolaiv – this is the first train since February 24. I don't know the number of people who used this train or needed it, but I know this event is highly significant. It symbolizes the return of a semblance of normal, and we pray for the day when the "normal" returns to Ukraine's land, especially the territories that have been under occupation since 2014.

Today was an important day as the UN General Assembly called for Russia to be held accountable for its conduct in Ukraine, voting to approve a resolution recognizing that Russia must be responsible for making reparations to the country. The importance of this resolution is that it establishes the need to "undo the wrong," which is a God-given principle of ransom. We are looking forward to the day when justice is restored.

We are also hoping for justice when we hear that over 11,000 children have been forcefully taken to Russia since the beginning of the invasion, and these are only the children whose names are known. So far, Ukraine has been able to find and bring back only 69 children. The rest may be put up for adoption or sent to orphanages throughout Russia. The total number of Ukrainians deported by Russia is over 1.6 million.

Day 264 • November 14

With the holiday season approaching, I have mixed feelings. On the one hand, we need to cherish all moments of joy. Afterall, what can be a greater reason for joy than Christmas? Yet it is hard to celebrate when you think about those who won't be able to feel festive. I remembered the initiative that makes sure that the children of the soldiers who gave their lives defending Ukraine get presents from St. Nicholas (a traditional Ukrainian holiday season figure who brings gifts on the morning of December 19). Each child can write a letter to St. Nicholas asking for a gift, and they do their best to make the dreams come true. They started the initiative in 2017, and this year the number of children in their care significantly increased because of all the lives lost since the beginning of the full-scale war. If you want to support this initiative, I will leave their information in the comments.

Day 269 • November 19

Since February 24, Russia has launched at Ukraine 4,000 missiles of various types. Unfortunately, they still have enough missiles to make our lives miserable. The missile attacks change nothing in the military sense at the front lines and have no other purpose other than terrorizing civilians. More missile attacks are expected this week. Please, pray for the protection of our people, for the power and connection to be restored as soon as possible. Pray for those who depend on the power supply – bedridden patients on ventilators, people undergoing surgery, the miners trapped underground, and so many others. Also, as Russia has fewer high-precision missiles, they go for less precision, which may cause more damage to civilians as the missile deviates from the initial target.

Russia may be preparing to deport over 10,000 Ukrainian children from the Luhansk region. They announced a health inspection and created a list of children "in need of special healthcare." That's the scheme they used on other occupied territories. The children from the list are taken to Russian territory, and then they come up with made-up reasons why the children cannot return home until their parents come to pick them up. Then, these families are detained at the border and told they are not allowed to leave the territory of Russia. Please, pray for all the enemy plans to fail.

Day 277 • November 27

If Russia is not stopped, all of Europe (especially Poland and the Baltic states) is at risk, which is why we keep requesting military aid and begging the world to stand with Ukraine. We don't want anyone to experience what we are living through, and we pray for Russia to be stopped.

I don't think I've ever considered the world so small. I pray that we all become aware of how incredibly interconnected we are. May our hearts always be open to the needs and pains of our brothers and sisters, no matter what part of the world they come from.

Day 290 • December 10

During yesterday's strike, a missile hit a residential building in Kryvyi Rih, killing an older woman and a young family with a 1.5-year-old son. At the same time, the Russian propaganda said they sent missiles for humanitarian purposes. They say they never send rockets in the middle of the night and never aim at civil infrastructure. Their cynicism is incomprehensible.

Day 297 • December 17

ᛦ Let everything that has breath praise the Lord! Praise the Lord! (Psalm 150:6)

It's been 300 days since we woke up to the sounds of explosions. 300 days since we left home. 300 days of anxiety, uncertainty, and hope against despair. Russia started this war on Ukraine almost nine years ago, on February 20, 2014, but 300 days ago, with the beginning of its full-scale phase, the horror of war spread over all of Ukraine's territory.

In the past 300 days, we've grown a lot, and we've learned a lot.

We discovered that we are much stronger than we thought, and our strength grows when we are united. It is liberating to know that you can stand up for yourself, what you believe in, and what you hold dear.

We've learned that your most prized possessions can be fit into a backpack, and the most precious things are not things.

We've learned that you don't have to know a person for a long time, or you don't need to keep in touch on a regular basis to call someone a friend – a simple "How are you doing?", "How can I help?" and "I will be praying for you" builds bridges between hearts in an instant.

We've learned to live in the present (it is ridiculous to make long-term plans when a missile can destroy them instantly) yet prepare strategically (in case of an extended blackout) and dream big. They say that only in Ukraine do people make plans not only for the apocalypse but also for the post-apocalyptic time as well.

We keep excelling at time management, managing to shower, do dishes, cook a meal, and do laundry, all within one hour in case the power goes out.

We've discovered that laughter can also be a weapon, so we come up with more witty comments about our enemies because you cannot be afraid of something you are laughing at.

We've learned to comfort our children when we are torn on the inside, especially when they ask questions no child should ask.

We've realized the meaning of the phrase "Home is where your heart is" because the millions of our people who had to seek refuge abroad left their hearts in Ukraine, so they keep aching.

We've learned to trust the Lord to take care of our loved ones, especially when there is no cell phone reception and we know that an air-raid warning has been issued for all of Ukraine.

We've grown more numb to the pain yet less tolerant of the lies and injustice. It will take decades for our nation to heal, but I pray that we will never forget how we survived this genocide. I pray that we (and the world) will remember these lessons we are learning the hard way.

We've learned that we have a whole army of prayer warriors who stand with us and persevere in faith, and the enemy will never be able to break this power.

Day 300 · December 20

It's Christmas Day.

Yesterday, Russian terrorists heavily shelled Kherson, killing sixteen people and leaving over more than 64 people severely injured. Despite continued shelling in Kherson today, people line up at the hospitals to donate blood. This may be the most beautiful expression of the true Christmas spirit.

Day 306 · December 25

Oh, how I wish war had weekends and vacations. Thankfully, the Christmas weekend was relatively uneventful and most people had electricity for at least a few hours. However, we are bracing ourselves for another massive missile attack before the New Year or the Orthodox Christmas (January 7 – the more traditional day of Christmas celebration in Ukraine and the only one "recognized" in Russia).

Day 306 · December 26

Instead of festive fireworks, Ukraine shuddered from yet another massive missile attack. Hits were recorded in Kyiv, Mykolaiv, Kramatorsk, Zaporizhzhia, and Khmelnytskyi regions. Our air-defense forces shot down twelve missiles and a surveillance drone, but the damage was done, people were killed and wounded. Today, the Russians did not target energy infrastructure – it seems they randomly aimed at locations that could have crowds.

It was expected. It is infuriating. However, we know that we are stronger than their agony.

Day 311 - December 31

Resilience and the Seeds of Future Hope

A season to multiply: *The tulips begin to multiply and prepare for the following year. This invisible work of resilience is crucial. The commitment to goodness brings life into the world.*

Twenty thousand pairs of woolen socks were brought to Ukraine from Finland. The socks were knit by the people of Lahti in only one week! Seeing this care warms my heart better than socks.

Day 226 · October 7

Today we honor our home front heroes, those who daily eliminate the consequences of Russian aggression and fix what was broken. Sometimes I see pictures made within 24 hours of each other, where Ukrainian heroes mend craters and destruction brought by Russian missiles. We believe it's a reminder that the Lord will soon bring complete healing to our land.

Day 230 · October 11

There are reports about intense fighting breaking out in the Kherson region. There are no official reports yet, but the Institute for the Study of War claimed a couple of days ago that it is possible for the Ukrainian army to liberate Kherson within a week. Please, pray for Lord's favor and miracles upon miracles!

Day 234 · October 15

Sometimes I wonder how long it would take us to get used to peaceful life after the war. We've acquired quite a few habits over the past eight months, which seem to be forever ingrained in our brains. I watched a movie the other day, and the characters were going out in the evening, so my initial reaction was, "Is it safe to go out at night? Will they manage to get back home before the curfew?" Or I saw pictures of my friend (from another country) on her vacation and admired her bravery for leaving home and her family for longer than a couple of hours. Of course, our lives resemble ordinary most of the time, but the reality of the war pops in unannounced and leaves one flustered. I guess it's called PTSD (post-traumatic stress disorder), except our traumatic experience is not over yet, and we all are experiencing it as a nation.

Please, pray for Ukraine's healing. Pray for special healing for our soldiers, POWs, civilians going through torture in occupation. We will need a lot of counseling and rehabilitation programs for those groups. May the Lord grant wisdom and grace to those conducting them.

Hours after Putin's press conference, there was a missile strike on the civil infrastructure in Zaporizhzhia, and more artillery and missile attacks followed in the following days. Today, there was a report (based on *The Washington Times* sources) that Russia is not only purchasing new drones from Iran but also has a secret agreement to get Iranian-made surface-to-surface missiles to cover its decreasing supply of missiles.

The mayor of the temporarily occupied Melitopol (Zaporizhzhia region) said that the occupational authorities have forcefully mobilized about 3,000 city residents (which goes against the Geneva convention – the population in the occupied territory cannot be forced to enlist in the occupier's armed forces). Severe fighting continues in the Bakhmut and Soledar areas. About 2,000 Russian inmates charged with especially grievous crimes were sent there to fight, and they were promised amnesty for faithful service or death for retreating. The Zaporizhzhia Nuclear Power Plant employees in Enerhodar tell about a dire state of affairs. The territory of the NPP is mined, and the staff is tortured. A severe nuclear accident may happen at any time.

Does anyone need more proof of what kind of "peace" Russia is looking for? Yes, we all long for the war to end soon, but we long for justice more. We want lasting peace for our children and grandchildren, not a pause before they choose to strike again. You wouldn't normally force "peace" between a bully or an abuser and their victim unless there is sound proof of repentance and a change of heart. Russia is as bloodthirsty as ever, so we must keep fighting and resisting this evil.

Day 235 · October 16

I dream of the coming days when we will recount these events and praise God for His faithfulness. Our children and grandchildren will know of His miracles. Please, keep praying with us to witness His greatness and steadfast love.

Day 239 · October 20

As I was cooking dinner tonight in the dull light of a flashlight, I had time to reflect on this experience we go through as a nation. Yes, the blackouts are inconvenient, and we may get frustrated or start complaining, but it becomes worth it once we realize the ultimate goal we are enduring for. It is not for nothing. It is the price we pay for our freedom, for the chance to live and be a nation. It is better to endure the hardships for one winter than to spend a lifetime in Russian occupation.

I've said before that we learn to be more creative in our routine, but there is more to this experience. I think that we learn to trust others and rely on each other more. There was a simple situation today that made me think of it. We ordered large jugs with drinking water to be delivered to our apartment in Kyiv (we have some family members staying there). The company came at the agreed hour, but there was no electricity, and it would be torture to haul those jugs up the stairs. The company representative called me and asked permission to leave the jugs with the concierge (the doorkeeper lady) instead. To cut a long story short, those jugs stayed downstairs by the entrance for almost twelve hours until someone could bring them in, and no one stole them.

A few days ago, my cousin visited a private clinic to see a doctor who had to perform an exam using a flashlight because of a power outage. When it was time to pay the bill, my cousin didn't have enough cash, and the clinic didn't have the electricity to run the transaction with her card, so they asked her to pay the bill the next day once there was electricity.

I'm not saying there is absolutely no crime, and all Ukrainians suddenly became perfect citizens. No. But these stories show us that we depend on each other and are all in the same boat. It is inspiring to see cooperation instead of people taking advantage of each other.

Day 257 · November 7

Today, Ukraine celebrates the Day of Ukrainian Literature and Language. This day is a reminder that our language unites Ukrainians wherever we may live. Today, it is a threat to the invaders: in the temporarily occupied territories, they are removing and destroying Ukrainian books from schools, libraries, and even private collections. Ukrainian speakers are being persecuted and tortured for their language. Russian state propaganda claims that Ukrainian is a "made up" or "artificial" language or a "dialect of Russian." On this day, supporting the study and promotion of the Ukrainian language, millions of Ukrainians from all over the world write the radio dictation of National Unity. This tradition became even more significant this year because we need to feel our unity. And the text brought many people to tears because it was about the memories of a place we call home.

Day 259 · November 10

It is so important to have something to be looking forward to. I realized it this year when I had the chance to work on the soil. In spring, during the first darkest days, we were planting flowers and vegetables against all hope, which gave us our daily motivation. We had a stubborn resolve to see our flowers bloom in the fall. This fall, we planted new bulbs, and while the days get shorter and we have our share of daily struggles, there is a powerful motivation to see the bloom in springtime.

As I was thinking about it, I remembered that God placed Adam and Eve in the garden and told them to work it and keep it. Gardening does teach you to set your eyes on the goal and walk in faith until you reach that goal. And it's a good analogy for our time here on earth – we know what our ultimate future holds for us, but it takes small steps of daily faith to get there.

So, we do not lose heart. Though our outer self is wasting away, our inner self is being renewed day by day. For this light momentary affliction is preparing for us an eternal weight of glory beyond all comparison, as we look not to the things that are seen but to the things that are unseen. For the things that are seen are transient, but the things that are unseen are eternal.

Day 263 · November 13

It's become a popular saying on Facebook that to be Ukrainian means to not only be prepared for the end of the world but to also have some plans for the afterwards.

We joke, we make plans, we play cards and board games. We read by the candlelight or flashlight. We sing. We cuddle. We are anxiously waiting for the day of our victory and we pity those who don't understand why we won't give up.

It is hard. It is uncertain. It is frightening at times, but we know that we are not forsaken nor abandoned. The morning comes after a long night, the spring comes after a dreary winter, and our victory will come. May God's glory shine even brighter in the spiritual world as Ukraine is physically in a darkness.

Day 274 · November 24

Today, I talked to a couple of middle school students who took refuge in a country in Europe but came to visit Ukraine for a couple of weeks. They said they felt scared during the missile attack, and they were inconvenienced by the power outages, but they wished they didn't have to go back to that other country which is welcoming and convenient but still foreign. So, we agreed to pray for the war to be over, for the peace to return to all of Ukraine, and for all of us to be able to return home.

Day 281 · December 1

This holiday season is going to be really hard on every Ukrainian. With its approach, more and more of my friends post their Facebook memories from last year, saying it feels as if they come from a lifetime ago. The traditions we used to have, the things we used to look forward to, the people we used to spend this time with – some of these are gone forever or are too far now. To be honest, I have mixed feelings about the upcoming holiday season – I look forward to it yet dread it at the same time. I am thankful that our son is still at the age when any day can turn into a holiday if we are in a festive mood (he is an expert in coming up with random reasons for celebration). Still, I know that we won't be able to fully enjoy the celebration thinking about all the people who can't be with their loved ones or can't enjoy a festive meal or afford a Christmas tree. This is why I earnestly pray that in such disadvantaged circumstances, they will discover Jesus, who will become their true reason to celebrate.

Day 282 · December 2

Ukraine survived the eighth massive missile attack today. Over 70 missiles were launched, and our air-defense forces shot down over 60 of those! It's amazing! Our energy system keeps functioning despite the damage in the Odesa, Sumy, Kyiv, and Dnipropetrovsk regions.

Today, during the attack, at first, I was glued to my phone, anxiously checking the news, but then I felt the need to put the phone away and worship God. So, I was standing in the kitchen, praising God at the top of my lungs to the worship songs playing on my phone. How appropriate were the lyrics of one of the songs, which talked about singing loudly even when enemies were near.[xlvi]

What an incredible comfort to know that victory belongs to the Lord, no matter what our present circumstances may look like! And what a joy it was to read afterward about most of the missiles not reaching their intended targets. How great is our God! May His name be praised in all the earth! May He grant Ukraine victory and restore justice and peace in our land!

Day 285 · December 5

A Ukrainian poet and translator, was volunteering at the Lviv railway station, handing out hot drinks and food to those fleeing from the east, when he discovered that the greater need the refugees had was to tell their stories. That's how he began working on what he calls a Dictionary of War, a collection of short stories he heard.[xlvii] "It is pure documentary," he says. "There is nothing imagined, nothing fictionalized, nothing created by me in this text, but there came a moment when I understood that this was also poetry." Some of these stories are chilling, some are poignant, but all speak volumes.

Art can have different forms. Banksy, the anonymous British graffiti artist, created murals in Ukraine to show solidarity and bring hope. He is also selling a series of rare screen prints to raise money for an organization helping civilians affected by the war in Ukraine.

I am inspired by an award-winning pianist and singer who organized a Christmas concert, "Our Christmas Gift: A Benefit Concert for Ukraine," in Penang, Malaysia. They raised over RM 20,000 (over $4,500!), which would provide food and household detergents for 229 families or 916 people in Ukraine for one week! We are forever grateful.

So, the next time you hear someone say that artists should stay away from any conflict, or when you think that you cannot make a change because you are not a person of influence, I pray that you will be inspired by people like her or other artists who use their God-given talents for His glory.

Day 291 · December 11

It's Sunday, and many of my friends will light the fourth Advent candle today.

In Ukraine, we light candles every day when the power goes out, and whenever we are forced to slow down because of the blackout, we enjoy family time with our loved ones and hope and pray for peaceful days to come.

Tomorrow, Ukraine will celebrate St. Nicholas Day (according to the Orthodox church calendar). Tomorrow morning Ukrainian children will look under their pillows in the hope of finding a small present there. However, the main dreams of our children won't fit under a pillow – the dream of being reunited with their fathers (who serve in the army or weren't allowed to leave the country), the dream of returning home, the dream of our country being completely liberated from the Russians.

This year, we'll have to be creative with finding room for a Christmas tree in our grandma's house (as every corner of it is filled with boxes of our belongings). This year, we'll skip our tradition of making Christmas cookies, but I know that we'll be making special memories that will be shared with our grandchildren and great-grandchildren. I pray that this year each of us will experience the miracle of God coming near.

"And the Word became flesh and dwelt among us, and we have seen his glory, glory as of the only Son from the Father, full of grace and truth" John 1:14.

Day 298 · December 18

There are so many more things we've learned, from our endurance and mental resilience to the national identity and worldview, but the main thing we've learned is that we are not ready to give up. So, we will keep standing on the promises of the Lord, we will keep relying on His mercy and grace, we will recount the stories of His faithfulness, and we will keep eagerly waiting for the day when he restores peace and justice in all of Ukraine.

Day 300 · December 20

Tonight, when I am overwhelmed by these (and many other stories), I pray that God would heal the hearts broken by the war and grant us our biggest dream, the dream of a free and peaceful Ukraine that doesn't have to live in fear. Perhaps then we'll learn to dream again.

Day 303 · December 23

The National Philharmonic of Ukraine - Day 291, December 11, 2022

Chapter Seven

Another February
Can't Break Us[xlviii]

January 1 - February 28, 2023

Joy: Sixteen children kidnapped by Russia in the Kherson region returned to Ukraine. The youngest is only eight years old.

Exasperation: The International Olympic Committee and a bunch of officials support the participation of Russian athletes in the Olympics under a neutral flag. Do they know that many Russian athletes are military officers? Do they know how many Ukrainian athletes died from the Russian aggression? It must be clear that those who do not speak against the war waged by Russia support it. It is one way or the other. No magic neutral. If you see someone being raped in the street, you call the police, yell for help, and do something; otherwise, you are enabling the rapist. But some people still believe in "being neutral," and I pray that they won't have to bear the consequences of their "neutrality."

Gratitude: The support we've received from Poland, Latvia, Lithuania, and Estonia always moves me to tears. Their boldness and willingness to stand with Ukraine are inspiring. Latvia would not participate in the Olympics if there were Russian athletes. Poland keeps persuading our allies to send military airplanes to Ukraine. Lithuania encourages the western governments to provide Ukraine with all necessary weapons. Estonia has sent all its 155 mm howitzers in military aid to Ukraine. These countries are examples of standing up for what you believe in, no matter the cost.

Outrage: The occupational forces are demolishing a building in Mariupol where 200 people were killed. It was one of the largest gravesites in Mariupol, and it was destroyed to get rid of the evidence as if demolishing could erase the horrors from the memory of those who witnessed it.

Delight: Volunteers rescued a cat that spent two weeks in the ruins of a destroyed apartment building in Dnipro. In another city, Chasiv Yar (Donetsk region), volunteers rescued a dog from under the rubble of a building destroyed a few days ago. If we still care for animals, we are still capable of love.

Horror: Kramatorsk was shelled again (after last night's attack). More residential buildings were destroyed, and more people were killed and injured.

Anxiety: Russia is preparing yet another massive missile attack. There have been shipments of drones and signs of activity in the Black Sea.

Hope: The children of Ukraine will be the generation that remembers the importance of acting upon your convictions. A station for making nets that camouflage equipment is casually set up in a school hallway, with kids freely working on it during the breaks and after-school activities. Kids praying mature prayers of protection for their friends and loved ones. May the Lord bless these children to be the generation He wants to see.

These are just a few of the emotions I went through today. An ordinary day, the 344th day of the full-scale stage of the 9-year-long war that takes its roots hundreds of years ago.

Day 344 • February 2

Hope Based in Past Memories

A season to plant: *Planting tulips is an expression of hope, based on past experience. After a bulb is placed in the ground, half a year passes before the gardener knows whether their hope is realized.*

January 27 is the International Holocaust Memorial Day. It is vital for us, the human race, to know and remember, no matter how sensitive matters may be. If we remember the horrors of the past, if we don't disregard them as distant history, if our hearts remain sensitive to the pain of those who went through the unspeakable, perhaps that would prevent us from repeating such crimes.

Holocaust is a mournful page of Ukraine's history. At the start of the war between Nazi Germany and the USSR, Ukraine had the largest Jewish population in Europe – 2.7 million people. According to historians' estimations, Ukraine lost over 1.5 million of the Jewish population.

As I read stories about the Holocaust, the Nazi occupation of Ukraine, and the accounts of ordinary people who did extraordinary things to prevent this genocide, even if for just one person or one family, I need to remind myself that I'm not reading current news. It's shocking to think that so many aspects of those cruel days could be taking place in the heart of Europe today.

Genocide becomes possible when ordinary people, perhaps even kind-hearted and well-meaning people, allow propaganda to corrupt their thinking, when they choose to turn a blind eye and become passive bystanders, or even find justification and rejoice in the crimes committed.

May the Lord have mercy. May He help us remember. May He stop the genocide in Ukraine and other nations suffering today. May the words "never again" become our reality on this side of eternity.

Day 338 · January 27

As we approach the one-year anniversary of the current invasion, it's getting harder to come to terms with the fact that this war will not be over soon. Some experts talk about two-three years, while others emphasize that pushing Russian troops out of the territory of Ukraine will not stop this war unless deep changes take place in Russia. Our only hope is in the Lord, who knows His plans and His timing.

When there are no victorious reports from the frontline, it is easy to grow weary and start doubting if our prayers make any difference. However, we must remember that God is at work even when we don't see or don't notice it.

Day 340 · January 29

I know that there are no coincidences for God. Everything happens at His timing and at His will. When I read some war accounts, I wonder what God had in mind. I am not asking why, but I wonder how this fits into His greater plan. That is one of the questions I would like to ask God when I see Him.

But now, while my knowledge is limited on this side of eternity, I choose to see the pieces of the puzzle that bring glory to His name.

Day 347 · February 5

A year ago today, we woke up in our apartment in Kyiv around 5 am to the sound of explosions. "Yes, this is it," was a message from a neighbor in our building's chat, and everyone knew what they meant.

A year has passed, but I still can't describe the mixed feelings rushing through my brain as I was still sitting in my bed. There was anger, fear, anxiety, but there was also a relief because we no longer had to live in anticipation and could finally face the inevitable. We prayed right there, trusting God to see us through this trying time. Some of the memories of that morning are still too painful to revise – for example, writing our son's information on his arm with a permanent marker in case something happens to us as we evacuate. My hands were shaking, but I was trying to look calm and excitedly chatted to him about getting a fun "tattoo." Or walking through our apartment, wondering what we should take and what would be left behind. One of the last things we grabbed was a bunch of children's books we had bought for our son a few days before that he didn't know about. Those books kept him busy the first few days while we were too shocked to be present.

However, one event that morning shaped us for what was to come. In all the uncertainty between making decisions and getting in touch with the family, there was a message from my son's school. They invited the families from our school to meet for an online prayer. We joined the Zoom call from our car. As we were leaving Kyiv, heading down an unfamiliar route, we prayed with our friends. Someone shared from the Scripture – Psalm 27, Psalm 31, verses from the prophets. Slowly, I felt the peace of God replacing anxiety in my heart. I felt covered by His grace and had the courage to walk with Him wherever He was taking us. That prayer meeting was the most meaningful thing that could happen. It also inspired Ivan to start a prayer meeting for our church that still meets daily to intercede for our country. Today, one year later, we met for another online prayer with my son's school. We laughed, we cried, and we cherished the chance to see each other again.

Reflecting on the day that marks the 1-year anniversary of the full-scale war, I noticed it being filled with the spirit of gratitude. In the prayer meeting, in my friends' posts on social media, and in the official addresses, I could sense gratitude. Gratitude for being alive. Gratitude to those who gave their lives for us to be here today. Gratitude that our worst fears from one year ago didn't come true. Gratitude for the support we've seen. A solemn sort of gratitude as we mourn our losses, knowing that the war is far from over. However, as long as we can be grateful, love others, and be compassionate, the enemy will not prevail.

"Not by might, nor by power, but by my Spirit, says the Lord of hosts" (Zechariah 4:6). This was one of the verses that came to me during those first days of this invasion. It's been with me throughout this year. Not by military strength, against all the expectations and prognoses, Ukraine stands with God's Spirit and your prayers.

Thank you so much for praying for us today. Thankfully, there was no massive attack today, but the enemy hasn't given up, and we aren't blissful about the days to come.

Day 366 · February 24

While I thought it would be traumatizing to revisit the past year's events, God was faithful to remind us about His power and mercy. A few documentaries were presented for the invasion anniversary. They mainly focus on the events of the first weeks since those military operations can be openly discussed now without threatening the ongoing operations. In one of the documentaries, they talk about the defense of Kyiv. The Russians hoped to deploy their troops in the heart of Kyiv, quickly seize power and victoriously march through the streets within a few days of the invasion. However, our air-defense forces outsmarted them and made the aerial operation impossible. They tried surrounding Kyiv by land, and one of the crucial battles was in the town of Moshchun. That's where Russia lost most of its elite forces. As one of the military commanders said, that victory was possible because Ukrainians were fiercely fighting for their capital city and because nature provided essential aid – the Irpin river flooded the area and prevented the advance of the Russian army. We know who rules over nature and makes rivers flood – we know who stands behind this victory.

This story encouraged me and reminded me that God was with us even when everything looked hopeless, so we shouldn't doubt him now.

Please, keep praying for our soldiers, especially in the Bakhmut area. Pray for more supernatural interferences. And pray for the world leaders to choose truth and life.

Day 367 · February 25

The Experience of Survival

A season to make roots: *Having planted our tulip bulbs, we move forward into the busyness of preparing for winter. This is a practical time, built around survival.*

We had our first power outage since Dec 31st today. Thankfully, it wasn't a long one. Because of the warmer weather, there's a drop in energy consumption, and we've had a few sunny days, which helps to increase energy production by solar power stations. Even though a temperature drop is expected over the weekend and the Russians may try another massive attack (Ukraine will celebrate the Orthodox Christmas on January 6/7), we treasure every moment of this blessing. Even though we have mostly adjusted to the scheduled blackouts, I realized how stressful it is to follow that schedule and what a refreshing surprise we've had over the holidays. They've updated our schedule for power supply – for every eight hours of the day, we are guaranteed two hours with electricity, two hours without electricity, and the fate of the remaining four hours will be determined by the situation in our energy system. It may be challenging, but we believe it's an opportunity to learn to be more mindful and responsible with the resources entrusted to us.

Day 314 · January 3

It's Christmas Eve for the Orthodox Christians in Ukraine. It's traditional Christmas time. During the Soviet time, it was a forbidden celebration, but thankfully our people managed to preserve the traditions and the spirit of this holiday.

Our day was interrupted by an air-raid warning extending over the whole territory of Ukraine. That's all you need to know about the "ceasefire." Thankfully, there was no massive attack, but the heavy shelling continued throughout the front line.

Day 317 · January 6

In the past few days, we had a pattern of two hours of electricity followed by a six-hour blackout. Some of those two-hour slots of electricity would start at 4 am or at 10 pm, which makes them barely useful. Thankfully, it looks like our internet provider found a way to maintain its services during extended blackouts, so at least we have a connection to the outside world. We just keep reminding ourselves that with every passing day, we are closer to spring.

The weather in Ukraine remains cold (-10°C/14 F at our location). Being outside isn't very pleasant now, and I can't imagine being in trenches. Unfortunately, there are cases of frostbite among soldiers, so even those not wounded can lose a toe or a finger. The groups at the forefront can't make fires, to not draw the enemy's attention. They have to rely on "trench candles." Please, pray for God's mercy on them.

Pray for Soledar and Bakhmut – the most intense battlefields in the Donetsk region. Pray for Kherson that's under constant shelling (they hit a perinatal center today, which set the building on fire, but thankfully there are no casualties). Please, pray for military aid to be sent to Ukraine without any delays and for the enemy to leave.

Day 322 · January 11

There have been no significant changes at the front lines, but no big news doesn't mean that personal tragedies are on hold as well.

Fighting in the Bakhmut area remains incredibly intense, with significant losses on both sides. The street fights in Soledar are unpredictable for both the soldiers and the roughly 500 civilians who stay there. You may not know this, but the name Soledar means "the gift of salt," so someone played on it and said that the fighting there is the battle for "the salt of the earth."

When the full-scale war started, they stopped the production of salt in Bakhmut and Soledar, and now it looks like the Russian army is fighting for access to the 200-kilometer (125 miles) long salt mines that have been in operation since 1881 and are one of the largest salt deposits in the world. These mines produced 95% of the salt consumed in Ukraine, so salt shortage was a serious issue in the spring of 2022. There is no shortage now – we have imported salt in stores, but I am reminded of the reality of war every time I reach for salt when cooking. Who knew that salt could be so different?

Day 323 · January 13

As I was scrolling through the news today, I came across a few reports about the life of civilians in an active combat zone or recently de-occupied territories. Life there is often reduced to survival, and human dignity is shattered more and more with every artillery shelling.

Many small villages are far from major routes, which makes them less attractive to the enemy, but it also makes it more difficult for the volunteers to reach them. That's why every package and truckload of humanitarian aid is welcomed with tears of joy and child-like wonder. Those people do not want to evacuate because of the fear of feeling abandoned or being a burden. Their current conditions are no better, but at least they have familiar surroundings. When they greet volunteers, they thank them for coming and say, "We thought everyone had forgotten about us, but here you come. Please, do not forget us!" Even living through hell, their greatest fear is not death but being forgotten and abandoned.

Day 332 · January 21

The Ukrainian army had to retreat from Soledar. We believe it is temporary. Our troops accomplished the task of exhausting the enemy and took the maneuver to save personnel. Our prayers are with the civilians remaining in the city.

As I'm writing this, the air-raid sirens are going off in many regions of Ukraine. There are reports of kamikaze drones taken down and more drones going toward objects of critical importance. Often, they will send drones to test our air defense, and then missiles come next. Lord, have mercy.

Day 336 · January 25

Last night, when I was going to bed, kamikaze drones were attacking Ukraine. I would doze off, wake up and check the news, then try to fall asleep again. This morning, I woke up startled by airplane noise. Our eight-year-old son gently patted me on my head and said, "Do not be afraid. Those are airplanes. They've flown over our house a few times already."

However, I knew that the airplane sounds meant that Ukraine was under another massive missile attack. After the night attack with 24 kamikaze drones (all shot down by our air defense), Russians fired 55 missiles, 20 of which were headed to Kyiv. The air-raid warning lasted for over four hours. Our air-defense forces took down 47 missiles. Eleven people were killed in these two attacks. Damage was done to our energy system, especially in the Odesa region.

But we learn to live through the attacks and despite the attacks. We might not always be rational, but we take necessary precautions and refuse to give up our moments of life to the terrorists.

This morning, during the attack, our neighbors in Kyiv casually mentioned the sounds of explosions while discussing a solution to the internet connection issues in our apartment building.

Day 337 · January 26

It would be accurate to say that this day was one long air-raid. The first kamikaze drones came in the middle of the night. Then a couple of waves of missiles throughout the day and another wave of kamikaze drones at night. It annoys us, ruins our plans, and adds to our anxiety, but it cannot break us.

According to preliminary reports, the enemy used 29 S-300 anti-aircraft guided missiles and 71 air and sea-based cruise missiles. Our defenders shot down 61 cruise missiles. They hit power infrastructure in six regions of Ukraine. Kharkiv suffered the most, but the enemy failed to achieve a total blackout. We praise God for His mercy and thank our allies for the reliable air-defense systems we received.

Day 352 · February 10

On a brighter note, we've been spoiled with a week without power cuts. Our energy system has achieved the necessary power generation level so the blackouts happen only due to power transportation problems (which is the case in the Odesa region and the active combat zone). However, we are not in a hurry to rejoice and relax as Russia hasn't given up on destroying Ukraine and terrorizing civilians. The next couple of weeks are going to be intense and challenging for everyone as Russians will try any trick possible to present some victory for the 1-year anniversary. They are also intensifying their informational and psychological attacks in international media to undermine the support for Ukraine, so make sure you verify suspicious or compromising information before sharing it. With more daylight, sun, and warmth, it is slightly easier to be hopeful. Lord, have mercy!

Day 357 · February 15

Last night I posted my daily update and turned off the laptop. As I was getting ready to go to bed, I saw a notification on my phone that all of Ukraine was under an air-raid warning. Another massive missile attack was underway.

Thirty-six missiles were launched at Ukraine. Our air-defense forces shot down only half (sixteen) of them because of the usage of Kh-type rockets, which cannot be intercepted with the current air-defense systems. This type of missile is meant to destroy aircraft carriers, and this is the type that destroyed the apartment building in Dnipro a month ago. The rockets hit infrastructure facilities in the Lviv, Kirovohrad, Poltava, and Dnipropetrovsk regions. One woman was killed, and seven more people were injured.

Thankfully, the attack did not damage the power grid, so blackouts were not needed. The experts said that with the aid received from our partners and the fearless hard work of our power engineers are now able to repair the damage faster than the Russians attack and destroy. It is a hopeful statement as we still have over a month of cold weather ahead of us, even though this winter did turn out to be very mild.

After last night's attack, a missile fragment landed in Moldova, close to the Ukrainian border. This is the fourth time it has happened. Please, keep praying for Moldova and for all Russian plans to fail there. Tonight, Kharkiv was attacked with S-300 missiles. This is another type of missile that our air defense cannot intercept. We'll learn more about the damage in the morning. The next massive missile attack is expected around February 22-24. Please, pray for special protection on those days.

Day 358 · February 16

The confirmed losses of the Russian army in February 2023 exceed the usual weekly losses by five times. The Wagner group has lost over 30,000 people in Ukraine (almost 9,000 of those in the fight for Bakhmut) – 90% of them were inmates hired to fight in exchange for the promise of release from prison.

According to the leader of NGO "Russia Behind Bars" (an organization providing legal and humanitarian assistance to citizens facing Russian investigations and the penitentiary system), Wagner Group will no longer seek volunteers from among inmates. Recent events point to the fact that this will now be the "privilege" offered by the Ministry of Defence. While the drafting used to be voluntary, now the Ministry of Defence comes with a list of names, and the inmates have no choice. The priority is given to those with military experience or specialization, but they admit that they will come for the rest of the inmates if there is a need. People are being treated as consumables – we've seen it before in Soviet policies, and we see it now in Russia.

Meanwhile, the Wagner Group will now focus more on Africa. It is easy to find information on the group's involvement in the Central African Republic. Their main goal is control over gold and diamond mines and other resources that can, in turn, be used to fuel Russia's aggression. There are reports of the Wagner Group being involved in the atrocities in the central African region, Wagner troops being accused of rape, the massacre of innocents, and alcohol-fueled human rights abuses like torture.

It's another evidence of how unrepented sin spreads and consumes more and more. God, save your people from these bloodthirsty men!

Day 359 · February 17

Today, Russia launched four Kalibr missiles. Two of them were shot down, and the other two hit a target in Khmelnytskyi. The rockets went dangerously low over the South Ukraine Nuclear Power Plant (in the Mykolaiv region). Their trajectory was not accidental, and the risk of them hitting a reactor and causing a nuclear disaster was high. Russia keeps terrorizing the world.

Day 360 · February 18

According to a recent poll, 95% of respondents believe in Ukraine's victory. We were convinced of this even last spring, but I guess we all long to know when this victory will come.

Today, Russian troops shelled a public transport stop in Kherson. 16 people were injured, and five died. My heart breaks for the people of Kherson who lived through occupation and now endure daily shelling. In fact, my heart breaks for the people in the Sumy, Chernihiv, and Kharkiv regions who are in similar situations. How much longer, Lord?

Many schools are switching to online format for the rest of the week for the fear of Russian provocations or upcoming attacks. Please, pray for our children – this kind of stress doesn't go unnoticed even if they don't show it.

Please, keep praying for Moldova. Ukraine's intelligence reported Russia's updated plans to destabilize Moldova. The Prime Minister of Moldova, Dorin Rechan, confirmed that Russia has plans to seize the airport in Chisinau to transfer troops to Moldova. May all enemy plans fail.

Day 363 · February 21

Today's weather was erratic, changing from a bright sunny warm morning to a windy and cloudy evening with cold rain. Perhaps the weather reads the news from Ukraine and changes accordingly...

Our power engineers did the impossible, and we haven't had a blackout in over two weeks. They say there will be no blackouts without further attacks on our energy system. However, some sources say Russians may change their tactics, and missile attacks would now target water supply and road infrastructure. Perhaps this change in tactics explains the extended periods between the missile attacks.

Day 367 · February 25

As I'm writing this, the air-raid warning is spreading over Ukraine. Kamikaze drones have been detected over the northern regions and Kyiv. Usually, missiles come after drones. We expected the attack on February 24, but it didn't happen. Apparently, the Russians naively believe they can surprise us with an attack on Monday morning. We trust in God's protection over our cities and in His hand over our air defense.

Day 368 · February 26

Please, pray for our soldiers. We had snow today; the trenches are full of water and mud. May God protect our defenders from Russian weapons, diseases, weariness, and despair. May He restore His justice and bring an end to this war.

Day 369 · February 27

When Hope Felt Distant

A season to cool: Winter buries the memory of the hopes that we had planted with our tulip bulbs.

As I was reading these reports throughout the day, they mixed up in my brain. Shelling of Kherson? Didn't it happen yesterday? Missiles on Kramatorsk? I remember reading about it before – could it be old news? Unfortunately, what used to be shocking at the beginning of this full-scale war becomes "old news" because of its frequency.

Day 320 · January 9

Today is another tragic day for Ukraine. Another massive missile attack. The first explosions in Kyiv came unexpectedly early in the morning before the air-raid sirens went off. Most likely, that resulted from ballistic rockets that cannot be traced or shot down by our air defense.

Then, a three-hour long air-raid in the afternoon. One of the missiles hit a multi-story residential building in Dnipro, my husband's hometown. One entrance block is completely destroyed, with people buried under the rubble. The attack came on Saturday afternoon when most people would be spending time at home with their families.

I saw just one short video clip from the disaster site. I couldn't watch more. It contained the blood-chilling cries coming from under the rubble. As of now (11 pm on January 14), 12 people (including one child) died, 64 (including 14 children) were injured, and 37 (including six children) have been rescued. The rescue operation continues. According to the estimations, this entrance block had 72 apartments, which means about 200 residents, including 50 children. People joined the emergency services in clearing up the debris and pulling away the destroyed vehicles. There's a video of a girl, maybe five or six years old, picking up rubble. Some people are still trapped in their apartments, so they use flashlights to signal the rescuers. The evil of this scale leaves you numb because if you allow yourself to process it, you risk falling apart. They think that massive missile attacks can wear us down to submission, but instead, they only cause more resolve and a deeper thirst for justice. We beg God's avenging justice to fall on every human being who planned these operations, put them into action, or rejoiced in the outcome. May the Lord act in His endless wisdom, and may the guilty repent and turn from their wicked ways before it's too late. Lord, have mercy on your children!

Please, pray special prayers for Dnipro tonight. This city became home to many people displaced from the occupied territories, and they are forced to relive their traumatic experiences. The apartment building that was hit today was the home of about 1,000 people, and most of them will need to find a new place to live as the whole building is no longer safe. Please, pray for supernatural strength and wisdom for the rescuers. Pray for God's comfort and His presence with the grieving. May Jesus be near and real to the people of Dnipro.

Day 325 · January 14

There was something I wanted to say when I sat down to write tonight's post, but my mind went blank when I checked the most recent news.

Tonight, Russia shelled Kramatorsk and hit an apartment building in the city center. Two entrance blocks were destroyed, and the eyewitnesses say you can hear people screaming from under the debris. The rescue operation continues, but we already know that at least two people were killed and seven injured.

I don't know what to say. Over this past year, I often went to the books of prophets. It is my favorite part of the Bible (if you can even choose one) because of the raw honesty and because you hear God speak there. Tonight, I am thankful for the book of Habakkuk, which starts with despair and ends with words of faith and praise. May the Lord bless us to follow Habakkuk's example.

"O Lord, how long shall I cry for help, and you will not hear? Or cry to you 'Violence!' and you will not save? (1:2) Though the fig tree should not blossom, nor fruit be on the vines, the produce of the olive fail and the fields yield no food, the flock be cut off from the fold and there be no herd in the stalls, yet I will rejoice in the Lord; I will take joy in the God of my salvation (3:17-18)."

As a child, I never understood why my grandma thought it was important to remember the date when the Soviet Union was invaded by Nazi Germany and many of its Axis allies. It was one of the dates from a history book to me. I understand her much better now. As we approach the 1-year mark, every day, I ask myself, "What was I doing on this day a year ago? Did I know what was about to happen?" I know that these memories will haunt us for years, and the month of February will always trigger anxiety until Russia is a threat no more.

Around this time last year, we felt the approach of doom. We had our emergency backpacks ready, downloaded maps on our phones (in case there was no internet), and made sure the gas tank in our car was at least 3/4 full at all times. We worked out an action plan and knew what to do if the invasion started when we were away from home, or if there was no cell phone reception. I remember hushed conversations during coffee breaks when everyone was thinking about the same questions, but few dared to speak them out loud. On Fridays, I volunteered at my son's school, and I wished I could be there every day to make sure I was with him if anything happened.

Around this time last year, we came to visit my grandma. It was unbearable to stay home and keep checking the news, so we went for a walk. There is a 600-year-old oak in this village. It is one of the tourist landmarks, located on one of the oldest streets by an old cemetery. We spent the whole day walking around, and just for a moment, it felt like all the news and prognoses were just a product of one's sick imagination, and invasion would not happen. In just under two weeks, we returned to the village, leaving behind our home and taking our son to safety. We had hoped it would be for a few weeks, perhaps a few months, but a year has already gone by, yet so many of those concerns remain.

Please, pray for our defenders as the fighting intensifies. Pray for the people in the temporarily occupied territories. Pray for those far from the combat zone but still shelled daily by the Russian terrorists – the Chernihiv and

Sumy regions, Kharkiv, Zaporizhzhia, the Dnipropetrovsk region, and Kherson. Pray for all of us to keep fighting the good fight.

Day 350 · February 8

I often think about the children who live through this war. Their experiences are different, and they all cope differently, but I keep praying for their hearts not to be scarred by this brutality.

I think about the children of war every time I look at my 8-year-old son, whenever we sit down to our homeschool lessons (the option we chose instead of returning to Kyiv), every time he talks about the friends and things he misses, every time he prays for all of his classmates to be safe and for all of them to be reunited in their school. No child deserves to know what war is, but I know that the Lord will restore justice, and He will wipe away the tears of Ukrainian children.

Day 355 · February 13

Nine years ago, February 18, 2014, was Tuesday, a lovely sunny day with a breath of spring in the air. I returned from my "future mothers" class, made myself a cup of tea, and came to the window to enjoy the beautiful scenery – our rented apartment had a fantastic view of the skyline of the right bank of Kyiv. Instead of the peaceful panorama, I saw black smoke rising from the downtown area and rushed to check the news. The Revolution of Dignity entered its darkest stage. A peaceful demonstration (about 50,000 people) marched from the fortified Maidan (Independence Square) to the Parliament building to support opposition demands for a new constitution and government but was met with special police units, stun grenades, and guns. Snipers were involved. The Metro was stopped. People were leaving work early to join in the fight. Over the next two days, over 100 people would be killed in this massacre. We'll call them "The Heavenly Hundred" (since the resistance forces at Maidan were divided into hundreds/centurions).

It was one of those times when you know that everything hangs in the balance. The circumstances looked hopeless. Our small group met for a prayer meeting at our place, and it reminded me of the disciples of Jesus meeting in the upper room after the crucifixion. We earnestly prayed, not knowing if our prayers would be answered. In a few days (which seem to have lasted a lifetime), we were amazed by the outcome – then-president

Yanukovych fled the country, and his parliament representatives gave up and accepted the demands of the protesters. Justice was being restored. We were mourning the losses and trying to make plans for the future, all the while Russia was initiating its occupation of Crimea.

February 2022 bore a strong resemblance to February 2014. Someone said that February is the shortest month of the year but is unbearably long for Ukrainians. It's also interesting that the name of February in Ukrainian means "furious" (referring to the traditionally severe weather conditions), so these events seem to have chosen February on purpose. I'd vote for a new name for this month if only it could help restore justice, undo the pain, and bring back all who have given their lives for Ukraine's freedom since 2014.

Day 360 · February 18

Russia continues blackmailing the world with nuclear threats to prevent president Biden's visit to Europe.

Iran has enriched uranium to 84% (purity of 90% is needed to produce nuclear weapons).

China is considering providing lethal aid to Russia.

The occupational authorities in Mariupol destroy Ukrainian books.

Ukrainians keep fighting for freedom and life.

We keep praying.

Day 361 · February 19

Defiance in the Face of Aggression

A season to grow: *In spite of the sometimes-returning onslaughts of fading winter, tulips start growing below the surface. This is a time of defiance and hope.*

You know, one of the traditional new year's wishes I remember from childhood is the wish, "May everything bad stay in the year that passes, and may all your wishes come true." How I wish that were true.

Last night, as soon as we welcomed 2023 at midnight, the Russians launched a massive drone attack (yes, it was another attack after the missiles earlier in the day). All of Ukraine was under the air-raid warning. I heard something that sounded like a distant thunder (there are no thunderstorms in Ukraine in winter), and then there was the sound of airplanes flying over us. As infuriating as it was, thankfully, the Russians achieved nothing with their attack.

Our air-defense forces shot down 45 drones! Our people kept celebrating – we have a curfew, so there were no people in the streets, but people opened their windows, went out to their balconies, and sang the anthem of Ukraine and patriotic songs. There was a video of our soldiers shooting down a drone to the sounds of people singing. We have also been blessed with 48+ hours without power cuts. The large industrial enterprises (main energy consumers) were asked to suspend their operations for the holiday so that people could have electricity in their homes. It's a luxury and a true Christmas gift to all of us! Unfortunately, some cities, like Kherson, couldn't enjoy it because the shelling on New Year's Eve damaged the power lines.

As I'm writing this, Ukraine is under another night attack from the air. Twelve drones have been shot down over Kyiv, and ten more – in the Dnipropetrovsk and Zaporizhzhya regions. We don't know how long this attack will last and what its outcome will be, but we know that they will never achieve their goals.

Day 312 · January 1

Last night's attack was exhausting but, thankfully, futile. All 39 kamikaze drones were shot down. Our close relative, who lives in Kyiv now, said it was one of the scariest nights for them because they could hear the drones flying over our district, and the only calming sound they were looking for was the explosions from our air-defense systems. In tonight's address, our President said the night drone attacks might become a regular occurrence throughout the next week as the Russians have received a new shipment of drones and want to exhaust our people and our air defense.

Day 313 · January 2

While my heart burns with anger, it also swells with gratitude. All the missile attacks have not broken the spirit of Ukrainians – 85% of people believe that we must not give up our territories to compromise with Russia. We learned our lesson in 2014 when Russia occupied Crimea and parts of regions in the east of Ukraine – they will not stop unless they are stopped.

Day 314 · January 3

There is another miracle that is undeniably the hand of God. Ukraine is under a bit of a cold front now, and we know that the Russians often plan their massive missile attacks on the days like this to leave people without electricity and heat. However, they haven't attacked yet, and the temperature is expected to rise to a few degrees above freezing by the end of the week. However, the interesting phenomenon I mentioned can be seen on a temperature map. I saw this map shared a week ago, but I dismissed it because I thought it was fake. So, we all know that Russia had been using natural gas as leverage to get European governments to make favorable decisions. This year, they cut the gas supply and hoped all of Europe would freeze this winter. Well, if you look at the map, you'll see that the cold front miraculously stays within Russian borders. Yes, there has been a temperature drop in Ukraine and the Baltic and Scandinavian countries, but it's mild compared to what Russia is experiencing. And the southwest of Europe keeps enjoying the unusually warm winter weather. Isn't this a miracle? Doesn't it remind you of the Old Testament times when God would prominently show His hand to call nations to repentance?

Day 320 · January 9

Every day we are bombarded with tons of information – Russians preparing for another attack, western governments discussing the provision of military aid to Ukraine, mobilization, the situation at the frontlines, economic challenges, prognoses of how much longer the war is going to last... Add this to the common everyday challenges, and you get a mixture that sends you on an emotional rollercoaster even after eleven months of itself full-scale war.

I wish we knew how much longer. However, I remind myself of the words that are said to belong to Viktor Frankl, Austrian psychiatrist and Holocaust survivor, "[In the concentration camp], the first to break were those who believed that everything would end soon. Then – those who didn't believe it would ever end. Survivors are those who focused on their affairs, without waiting for what else might happen." So, as I remind myself to focus on the affairs at hand, I also remind myself not to postpone my life "until the war is over," even though it is so tempting to go into this hibernation mode and suspend all your activities until life returns to the usual "normal."

We remind ourselves to live in the present, love in the present, and use our present circumstances with gratitude. Today, our son mentioned the story of Thomas asking to place his fingers into Jesus's wounds, and we talked about the response of Jesus, "Blessed are those who have not seen and yet have believed" (John 20:29), which then took us to the question of how we can experience God in our life. It was such a great encouragement to listen to Ivan list one event after another that testified about God's faithfulness. Focusing on Him and His greatness is a powerful encouragement, even in dire times.

Day 333 · January 22

There is another story I smile about. It might be one of those I'll be sharing with my grandchildren in my old age. A few months back, during one of the massive missile attacks, I got a sudden urgency to order some painting supplies – I've never tried painting, but these attacks gave me the courage to try. I was laughing at myself, using the last minutes of a weak internet signal to place an order. The next day, I got a message from the online store, "We are sorry for the delay. We had no electricity for over 20 hours and couldn't process your order earlier, but your supplies are on their way. Ukraine will be victorious." At that moment, I felt how deeply interconnected we are in our experiences and hopes.

January is almost over, and daylight has gained almost one hour. This crazy winter that started eleven months ago will soon be over, and the Russian terrorists will never be able to break us.

Day 337 · January 26

By this I know that you delight in me: my enemy will not shout in triumph over me.

Psalm 41:11

I often say that this war takes us on a wild rollercoaster ride, often leaving you dizzy and nauseous. You try to find balance but end up swinging from despair to hope, from helplessness to eagerness, from passivity to restlessness...

I guess we all follow one rule – do what you can. Do what you can, no matter how big or insignificant. Take care of those in need, and if you feel like this task is too big, then start with taking care of yourself and your family. Support the army – donate to the military funds, bring supplies requested by volunteers (for example, candle wax from used-up candles can be repurposed for trench candles), offer your hands making masking nets.

Support Ukraine's economy – work and pay taxes, buy goods from local vendors, provide for your family and neighbors. Offer emotional support to those who lost their loved ones or those separated from their loved ones – check on them, bring them food, take them out for a walk, and be there for them. Invest in Ukraine's future – become an expert in your field, acquire new skills, find opportunities to apply yourself, bring up a new generation of Ukrainians.

Defend Ukraine in your line of duty – guard your mind and heart against informational and psychological attacks of the enemy, spread the truth, raise awareness, debunk false news, even if your audience is limited to your household or neighborhood.

Keep your faith and keep interceding for those God puts on your heart.

Do what you can.

The things I listed above are examples of what I've seen around us in the past eleven months. There are days when I can do a few things from this list, and there are days when I manage just the bare minimum. I remind myself that it's okay to feel low and weary as long as you remember to do what you can. There was a silly motivational quote circulating on the internet a couple of years ago, "Run towards your dreams. If you can't run, walk toward your dreams. If you can't walk, crawl toward your dreams. If you can only lie flat, then lie facing your dreams." All Ukrainians share in one big dream, and it's the one we'll be moving towards, even if we can only crawl or lie flat. We will do what we can.

Day 341 · January 30

I open the news and see destroyed buildings, reports of thousands dead and injured, displaced people warming up by a street fire, and miracle rescue stories. The only difference is that today's stories are not from Ukraine, and this pain was not caused by a human hand. The powerful earthquake took over 3,000 people's lives in Turkey and Syria, and the number keeps rising.

Such natural disasters cannot be stopped or prevented by people. I am convinced that they are God's megaphone, trying to shake us out of hibernation and make us aware of the fragility of human life and the need to value the time we are given.

Please, pray for Turkey, Syria, and other affected locations. Ukraine is sending a rescue mission there – our rescue squads have extensive experience pulling apart the rubble. Turkey was among the countries that welcomed refugees from Ukraine (especially the southern regions of Ukraine) – please, pray for their protection.

Day 348 · February 6

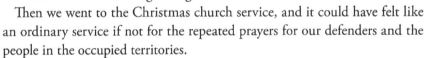

Celebration,
While Aware of the Costs

A season to bloom: *The crowning season for the tulips arrives as their flowers reach to the sky. But celebration is vulnerable – the tulip has used huge amounts of the bulb's resources in the hope of future goodness.*

It was a great Christmas day. It seemed so ordinary. We took my son and niece caroling in the morning, and it was almost like any other year, except everyone would get extra emotional and add wishes for peace and victory to the traditional Christmas greeting.

Then we went to the Christmas church service, and it could have felt like an ordinary service if not for the repeated prayers for our defenders and the people in the occupied territories.

We continued with a great family time – a tasty meal, gift exchange, and fun games, just like any year. We would only sneak out to check the news and someone would quietly ask, "Have they done anything? Has there been anything massive?"

I am incredibly thankful to God for these glimpses of the ordinary. It's a priceless treasure. I'm also grateful for this urgency to live and appreciate life – it's not something I would choose to experience, but it's an experience I'm thankful for.

Thankfully, there were no large-scale provocations today. The enemy kept shelling Zaporizhzhia, Kherson, and the Kharkiv region. They continued attacks on Bakhmut and Soledar as well as along the frontline.

Ukraine's energy system is under control with scheduled blackouts during the day, and no power cuts at night due to consumption decrease. However, the situation may change at any moment because of the temperature drop (to below freezing) or if Russia chooses to attack our energy infrastructure again. Please, keep us in your prayers.

Day 318 · January 7

On a brighter note, 50 more defenders of Ukraine returned from Russian captivity today during the first POW swap of 2023. May all POWs and those considered missing-in-action return home to their loved ones soon.

Day 319 · January 8

We believe God is already at work, and His creation is fulfilling His orders. Our new allies at the Belarusian border are beavers![xlix] Their dams created miles of thick mud, waterlogged fields, and burst river banks in the northwest of the country, which is a significant obstacle for any new front in Moscow's invasion. This makes it easy for Ukrainian forces to channel the movement of Russian troops into specific areas where they would be shelled by artillery. We pray for more supernatural intervention.

One of the chaplains shared about the miracles he witnessed in Bakhmut. As he prayed with and for the soldiers, he would give them badges "God protects and grants victory." He also met two paramedics who asked for a badge "With God for Ukraine," so he gave them his own. The paramedics got in their car, and at that moment, an artillery shell landed about 2 meters (6 feet) away from them, and then another one. Neither of the shells detonated, but the car was covered with soil and debris. The paramedics got out of the car shaking and said, "Thank you, chaplain, for coming here. God does protect." One of them said he would keep the badge as a testimony of God's protection and would share this story with his children and grandchildren. Everyone who witnessed the event kept saying that it was the hand of God because it was a miracle that two shells in a row did not detonate and caused no harm. God is very present at the front lines. May all Ukrainian soldiers experience His saving grace.

Day 324 · January 13

I don't think there's a day when I don't think about how this war affects children. And it breaks my heart to know how deeply affected they are, even those who haven't witnessed the horrors but whose lives have been torn anyway. Refugee children who pull double duty, studying in their local schools during the day and catching up on the Ukrainian program at night because they don't want to miss a thing because they want to return as soon as the war is over. One of my online students (currently in a European country) missed our online class because of a phone call with his dad. The student apologized, but I felt like I was the one to apologize for interrupting this precious time.

A fun activity with my online students, a game "If you could go anywhere in the world, where would you go?" turns into one emphatic answer – "Home!" And instead of listing exotic geographic locations, the students start listing the reasons why they want to return to Ukraine – "because my dad is there," "because I miss my friends," "because I want to sleep in my bed."

Our son praying at night, asking God to protect the soldiers and stop the war, telling Him that he "really, really, really, really, really wants to return home."

I try to hold my tears when I think about our children.

Day 339 • January 28

Last week, I saw a video of a soldier emphatically thanking for the prayers. He showed a muddy road he took at night without headlights (to be invisible to the enemy). When he returned there in daylight and checked the tire tracks, he was amazed. There were mines on the side of the road, just a few centimeters from where his tires were. One landmine was in the middle of the road, and his car passed over without setting it off. He showed that spot and asked to keep praying because he was confident that prayers make a difference.

Day 340 • January 29

The value of human life is one of the fundamental questions shaping our worldview. We've seen a lack of that value in the Russian authorities – 130,000 Russian soldiers killed (they say at least as many have been wounded), thousands of Ukrainian soldiers, and over 20,000 civilian casualties, including 7068 deaths (the actual number is significantly higher as the victims from the temporarily occupied territories are not included in this number). That bloodthirsty mindset has destroyed millions of lives, and that's why it will not last. That's why it is bound to lose because it seeks only destruction and sooner or later will consume itself. There is still time for repentance, but my faith isn't strong enough to believe that it will actually happen.

I also praise God for the hearts of our soldiers. They had every right to kill the enemy (that POW was trying to kill them when they took him captive), but they showed compassion and care instead. This already is a victory in itself, a victory of life over death, love over hatred, and God over the present darkness.

"For we do not wrestle against flesh and blood, but against the rulers, against the authorities, against the cosmic powers over this present darkness, against the spiritual forces of evil in the heavenly places" (Ephesians 6:12).

Day 345 · February 3

The doctors pulled out an unexploded armor-piercing projectile from a soldier's body. It burned through the skin and into the body, but the doctors managed to get it out. I guess Ukrainian bodies are harder than armor.

The Russians attacked Kharkiv this morning, damaging a city center and a couple residential buildings. Four people got injuries – thankfully, the buildings did not collapse. An older woman was brought out of the damaged building on a stretcher. As her relative explained, the lady can barely move and left her bed to wash her face this morning when the missile hit. There was debris on her bed, but she was unharmed.

A Russian bullet scraped the helmet of a Ukrainian defender somewhere near Izium but caused no damage.

When I get overwhelmed by the tragedies of war (because it consists of millions of personal tragedies), when it gets harder to make sense of life, I look at these glimpses of hope and am reminded of the thousands of reasons to praise His name.

Day 347 · February 5

A highlight of the day is a POW swap. One hundred military personnel and one civilian were brought home to the territory of Ukraine. Among the freed soldiers are National Guardsmen, border guards, and soldiers of the Armed Forces of Ukraine. Ninety-four of them are defenders of Mariupol, including 63 soldiers from Azovstal. We keep praying for all the defenders who were taken captive to return home safely.

Day 358 · February 16

As we mourn the Heavenly Hundred and the beginning of this "special military operation" nine years ago; as we relive the pre-invasion days in our memory and anticipate possible provocations and massive missile attacks in

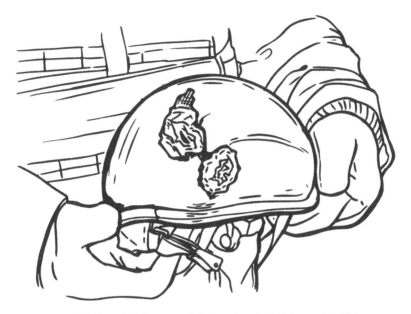

The helmet of a Ukrainian defender - Day 347, February 5, 2023

the next couple of days, it is easy to give in to gloom and despair. That is why today's visit of the President of the United States was a powerful encouragement to many Ukrainians and a slap in the face of the Russian dictator.

This was the first visit of an American president in 15 years and a visit to a country at war. In fact, air-raid sirens went off as soon as the information about his visit became public, but they did not ruin the day. This official visit during one of the most intense moments was a powerful statement of support and responsibility, and you cannot overestimate the importance of this visit. We know that the people of the US stand with us, and we are incredibly grateful for all the support, but seeing it confirmed on the highest level is a great encouragement, especially as the Russian propaganda tries to convince us that "the West" has given up on Ukraine.

We've had American presidents visit Ukraine before. A few weeks before Ukraine's independence was proclaimed in 1991, George Bush Sr. visited Ukraine and delivered the famous "chicken Kyiv speech," cautioning against "suicidal nationalism" (i.e., independence). Bill Clinton visited Ukraine a few times during his presidency. One of his visits was related to signing the denuclearization memorandum, according to which Ukraine had to give up its nuclear weapons (yes, Ukraine had nuclear weapons after the collapse of the Soviet Union and was the third largest nuclear power in the world) in exchange for the territorial defense guarantees from Russia and the US. Next, George W. Bush visited Ukraine in the spring of 2008 (a few months before Russia invaded Georgia) and focused on the need for Ukraine and Georgia to be allowed to start the process of joining NATO despite resistance from Russia and skepticism from some European countries. Unfortunately, this never happened and we see the consequences today. Looking back, we know how those visits turned out. We pray that today's visit of the President of the United States will one day be viewed as a historic event that helped Ukraine gain its victory.

The day ended with more encouraging news. Russia launched missiles at Kharkiv, but none of the rockets landed on Ukraine's territory. They exploded midair over the Russian territory (Belgorod) due to malfunction or Russian air defense shooting down their own missiles. Whatever the reason for that is, we praise God for it.

Please, keep praying for Ukraine over the next week, as this may be a crucial time. May God reveal His glory and power.

Day 362 · February 21

Remembering that this war started nine years ago, February 26 is the Day of Resistance to the Occupation of Crimea. On this day in 2014, a rally was held in Simferopol (Crimea) in support of Ukraine's territorial integrity. At night, Russian special forces in military uniforms without insignia seized the parliament's building, and a sham referendum took place two weeks later. The rally participants were persecuted. Over the past nine years, 180 people have become political prisoners of the Kremlin; of these, 116 are Crimean Tatars. The beautiful Crimean Peninsula has been turned into a military base and a place with little respect for human rights. Appeasement only increases the appetites of the aggressor. May Crimea be free and prosperous again.

Day 368 · February 26

Loss and Lament

A season to regenerate: *Far too quickly are the days of the beautiful flowers gone. The tulip begins to replenish its stores under the ground. This stage is not lovely to look at, but if the stage is cut short, tulips are at risk of dying.*

We often say that this war is a war of worldviews. Perhaps it explains why some news reports are so shocking to us – they don't fit into our worldview and value system.

The defenders of Bakhmut, even the experienced ones, are shocked by the mounds of Russian bodies left in the open field. Their fellow soldiers crawl over them or even use them as a shield when attacking Ukrainian positions.From the intercepted conversations, we know that Russian soldiers are often mistreated and abused by those higher in rank. A couple of days ago, there was a story of a mobilized Russian conscript who committed suicide after being robbed and violated by Kadyrov servicemen.

It is heartbreaking to see this happening to a nation, and it's even more heartbreaking to know that these are the consequences of their corrupt choices and compromising decisions generation after generation. Someone said it's essential for Ukraine to win as it would give Russia a chance to rethink its values and undergo cleansing and much-needed change. We pray for it. We pray for Ukraine's victory to bring a lasting change for the better, not just in Ukraine but also in Russia and other nations.

Day 315 · January 4

When I think about this war, I lose it every time it comes to children. Our son was born in 2014, so he has never had a war-free day in his life, even though it wasn't personal for him until last February. I still shake when I remember how we woke him up that day and explained that we had to leave our home. I'm angry that he is missing out on lots of childhood experiences, he misses his friends, but I know that at least he's safe with his parents in a warm house, and that's something that many children can only dream of.

Since the beginning of the full-scale war, at least 453 Ukrainian children have been killed. Eight-hundred-seventy-seven have been injured. Just imagine these numbers! Almost 14,000 children have been deported to Russia – most of them are orphaned or were separated from their families under false pretenses. Thousands of children remain in active war zones or temporarily occupied territories.

Human rights activists are increasingly worried about the active militarization and brainwashing of children in the occupied territories, especially Crimea.[1] It will take decades to overcome the consequences of such "education." And our children, who have to live through this war now, will have to deal with so many other effects of war even decades after it's over – from overcoming personal trauma and PTSD to rebuilding the economy to getting rid of the pollution brought by this war. Ukraine is the most heavily mined place in the world, with the mines covering over 250 thousand square kilometers (almost 100 thousand square miles) of land. That's over 1/3 of Ukraine's territory and more than the territory of Romania or Great Britain.

Thinking about the opportunities our children miss now and the challenges they will have to face in their adult years just breaks my heart. That's why I am incredibly grateful to everyone who brightens the days of our children.

Day 319 · January 8

Intense attacks on Bakhmut and even more intense attacks on Soledar (about 15 km/10 miles to the northeast of Bakhmut). The Russians come one wave after another, trying to capture the almost completely destroyed city.

The shelling of a market square in Shevchenkove (Kharkiv region) killed two women and left six civilians injured, including a thirteen-year-old girl.

The shelling of Ochakiv (Mykolaiv region) left fifteen people injured, including a two-year-old.

Kherson is shelled dozens of times every day (Kherson region was shelled over 77 times yesterday). During today's attack, they hit an intersection in a residential city block, which set one of the buildings on fire. One person was killed.

During a missile attack on Kramatorsk (Donetsk region, about 50 km/30 miles from Bakhmut), they hit a car that was moving on the road, killing its passengers.

I'm incredibly grateful that we see glimpses of hope among these heart-wrenching reports. Ukrainian combat medics performed a unique surgery to remove a grenade (!) from a soldier's body. It's a miracle that it did not explode.

Day 320 · January 9

Our thoughts remain with the city of Dnipro. The missile that hit the residential building was an X-22. Our air-defense forces have no weapon against this type of missile. Since the beginning of the war, Russia has launched over 210 missiles of this type, but none could be intercepted. That's why our government, diplomats, and citizens have kept asking for modern air defense systems since February.

As of now (9 pm on January 15), over 24 hours after the hit, the report is about 30 dead, 75 injured, and 30 to 40 people still missing. The rescue operation continues nonstop. They have teams of SAR dogs working on the location and set up minutes of silence to try to hear people under the rubble. That's how one woman was rescued this morning – they heard a sound last night but couldn't get to her until morning. She spent the whole night in freezing temperatures and couldn't call for help because she was born mute and deaf. They are still searching for her husband and their one-year-old baby.

As we live in the age of the internet and social media, any disaster can become personal if you care to listen. Sometimes I wish we couldn't learn their stories.... Two young women, dentists, volunteers were simply passing by, killed by the missile. They both have young children. A family was getting ready to go out. The kids were already outside while the parents were finishing something up at home. They are still looking for the parents, and the kids are in the hospital. Six months ago, this family moved from Nikopol (Dnipropetrovsk region) to escape the constant shelling.

A soldier was fighting in the Bakhmut area. He rushed home when he learned that the apartment building his mom lived in was hit. While on his way to Dnipro, he received a message that his mom miraculously survived –

she was saved by a piece of the wall in a kitchen corner, the only corner of the apartment on the 9th floor that remained.

As if this isn't enough, today, Russians shelled Kherson – the Red Cross building, a rehabilitation center for disabled children, critical infrastructure facilities, and residential buildings. Seven people were injured.

Our intelligence services warn that Russia used only half of the prepared missiles, so they may repeat the attack soon. And we never know which "object of strategic importance" they may hit next time – a maternity ward, a shopping mall, or another apartment building.

Day 326 · January 15

It's the third day of the rescue operation in Dnipro after a Russian missile hit a multi-story apartment building. As of now (11 pm on January 16), we know about 40 people (including three children) killed, 77 people (including fourteen children) injured, 39 people (including six children) rescued, and 25 people still missing. The chances of finding them alive after so much time under the rubble are slim, but we know that nothing is impossible for God.

Day 327 · January 16

The rescue operation in Dnipro is over. They have finished picking apart the rubble. Forty-five people (including six children) were killed. Fifteen bodies still need to be identified. Twenty people (including four children) are still missing. Unfortunately, they may never be found after such a powerful missile.

Someone organized a memorial to the Dnipro victims by a monument for Lesia Ukrainka (a Ukrainian poetess) in Moscow. They brought a picture of the destroyed building and candles. People were bringing flowers. It was in one of the districts further away from the downtown area, and people were few, coming spontaneously, so it went under the police radar. However, police arrived in the evening and detained those passing by the memorial. It was not a political rally. It was an act of mournful compassion. Apparently, empathy is considered illegal in Russia and, unfortunately, remains a totally foreign concept to many. I must admit I did not expect to see a show of solidarity in Russia and am grateful to the brave people who genuinely care. May the eyes of many be opened, and may the truth shine brightly in the deep darkness brought upon Russia.

The situation in our energy system is dire. As the strike on the apartment building in Dnipro took most of the attention, everything else lost its importance. But that attack destroyed four power-generating blocks, three major substations, and a power line, which caused a severe energy deficit. In the place where we are now, the scheduled blackouts look like two hours with electricity followed by six hours without. If your laundry cycle needs more than two hours, you are presented with a challenge. But all of this is a mere inconvenience.

Our US partners promised it would take ten weeks to train Ukrainian soldiers to use Patriot systems. That's something unprecedented as a minimum training time used to be ten months. We pray for this miracle to happen. We pray for more air-defense systems to be sent to Ukraine. We pray for modern tanks (such as German-made Leopards) and long-range artillery systems to be sent to Ukraine to stop Russia before more evil is done.

Day 328 · January 17

May the Lord give strength to our people... This morning started with yet another tragedy far from the frontline. A helicopter crashed into a preschool (kindergarten) building in Brovary (one of the suburban towns near Kyiv). The aircraft carried the Minister of Internal Affairs and other officials of his ministry (a total of nine people). It was supposed to be a quick trip to the Kharkiv region. At a little past 8 in the morning, people saw the helicopter circling, catch fire, and crash into the building. As of now, we know about fourteen people who have died (nine of them were in the helicopter). Among them is a mother and her daughter – she was just dropping her off at the preschool. Twenty-five people, including eleven children, are in the hospital, and five of them (including three children) are in severe condition. Among the injured, there's a pregnant woman with a big wound on her back and a father and his daughter with severe burns on 30% of their bodies.

This tragedy right after the tragedy in Dnipro seems to be more than one can handle. They are investigating the causes (pilot's mistake because of the fog, engine problems, or sabotage). However, I must agree with President Zelensky's words that every death and every tragedy after February 24 is not an accident but the result of the war. The stress, exhaustion, anxiety, poor sleep, and poor medical care – these have been our companions since February 24, and none of these is known to prolong someone's life.

May the Lord comfort those who mourn today.

Day 329 · January 18

We had a lovely sunny day today, so I took my son for a walk instead of one of our homeschool lessons. The birds were chirping, and it felt like spring (in the middle of January!), and it unexpectedly triggered so many memories.

When we came to this village on the first day of the invasion, there were many uncertainties, so we tried not to go too far from our yard. Sometimes, we would go to a small dried-up pond nearby, where we ended up today. I was overcome with the feelings of those early days of March 2022, the memories of the first missile attacks on Kharkiv and Kyiv... This winter has been challenging, and we're looking forward to the spring, but today showed me that it may not necessarily be easier since we'll have to come to terms with the fact that the full-scale war will have passed the one-year mark.

This week, I was thinking about children – many of them displaced, living through sirens and learning to deal with anxiety and loss, many of them separated from their families (men are not allowed to leave the country during the martial law), many of them have witnessed the horrible things they should never have seen. This new generation of Ukrainians is going through severe challenges, and we pray that the Lord uses it all for His glory. May this fire refine their hearts but not destroy them. May the Lord have mercy and be their comfort.

"The Lord your God is in your midst, a mighty one who will save; he will rejoice over you with gladness; he will quiet you by his love; he will exult over you with loud singing" (Zephaniah 3:17).

Day 331 · January 20

There are too many flashbacks from January 2022. Last year, the western intelligence services were warning about the imminent invasion. There were the first shipments of weapons, and we were slowly coming to terms with the things we didn't want to believe were possible. Now, we've heard a few western officials say that the next few weeks may be crucial in determining the outcome of this war. It makes sense – Russia will try to achieve something that could be presented as a small victory for the invasion anniversary. Even a few months back, many officials were talking about the big attack Russia could be planning for the end of January or February. Our army is constructing fortifications along the northern border in case Belarus gives in and officially joins Russia.

Our intelligence service said that Russia is planning a big spring campaign, and if they fail, it will crush the current regime. Meanwhile, they keep shuffling the army commanders, and their mobilization is at full speed. Please, pray for God's mercy and divine interference.

It's devastating to think about the losses this war brought, and I'm not talking just about the deaths and injuries but also about the crushed dreams and long-term consequences. They say it will take over ten years to clear the territory of Ukraine from mines and other explosives – how many lives will be lost in this process?

I read about a dairy farm 30 kilometers (20 miles) from the Russian border. They used to have 600 cows and a promising family business. The occupation took its toll – the roads to the farm were destroyed, making it impossible to bring supplies. Now, they are down to 170 cows and a few calves born during the occupation. The front legs of the calves are shorter than the back ones because the mother cows were severely malnourished. The war doesn't care who you are, and these baby calves make me wonder about the scale of the consequences that escape our immediate attention.

Day 334 · January 23

Today, there was a large prisoner swap. One-hundred-sixteen Ukrainian soldiers were exchanged for 63 Russians. Ukraine also managed to return the bodies of foreign volunteers killed by the Russians.

It is a great joy every time. Our officials would usually post video clips and pictures of the first moments of the meeting with the released soldiers. Every time, the released would look thin and exhausted, with shaved heads and painful looks in their unbroken eyes. A few weeks ago, after one of the swaps, my mom noticed that all of the soldiers were given a small bag, and in one of the videos, she saw them eating something that was in those bags. "They must have been starving this whole time," she pointed out. I agreed with her because you couldn't think otherwise when you saw their skinny bodies. However, this reality struck me anew today.

In one of the pictures shared today, you could see a tall thin man holding an apple and looking at it in bewilderment. The newly released prisoner of war said it was the first time he saw an apple (or fresh fruit) in 11 months and was even scared to taste it at first! We've always known that the Russians treat our soldiers horribly, we never expected them to be well-fed, but somehow this soldier's amazement at the apple brought it to a whole new level. I was even more shocked to discover that this prisoner in the picture is a Ukrainian restaurateur and a successful marketing director who joined the army back in 2015 and was taken captive last March as he was defending the Kyiv region. I didn't know him in person, but I followed him on Facebook several years ago when he opened a restaurant after the Revolution of Dignity and when he started sharing his "Notes of a conscript" after joining the army. This is why I was shocked that he looked nothing like himself in the picture, and even some of his close friends couldn't recognize him.

All released soldiers are taken to the hospital for treatment and rehabilitation. Please, keep praying for our POWs and the softening of the Russian hearts.

The situation at the front lines is intensifying, and the Russians have started drafting female prisoners, having lost dozens of thousands of prisoners in the attacks near Bakhmut.

Day 346 · February 4

It's been almost a year since the beginning of the full-scale aggression on Ukraine. The experts say the next three months are going to be very intense and trying, with Russia preparing a massive attack in several directions. The promised military aid will most likely arrive at the end of spring (and that's an optimistic timetable) and will be used in Ukraine's counteroffensive. I can't help but think about the cities and villages that will be destroyed and possibly occupied during this time. Lord, have mercy and stop the invaders.

A captive Russian soldier confessed that they had been given an order not to take Ukrainians captive and shoot even the unarmed who raised their hands in surrender.

The first trial of the Russian soldiers who refused to fight against Ukraine was held in the temporarily occupied Sevastopol (Crimea). The defendants are cousins who refused to fulfill a commander's order. They were sentenced to over three years of correction colony. Please, pray for these men and pray for more Russian soldiers to refuse to fulfill the criminal orders of their commanders. May justice be restored.

A strong storm in the Black Sea made the Russian warships return to the harbor. Unfortunately, the weather didn't stop the Russians from attacking

A freed prisoner of war with an apple - Day 346, February 4, 2023

Kharkiv with missiles. There were six hits in the downtown area and a fire at one of the industrial facilities.

O Lord, do not delay!

Day 349 · February 7

Sometimes, when you read the news, you feel like the whole world is in turmoil. We read about rumors of war, famines, and earthquakes and cannot help but wonder if that's what Jesus had in mind when he warned his disciples in Matthew 24. His words both terrify and encourage, "you will be hated by all nations for my name's sake. And then many will fall away and betray one another and hate one another. And many false prophets will arise and lead many astray. And because lawlessness will be increased, the love of many will grow cold. But the one who endures to the end will be saved. And this gospel of the kingdom will be proclaimed throughout the whole world as a testimony to all nations, and then the end will come" (Matthew 24:9-14). While it's tempting to arrogantly think that Jesus was talking about Ukraine, I remember that He was talking to his disciples about things many of them might witness in their lifetime. If we shift focus from ourselves and look at the big picture of history, we will see many time periods that match these words. However, the main message of Christ hasn't changed in the past two thousand years, "Therefore you also must be ready, for the Son of Man is coming at an hour you do not expect" (Matthew 24:44). Let us keep watch, be conscious and ready at all times, and let us be faithful until the day He comes.

The world needs our prayers. Turkey and Syria are still trying to come to terms with the aftermath of the earthquake – the death toll exceeds 25,000 but rescuers are still finding life and sharing incredible miracle stories. May those hurting meet Jesus face to face in their suffering, and may His name be glorified in all the miracle stories.

Day 353 · February 11

It's Valentine's Day, and while my Facebook feed is filled with cards, flowers, hearts, and messages of love, I keep thinking about what love is. The Bible tells the greatest love story one could imagine. The greatest act of love did not include flowers or chocolate but consisted of a crown of thorns, a broken body, a cross, and blood poured out for the salvation of many. It was not pretty, but it was precious.

However, God's love does not stop there. He gives us a responsibility to love, "A new commandment I give to you, that you love one another: just as I have loved you, you also are to love one another. By this all people will know that you are my disciples, if you have love for one another" (John 13:34-35).

He calls us to imitate His love to the fullest, to love others more than we love life itself. "Greater love has no one than this, that someone lay down his life for his friends" (John 15:13). This is the kind of love we've been witnessing for the past year (for the past nine years, to be exact). Millions of people standing up to the enemy, uniting in their effort to restore justice and protect their loved ones and complete strangers. Thousands of them have laid down their lives. I am well aware that not all of them knew Jesus, but it didn't prevent them from following His example and loving to the greatest extent possible.

As I stand in awe of this love, I remember one more responsibility given to us by the Lord and articulated by Apostle John, "Let us not love in word or talk but in deed and in truth" (1 John 3:18). Letting love seep through our actions, seeking truth in all circumstances, and bringing glory to the Giver of Life – that is the least we can do in response to this great love we have been given.

Please, cover Ukraine with your love and prayers. Pray for the families of those who had laid down their lives fighting against the Russian invasion. Pray for God's comfort and healing. Pray for the families who have been separated for almost a year because of the war. Pray for comfort in loneliness and for love to be stronger than distance. Pray for the disadvantaged and most vulnerable groups – the orphans, the elderly, the sick – who are often left behind. May they feel God's presence, and may His love reach them through the loving hands here on earth. Pray for God's love to grow stronger in His children.

Day 356 · February 14

The day was nice and sunny, so we went to a local playground to enjoy some fresh air with hope of meeting some kids. One of the biggest challenges for our son is that there are no children nearby, and he misses his old friends. We were lucky to meet a family at the playground. While the kids were playing, we started talking with their mom. The brief phrases were both unique and universal at the same time, as usually happens when you speak with someone who shared your experience.

... You aren't local, are you?... We left Kyiv early in the morning on the 24th (Feb 24, 2022) after the first explosions. Our bags were packed, and we were ready because we had the feeling it would happen... We were convinced we came here for two or three days, maybe a week, but it will be a year in a few days... Did you wonder what to do with school? Online education is the worst, and homeschooling is challenging, but these two are better options in our situation... We were hoping to find some afterschool activities, like a club or music lessons, but it would require a trip to another town, and it's too much with everything that's going on... We are reluctant to make any long-term commitments here because we want to believe we'll be able to return home soon, but that's what we've been telling ourselves for the past year...

All of these phrases were spoken by that other mom, yet they describe our situation almost word for word. The past year's pains, anxieties, and hopes resonate in each Ukrainian heart.

Meanwhile, the UK Defence Secretary says that 97% of the Russian army is now committed to Ukraine, with an attrition rate very, very high (First World War levels of attrition), their combat effectiveness may have been depleted by 40%, and nearly two-thirds of their tanks have been destroyed or broken." Yet the UK defense and security think tank believes war will likely continue into at least next year (2024).

Day 357 · February 15

It is amazing how my memory chooses to keep some ordinary events that didn't mean much at the moment. For example, the first weeks of the war are a blur. I don't remember anything specific from days a week or a month ago, but I remember the days before the invasion in great detail.

A year ago today, I spent most of the day reading the news and crying. It felt similar to mourning. Perhaps, it was my moving from bargaining to acceptance. On the evening of that day (Wednesday, February 23), we had an important doctor's appointment that we had rescheduled a few times. I was worried about whether we would make it before the invasion. We had to travel to the other side of the city to see the doctor. While waiting for her in the hallway, we heard an airplane flying low over the hospital building – the military airfield was only a few kilometers away. In less than twelve hours, that military airfield would be attacked by the Russians – it was an air assault meant to be the primary steppingstone to surrounding Kyiv. As we left the hospital, the streets were packed with traffic, a usual occurrence in Kyiv. The navigator showed that it would take us almost two hours to get home. My heart kept racing, and my only prayer was, "God, help us get home before the invasion." It seemed that the air in Kyiv was thick and heavy with the anticipation of doom.

We tried our best to keep the usual activities. We bought groceries that day. Preparing the grocery list, I kept second-guessing every purchase, wondering if we would have the chance to use it, but Ivan kept encouraging me to go about it as usual. Most of the groceries we bought that day stayed in our fridge untouched.

We did get home before the invasion. I was even going to take my good friend to the airport later that night, but she found someone else to do it. I was sad I didn't get a chance to say goodbye, but we hoped she would return soon. She was the first to message me in the first hours of the full-scale war. And her plane was among the last ones to leave the airport. Soon, all runways were blocked to prevent the Russian planes from landing.

That night, we went to bed as usual. We kept joking that everyone was hesitant to take a shower those days because everyone was afraid to be "indecent" at the moment of invasion. At that moment, we were still unaware of how many times we would choose to use humor to overcome our fear.

We've seen so much pain in the past year, yet we know that more months of this pain are still ahead of us. We now have no illusions about the nature of our enemy and have no false hopes for its humanity. However, this year has changed us. A dear friend of mine phrased it perfectly, "The cost is unspeakably horrible. But we have also gained so much. Strength, unity, hope, and dependence on God. Love for the Ukrainian language. Awakened churches and people hungry for God. A country full of volunteers. Incredible support and friendship from our neighbors in Europe and much of the rest of the world. A new openness, support, and willingness to sacrifice for each other. Gratitude for small things. Countless reminders of eternity and what is truly important."

As I go to bed tonight, I am surprised by how different my feelings are from one year ago. And it's not just me. I was surprised by how many people make plans for tomorrow, the day after tomorrow, and weeks and months ahead. We know that God is with us, and we are confident that He will not leave us nor forsake us, for we've already seen proof of that. The fear, cruelty, and war did not kill our desire to keep living. And this already is a victory in itself.

"We are afflicted in every way, but not crushed; perplexed, but not driven to despair; persecuted, but not forsaken; struck down, but not destroyed... For this light momentary affliction is preparing for us an eternal weight of glory beyond all comparison, as we look not to the things that are seen but to the things that are unseen. For the things that are seen are transient, but the things that are unseen are eternal." (2 Cor 4:8-9, 17-18)

Day 365 • February 23

One of the publications made a photo collection that captures the past year's key events. I got to the third or fourth picture.[li] I couldn't bear the pain of memories. I know that art helps us process trauma. There have been a few movies made about the 2014 invasion that we watched and cried our eyes out in the movie theatres. I know that one day we'll be able to watch movies about this one, but it's still too raw.

Last night's attack was limited to kamikaze drones. Out of 14 drones, 11 were shot down. The remaining three caused explosions in Khmelnytskyi. They took the lives of two emergency rescuers helping out at the site of the attack when the Russians decided to repeat the strike. Thankfully, there were no missiles. Russia cannot produce many high-precision rockets, and they have used up most of their missiles, so they are more moderate with the rockets now.

Day 369 · February 27

Resilience and the Seeds of Future Hope

A season to multiply: *The tulips begin to multiply and prepare for the following year. This invisible work of resilience is crucial. The commitment to goodness brings life into the world.*

Meanwhile, our energy system is well-maintained by our power engineers, and there has been slight optimism about how we may go through this winter. The temperature remains abnormally high (+13°C/55°F today), so we discovered tulip buds in our flower beds, and there were reports of Sakura (cherry trees) blooming in one of Kyiv's parks. The weather forecast also promises temperatures just below freezing and not lower than -12°C/10F until the end of the month. God is merciful.

Day 313 · January 2

Over this past week, I noticed how much we care. After 11 months of tragic news and pain, we care and cry for the people we never knew. We feel their pain, and it gives me hope. When the Russian soldiers were committing atrocities in Bucha and Irpin, they were intentionally cruel. They wanted to shock us, they wanted us to drown in pain, despair, or hatred, but they failed. Because we still care, we still cry with those who cry and rush to help those in need. I praise God that He has been guarding our hearts, and I pray for His healing.

Please, keep praying for our army. Russia may be planning a series of attacks at the frontlines or the Ukrainian border, and we need more military aid. Today (January 19), nine European nations – the UK, Poland, Estonia, Latvia, Lithuania, Denmark, the Netherlands, Czechia, and Slovakia – signed a joint statement known as the Tallinn Pledge, committing to providing Ukraine with the support that it needs to liberate all its territory currently occupied by Russia. Tomorrow, on January 20, the eighth summit of Ukraine's defense partners will take place at the U.S. air base in Ramstein,

Germany. Important decisions may be made and announced there, including Germany's decision to provide modern Leopard tanks to Ukraine. A few countries have announced their desire to give the Leopard tanks they have, but they still need Germany's permission. Of course, we don't trust in "chariots" or "horses"; we know that our help comes from the Lord, so we ask you to pray for God's will.

Day 330 · January 19

"The Lord is good to those who wait for him, to the soul who seeks him. It is good that one should wait quietly for the salvation of the Lord" (Lamentations 3:25-26). As we wait for the great victory, it is vitally important to see God's faithfulness in the small victories. Today's news reports speak to me about God's faithfulness and the need to wait quietly for His salvation. Germany allowed the sale to Ukraine of 88 Leopard 1 tanks (in addition to 14 Leopard 2 tanks that had been promised before). Representatives of 40 countries are preparing their statement against the participation of Russia and Belarus in the Olympics.

Today's summit Ukraine-EU took place in Kyiv to confirm Ukraine's intention to join the EU and demonstrate Europe's dedication to supporting Ukraine as long as needed. The US announced another military aid package, which will include GLSDB (Ground-Launched-Small-Diameter-Bomb) rockets with a 150 km range. These would help cut off the supply routes from Crimea and other logistics. Lithuanians raised 1,006,000 euros for radars for Ukraine in one hour. Lithuanian IT company Tesonet doubled it for 2,012,000 euro. It was done within the fundraising campaign of the four biggest support organizations to buy Israeli-made modern radars to help protect the Ukrainian sky. I am speechless and forever grateful.

Day 345 · February 3

Many families with children remain in the active combat zone and refuse to evacuate.

A few days ago, I read about another soldier (a Ukrainian TV host who took up arms after the invasion) who rescued a two-month-old girl when her whole family was killed in one of the cities on the front lines. He wants to adopt the baby and is preparing the paperwork to finalize the process as soon as the war ends.

Stories like this are testimonies that we fight not out of hate but out of love, out of the desire to protect those we love, even if we never met them.

Day 351 · February 9

The last day of calendar winter is over. Going to bed, our son excitedly asked what would be different tomorrow because of spring. Unfortunately, we had to disappoint him with our answer. I wish a turn of a calendar page could bring great changes and undo the pain and the losses. However, we are grateful that the winter season is almost done with. Back in November, when the days were getting shorter, the massive missile strikes were intensifying, and the blackouts were getting longer, it took all we had to remain positive and hopeful. We didn't know how we would endure the long winter months. We thank God that He didn't abandon us, and what the enemy intended for resentment, He used for His glory.

I heard my son talking to his classmates during their online lesson tonight. The kids were excitedly discussing the books they had read (or had their parents read to them) and recommending new titles to each other. I had tears in my eyes and prayed for these young hearts to remain excited about books and eager to learn. In many interviews with the soldiers fighting on the front lines, when asked why they chose to fight, they say they do it for the children of Ukraine to live in a free country. I believe their answer sets a task for our home front – to bring up children worthy of their sacrifice.

Many of you might remember how dearly we love our son's school. The team of devoted Christians serving the children of Ukraine, teaching them to honor God in all areas of life, and doing so by their example. Since the beginning of the full-scale war, our school has been seeking opportunities to help our children serve those affected by the war. Last year, they had a "Read for Ukraine" challenge and encouraged the kids to record their reading minutes throughout March. They raised $8,600 for humanitarian aid ($1 was donated for every 10 minutes read by the student). This year, they continue the special tradition of "March is Reading Month" to raise funds for the volunteer military paramedics who are saving the lives of soldiers on the front lines. Our school's students aim to read for about 50 minutes per day (a total of 1500 minutes of reading by each student by the end of the month). I am so grateful that our kids have the opportunity to learn to serve others while fulfilling their deepest longing – helping their country.

Please, pray for our cities and our air defense. The central part of Ukraine is under a drone attack now.

Day 370 · February 28

Afterword

Dear reader,

Thank you for picking up this book. I appreciate you letting me share the story of the first year of the full-scale invasion of Ukraine as seen by an ordinary person caught up in these challenging moments. I hope it helped you learn more about what's going on in my country, but I also hope it could become an encouragement and an inspiration to you in whatever life circumstances you might be going through.

When I wrote my first war-related post on February 22, 2022, I never expected it to turn into something big. However, in less than two days, when Russia started its full-scale aggression, I received dozens of messages from people across the globe, asking me if I was alive, if there was anything I needed, and if what they saw reported by their media was true. That's when I realized I needed to keep writing daily updates, and it could be my input into Ukraine's victory. However, I still didn't know it would end up being a book.

In November 2022, I received a message from my good friend, who currently serves with Envision Berlin. They asked if I would be interested in publishing my posts as a book. I never considered myself an author (even though I dreamed of becoming one). Besides, at the time, Ukraine suffered from frequent attacks on the energy system, we had a sporadic power supply and almost no internet connection, so this offer sounded too good to be true. However, the perseverance and faithfulness of the Envision Berlin team could overcome these circumstances, and you are holding the product in your hands.

The final day covered by the book is February 28, 2023. Almost another year has gone by since then. Unfortunately, the war in Ukraine continues. Parts of the Kharkiv, Luhansk, Donetsk, Zaporizhzhia, Kherson regions, and Crimea are still occupied by Russia. Our cities are still shelled by the aggressor. Almost every day, people in all of Ukraine need to go into bomb shelters because of possible missile and drone attacks.

The first year of the full-scale war taught us many things. We discovered that we have a great army of supporters worldwide. We realized that a sense of humor and a little creative approach can help you deal with many hardships. We learned that we are more resilient than we ever thought. This resilience and resolve to resist the enemy keep us going.

The war is far from being over. I dream of the day when I will write my final post, saying, "Ukraine has finally gained its victory. Peace and justice have been restored. We can start healing now." Till then, join us in supporting Ukraine and praying for our people.

Let me conclude with a wish for you – May you always be able to notice tulips, even when your world is grieved with ashes.

Yours truly,
Ira Kapitonova

December 2023

Acknowledgements

You may have heard the saying, "It takes a village to raise a child." I must say, it takes a few villages to write a book! What you are holding in your hands now is the true product of a team effort. I even feel that it's not just my name that should be on the cover but a whole list of names. Fortunately, I have this acknowledgments section to express my gratitude.

Firstly, I would like to thank my *family*.
To my incredible husband, *Ivan*, thank you for always being my first reader and critic. Your unwavering belief in me and your constant encouragement give me the confidence to explore and create, even when I doubt myself. Thank you for your patience when I stay up at night writing and for your understanding in the mornings.
To my dearest son, *Andriyko*, you will always be my inspiration. The depth of your thoughts and the tenderness of your heart teach me how much I can learn and grow. I am grateful for your eagerness to contribute to this book, and I cherish every moment we share.

This book came to life through the enthusiasm and perseverance of *Envision Berlin* and a few exceptional people on the team.
Mike and *Elissa Picconatto*, our friendship goes way back to when I was a 16-year-old exchange student in a small town in Minnesota, America. You showed me an example of a godly Christian family, and you inspired me with your courage and dedication when you moved across the ocean to serve in Berlin. A lot of who I am today comes from what I observed and learned from you. Mike, when I received your message suggesting turning my daily posts into a book, it seemed impossible and too good to be true. Now, it has become a gemstone I will treasure in my heart forever.
Stephen Jones, thank you for performing the miracle of turning a collection of social media posts into a book. Your hard work and dedication are amazing.

It is so special how you took time to immerse yourself in my writing and then thoughtfully noticed the details to present the idea of the life stages of a tulip. Thank you for guiding me through the process and for helping me share the story of my country.

Justin Siemens, your ability to create images that match my words is truly remarkable! I am grateful for your creativity and commitment to designing the visual component of the book. It is breathtaking and adds so much value to the final product. I also appreciate your patience when I asked too many questions or was slow in providing the necessary pieces. I look forward to the day when I can welcome you and your family to Ukraine!

I would like to take this opportunity to thank two special communities who have become like a family to me.

YWAM Kyiv, I've had the privilege of working with you and learning from you. *Japhin* and *Marie John*, you are my heroes of faith, an example of people who live out their beliefs. Your resolve to serve in the nation you'd been called to, your willingness to exchange a classroom setting for a war zone, and your dedication to sharing the love of Christ with the people of Ukraine are admirable, even though I know you would say it's not you who deserves the credit. Your sacrificial love helped me keep my faith, especially during the first weeks of this full-scale war. I am honored to know you and to call you my friends.

I want to thank the *New Generation Christian School family* and *Maggie Palatova*. If I am ever asked to name events that became a turning point in my spiritual life, our school's online prayer meeting on February 24, 2022, hours after we woke up from explosions, will be at the top of the list. Your wisdom in guiding our community towards God and encouraging us to hold fast to prayer when the world as we knew it was collapsing gave our family a sense of direction. Thank you for being an example of loving God with all your heart, mind, soul, and strength.

I would like to express my gratitude to all the *kind people* who supported me on Facebook, without whom this book would not have been possible. I am truly grateful for each message and comment I received, and I value your unwavering support and prayers. Although social media might not have been designed for this kind of interaction, it has made it all worthwhile.

Lastly, I would like to extend my heartfelt thanks to the wonderful people who backed our book project on Kickstarter. Your belief in our cause and support has given me a voice and made this book a reality. Thank you so much for making it happen!

Marianna Kapliuk, my faithful supporter since our university years, it was around the second week of this full-scale invasion when you said that my posts should become a book, and then you went ahead and backed it once the opportunity presented itself. Thank you for always being there for me, even though distance may separate us.

Endnotes

i   *The Life Of A Tulip Bulb.* (2020). Tulips.Com.
https://www.tulips.com/bulbs_life_of

ii   In Ukrainian, the month "February" literally means "furious, fierce, ferocious, savage," and it felt like a very appropriate name for that month of the year in 2022

iii   Original work by Volodymyr Viatrovych, translation by Iryna Kapitonova

iv   Belam, M. (2022, April 21). Ukrainian Holocaust survivor, 91, dies during Mariupol siege. *The Guardian.* https://www.theguardian.com/world/2022/apr/21/ukrainian-holocaust-survivor-91-dies-during-mariupol-siege

v   Psalm 94:1-2,5,14-15,18-19,22-23

vi   A reference to John 15:13

vii   Андрєєва, В. (2022a). Офіційно зниклий безвісти, та насправді – в полоні. Історія 19-річного морпіха, який боронив Маріуполь. *Українська Правда.* https://life.pravda.com.ua/society/2022/07/11/249500/

viii Psalm 56:1a,3b-4

ix   The picture was by Andrii Yakovyn.

x   Psalm 34:1,4-5,17-19,21-22

xi   Андрєєва, В. (2022a). Офіційно зниклий безвісти, та насправді – в полоні. Історія 19-річного морпіха, який боронив Маріуполь. *Українська Правда.* https://life.pravda.com.ua/society/2022/07/11/249500/

xii   Spicer, J., & Dikmen, Y. (2022, July 21). Turkey says Russia, Ukraine to sign U.N. grain export deal Friday. *Reuters.* https://www.reuters.com/world/europe/turkey-says-russia-ukraine-sign-un-grain-export-deal-friday-2022-07-21/

xiii Ukraine: Russian soldiers filmed viciously attacking Ukrainian POW must face justice. (2022, July 29). *Amnesty International.* https://www.amnesty.org/en/latest/news/2022/07/ukraine-russian-soldiers-filmed-viciously-attacking-ukrainian-pow-must-face-justice/

xiv   Forrest, B., & Gershkovich, E. (2022, July 29). Explosion Kills Ukrainian
         POWs Held by Russian-Backed Forces. *The Wall Street Journal*. https://www.
         wsj.com/articles/explosion-kills-ukrainian-pows-held-by-russian-backed-
         forces-11659097747

xv   Балаєва, Т. (2022, November 6). *Чий Херсон*. https://projects.liga.net/kherson/

xvi   Сергій, Л. (2020). Про український борщ з історичними приправами.
         Українська Правда. https://www.istpravda.com.ua/articles/2020/11/3/158395/

xvii   *Кара Божа: В РФ сарана атакувала місто, з якого ворожі літаки бомблять
         Україну (відео)*. (2022, December 7).

xviii   Безстрашний мешканець окупованого Маріуполя вийшов у центр міста
         з українським прапором–Фото. (2022). *New Voice*. https://nv.ua/ukr/ukraine/
         events/u-mariupoli-misceviy-zhitel-viyshov-u-centr-mista-z-ukrajinskim-
         praporom-foto-novini-ukrajini-50257155.html

xix   Lukashova, S., & Petrenko, R. (2022, June 26). Missile strike on Kyiv
         causes fatality. *Ukrainska Pravda*. https://www.pravda.com.ua/eng/
         news/2022/06/26/7354718/

xx   Lachenkov, I. (2022, June 26). Дякую за переклад. @
         igorlachenkov. https://twitter.com/igorlachenkov/
         status/1540977196378062850?s=21&amp%3Bt=EGugVsMC4HGram6pRDbh7g

xxi   Psalm 69:1-4a, 13-22, 24, 27, 29-36

xxii   Russian Invasion of Ukraine Russia Continues Shelling in Ukraine's East as
         War Divides G20. (2022, July 8). *The New York Times*. https://www.nytimes.
         com/live/2022/07/08/world/russia-ukraine-war-news?smid=url-share#the-us-
         identified-18-russian-filtration-camps-for-ukrainians-a-diplomat-says

xxiii   Андрєєва, В. (2022b). Повернення з Мордору. Як депортованих
         українців витягують з Росії. *Ukrainska Pravda*. https://life.pravda.com.ua/
         society/2022/06/9/249026/

xxiv   *Костянтин Огнєвой Чорнобривці*. (2018, June 23). UkrainianCulture ! https://
         www.youtube.com/watch?v=f5c7_IBZYqQ

xxv   Psalm 27:1, 3, 5, 7, 9, 1,13-14

xxvi   Ministry of Defence, United Kingdom. (2022b, September 18). Latest Defense ...
         @*DefenceHQ*. https://twitter.com/DefenceHQ/status/1571373728008736769

xxvii   *My "Hell" in Russian Captivity*. (n.d.). https://www.youtube.com/
         watch?v=7MbGOFOTt-E

xxviii   Russia lost over half of its naval aviation in Saky airfield strike. (2022, August 19).
         New Voice. https://english.nv.ua/nation/saky-explosions-knocked-out-more-than-
         half-of-russia-naval-aviation-russia-military-news-50264381.html

xxix   Public Domain. Find the whole poem at https://shevchenko.ca/taras-shevchenko/
         poem.cfm?poem=30

xxx   ESZaporizhzhia / Twitter

xxxi   Guterres, A. (2022, August 11). Secretary-General's statement on Zaporizhzhia
         Power Plant. *United Nations Statements.* https://www.un.org/sg/en/content/sg/
         statement/2022-08-11/secretary-generals-statement-zaporizhzhia-power-plant

xxxii   Цьомик, Г., & Богдан, Р. (2022). *Виривали нігті, годували двічі на тиждень:
         Окупанти тримали в полоні на Харківщині 7 громадян Шрі-Ланки.* https://
         suspilne.media/283029-bogdan-2/

xxxiii   У Росії 40% техніки для оснащення нових підрозділів не боєздатна–ГУР.
         (2022). *New Voice.* https://nv.ua/ukr/world/countries/viyna-v-ukrajini-rosiya-
         zmozhe-sformuvati-noviy-pidrozdil-lishe-do-kincya-oseni-gur-50267570.html

xxxiv   Ministry of Defence, United Kingdom. (2022a, September 4). Latest Defense ... @
         DefenceHQ. https://twitter.com/DefenceHQ/status/1566285175830478850

xxxv   Топчій, О. (2022, April 9). *Українські військові збили російський літак без
         жодного пострілу: Як це вдалося.* https://www.unian.ua/war/ukrajinskiy-
         viyskovi-zbili-rosiyskiy-litak-bez-zhodnogo-postrilu-yak-ce-vdalosya-novini-
         harkova-11966724.html

xxxvi   *The Untold Story of "Carol of the Bells" · Ukrainer in English.* (2022, October 5).
         https://www.youtube.com/watch?v=jk6GZe15FRY

xxxvii   Медведєва, Н. (2022). *Біля кордону з Естонією росіяни забрали невідомо куди
         понад 1000 українських біженців – ERR.* https://news.liga.net/ua/politics/news/u-
         granitsy-s-estoniey-rossiyane-uvezli-neizvestno-kuda-bolee-1000-ukrainskih-
         bejentsev-err?fbclid=IwAR06hxn3o3-mXMlv5OlYtFUBBwIHsxZb68a9yTNH-
         LhkDfDCYD5wZt8-3-UM

xxxviii An interview with General Valery Zaluzhny, head of Ukraine's armed forces.
         (2022, December 15). *The Economist.* https://www.economist.com/zaluzhny-trans
         cript?fbclid=IwAR2mo31MOQnwZndhGjK7GaSAObNmVAMizEgJ71yYPkzEizobdic
         NHqHnMKY

xxxix   The symbol of Ukrainian fortitude–A kitchen cabinet with a ceramic rooster
         from the deoccupied Borodianka–Is now in the Museum Fund of Ukraine. (2022,
         April 16). *Maidan Museum.* https://www.maidanmuseum.org/en/node/2138

xl   *Кличко провідав "поранений" міст.* (2022, October 10). https://www.youtube.
         com/watch?v=3uEMob0BviU

xli   Чибісов, О. (2022). *Заважав здаватися: На Херсонщині російські мобілізовані
         вбили командира та передали зброю ЗСУ. Channel 24.* https://24tv.ua/
         velika-grupa-rosiyskih-mobilizovanih-zdalasya-polon-zsu-hersonshhini_
         n2176210#Як%20російські%20військові%20можуть%20здатися%20в%20
         полон

xlii   «Трупи скидали в Дніпро». Через інформаційний вкид росіяни билися
         між собою на Антонівському мосту–Політолог із Херсона. (2022). *New
         Voice.* https://nv.ua/ukr/ukraine/events/rosiyani-perestrilyali-odin-odnogo-na-
         antonivskomu-mostu-molchanov-novini-ukrajini-50283295.html

xliii   *Small Enough.* (2015, March 4). Nichole Nordeman. https://www.youtube.com/watch?v=KbIv--Nse5c

xliv   Davis, J. (2022, October 23). Meanwhile on … *@JuliaDavisNews.* https://twitter.com/JuliaDavisNews/status/1584054018145685504

xlv   Asow-Kämpfer wurden in Gefangenschaft Christen. (2022, March 11). *IDEA.* https://www.idea.de/artikel/asow-kaempfer-wurden-in-gefangenschaft-christen

xlvi   *Raise A Hallelujah (Official Lyric Video)–Bethel Music, Jonathan & Melissa Helser | VICTORY.* (2019, January 24). Bethel Music. https://www.youtube.com/watch?v=G2XtRuPfaAU

xlvii   Slyvynsky, O. (2022, June 9). A war vocabulary: Displaced Ukrainians share fragmented stories of loss, trauma, and absurdity. *Camper.* https://www.documentjournal.com/2022/06/a-war-vocabulary-aaron-hicklin-ukraine-lviv-kyiv-ostap-slyvynsky/?fbclid=IwAR3g9uufoFwYYWJs3OvFy6GG2xPB0GALh1kHY67Ly5M5DQobM_v3hrmBq2U

xlviii I wanted it to end with a life-asserting statement. Having lived through the first year of the full-scale invasion, we have accepted this new reality. We have come to terms with the fact that it will not be over soon, but that only means that we need to keep on fighting and resisting the enemy.

xlix   Barnes, J. (2023, January 13). Beavers save Ukraine from invasion. *The Telegraph.* https://www.telegraph.co.uk/world-news/2023/01/13/beavers-ukraine-russia-invasion-belarus-military-defences/?fbclid=IwAR0Wlg2mEJ-8lfJ76Zg-yACAIVKO1uhPSqTCLHKxhX3DydqPMI9XvQ5jOpg

l   Дорогань, А. (2023). «Я сьогодні кричу Америці: «Руки геть від моєї країни!» Як дітям у Криму нав'язують любов до Росії. *Крим Реалії,.* https://ua.krymr.com/a/krym-dity-shkola-rosia-viyna-militaryzatsia-propahanda/32210836.html?fbclid=IwAR1qDO42nuYQfmq3bYQOgtIQZgJMbBxFU8WF_DJFt2KRHm7HDPA0txPsuRc

li   Війна, яку почала Росія. Надія, яку здобула Україна (фотохронологія). (2023). *Радіо Свобода.* https://www.radiosvoboda.org/a/vtorhnennya-rosiyi-richnytsya/32279807.html?fbclid=IwAR06poGGFHyZwG6bYGz32-JH1e16ONlbPzf_SlFQ17sM7CV_WoP2D0Hpy30

Discover more books from Edmonds Press!

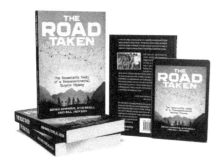

THE ROAD TAKEN
The Remarkable Story of a Transcontinental Bicycle Odyssey

In 1972, five college graduates set out on a remarkable transcontinental bicycle journey from North Carolina to Oregon. This true story of determination, camaraderie, and finding strength and kindness of strangers along the way invites the reader to remember or imagine the beauty of America and of finding oneself on the journey.

THE ISLAND
Adventures on Matinicus Island

After a young boy's father is lost at sea in the mid 1800's, his mother sends him to grow up on an Island off the coast of Maine. Toward the end of his life, Stephen Cronin recounted this true story. The Island has now been updated for contemporary readers.

Available at www.edmondspress.com

EDMONDS PRESS

Printed in the USA
CPSIA information can be obtained
at www.ICGtesting.com
LVHW040955300324
775944LV00033B/418